Edited by Veronica Beechey and Elizabeth Whitelegg

OPEN UNIVERSITY PRESS
MILTON KEYNES · PHILADELPHIA

Open University Press
Celtic Court
22 Ballmoor
Buckingham MK18 1XW

and

1900 Frost Road, Suite 101
Bristol, PA 19007, USA

First Published 1986
Reprinted 1988, 1989, 1991

This book is derived from Open University Course U221: *The Changing Experience of Women*.
Copyright © The Open University 1982. Adapted and revised material © the editors and contributors 1986.

British Library Cataloguing in Publication Data

Women in Britain today: issues and perspectives.
1. Women — Great Britain — Social conditions
I. Beechey, Veronica   II. Whitelegg, Elizabeth
305.4'2'0941   HQ1593

ISBN 0-335-15138-8
ISBN 0-335-15137-X Pbk

Library of Congress Cataloging in Publication Data
Main entry under title:

Women in Britain today.
1. Women — Great Britain — Social conditions — Addresses, essays, lectures.
2. Women—Great Britain—Economic conditions—Addresses, essays, lectures.
I. Beechey, Veronica. I. Whitelegg, Elizabeth.
HQ1597.W567 1985   305.4'2'0941   86-815

ISBN 0-335-15138-8
ISBN 0-335-15137-X (pbk.)

Text design by Clarke Williams
Typeset by Gilbert Composing Services, Leighton Buzzard, Beds.
Printed in Great Britain by St Edmundsbury Press Limited,
Bury St Edmunds, Suffolk.

Contents

Acknowledgments

Grateful acknowledgement is made to the following for material used and quoted in this book:

Chapter 1
Table 1 from R.D. Blood and N.M. Wolfe (1960) *Husbands and Wives: The Dynamics of Married Living*, Collier-Macmillan.
Table 2 from R.E. Dobash and R. Dobash (1980), *Violence Against Wives*, Open Books.
Table 3 from Oakley, A. (1974) *The Sociology of Housework*, Martin Robertson.
Figure 1 from Ferri, E. and Robinson, H. (1976) *Coping Alone*, NFER, © National Children's Bureau.

Chapter 2
Tables 1 and 2 from EOC *Sixth Annual Report*, 1981, General Household Survey 1982.
Tables 3, 7, and 11 from C. Brown (1984) *Black and White in Britain* The Third PSI Study, Gower Publishing Company.
Tables 4, 5, 10, 12, 13, 14 and 15 from *EOC Eighth Annual Report* 1983, reproduced by permission of Controller of HMSO.
Table 6, '100 Women', from Ursula Huws, *Your Job in the Eighties*, Pluto Press, 1982, p.15.
Table 8 from C. Hakim, *Occupational Segregation*, Research Paper No. 9, Department of Employment, reproduced by permission of the Controller of HMSO.
Table 9 from A. Cragg and T. Dawsin, *Qualitative Research Among Homeworkers*, Research Paper No. 21, Department of Employment (May 1981).

Chapter 3
Table 1 and 2 from I. Reid (1981) *Social Class Differences in Britain*, Grant McIntyre.
Table 3 from *Social Trends* 1984, Central Statistical Office.
Table 4 from *The Class of '84*, published by The Fawcett Society and National Joint Committee of Working Women's Organisations, 1985.
Table 5 from J. Harding (1982) *C.D.T. What's Missing? Studies in Design*

Education, Craft and Technology, Department of Education, University of Keele, Trentham Books.
Table 6 from Department of Education and Science 1975 *Curricular Differences for Boys and Girls*, Education Survey 21, HMSO.

Chapter 4
The Equal Opportunities Commission *The Experience of Caring*, EOC, 1980. Tables 1 and 2 from *DHSS Medical Staffing Statistics, 1984*, reproduced with the permission of the Controller of HMSO.

The editors are very grateful to Stephen Barr for his help and encouragement in the preparation of this book.

Notes on Contributors

Madeleine Arnot is a lecturer in the School of Education, Open University. She has contributed to courses in the sociology of education, women's studies and education. Her main teaching and research interests are class, race and gender relations in education and equal opportunities policies. Her recent articles focus on family and school relations, boy's education and coeducation. She has recently edited *Race and Gender: Equal Opportunities Policies in education*, Pergamon 1985.

Veronica Beechey is a lecturer in women's studies at the Open University and chairs the Changing Experience of Women course team. She is a co-editor of *The Changing Experience of Women* Martin Robertson (1982) and *Subjectivity and Social Relations* Open University Press (1985) and is currently preparing a book on women's part-time employment. *A Matter of Hours*.

Lesley Doyal is Senior Lecturer in Sociology and coordinator of the Women's Studies Unit at the Polytechnic of North London. She has been active in the women's health movement for many years and is currently finishing a book on what makes women sick.

Mary Ann Elson is a member of the organising collective of the Women's Health Information Centre and teaches medical sociology at University College, London and Royal Holloway and Bedford New College. She has done research on doctors' careers and the women's health movement in both the nineteenth and twentieth century and is currently working on a book on the history of women in British medicine.

Diana Leonard started her employed life as a science teacher, and then switched to do a research degree in anthropology while living in Wales and with small children. This resulted in *Sex and Generation: A Study of Courtship and Weddings* Tavistock (1980). She now teaches sociology at the University of London Institute of Education and is helping to establish a centre for research and education on gender there. She was seconded to the O.U. for three years to chair The Changing Experience of Women course. She is active in publications collectives which produce *Trouble and Strife* and *Explorations in Feminism*.

Mary Anne Speakman's main research interests are the training of pre-school childcare workers and the provision of pre-school facilities, ideologies of motherhood, and the experience of miscarriage and ectopic pregnancy. She has been involved with the Women's Liberation Movement since the late 1960's and has been mainly concerned with campaigns to extend nursery facilities and upgrade childcare workers' training and status.

Liz Whitelegg is a course manager in the Faculty of Science at the Open University, and was a core member of the team which produced the 'Changing Experience of Women' course. She co-edited the book which accompanies the course (*The Changing Experience of Women*, Martin Robertson, 1982). She currently spends half her time working on Women's Studies and the remainder working on Physics courses.

Introduction

Women in Britain Today contains a set of essays about important aspects of women's lives in contemporary Britain: women's experience of relationships within the family, their structural position in the labour market, girls' education, and women's experience of health and medicine. Originally the essays formed part of the Open University Women's Studies course, *The Changing Experience of Women*, but they have been adapted and updated here for a wider audience. Whereas *The Changing Experience of Women* is interdisciplinary in approach, drawing on and developing analyses within biology, literature, cultural studies, history and economics as well as sociology and social policy, this volume is more sociological. It is not, however, conventionally so, for the questions asked and the perspectives used within the volume have been strongly influenced by Women's Studies.

Women's Studies was a direct product of the feminist movement which re-emerged as a powerful social force in many advanced capitalist countries in the late 1960s and early 1970s. Over the past ten to fifteen years Women's Studies courses have grown phenomenally, especially within adult and higher education. Paradoxically, in a climate of educational illiberalism and a period of government re-direction of resources into science, technology and mathematics, Women's Studies has emerged as one of the few areas of growth within the humanities and social sciences in recent years, with courses proliferating and research centres beginning to be established.

At first the concerns of Women's Studies seemed fairly straightforward — to criticize the masculine bias of the established academic disciplines and to develop alternative perspectives and methodologies which were firmly grounded in women's own experiences. While there was never total agreement among people working in the area, 'women' were introduced as objects of analysis in a relatively unproblematic way. Now, however, the issues have become more complex, and many of the points of dispute mirror disagreements within other academic disciplines and areas of study. The category 'woman' is no longer thought to be unproblematic, and the concept of 'experience' which remains the bedrock of a feminist analysis for some writers is criticised by others for being subjectivist. The object of analysis for many has shifted from 'women' to 'gender', with the implication that both women and men should be regarded as gendered subjects.

The essays in this volume do not share a single perspective, but reflect some of the differences among feminists whose approach is broadly sociological. In

1

their essay 'Women in the Family: Companions or Caretakers?', Diana Leonard and Mary Anne Speakman analyse women's experiences within the family in some detail. They show how the family is an area of ambivalence for women, a place of emotionality and warmth but also of depression, isolation and loneliness. Above all the family is a place of women's work. The authors criticize conventional sociological approaches to the family for ignoring women's viewpoint, and for representing the family as egalitarian and marriage as companionable. The family in their analysis embodies a structure of male dominance, and marriage is seen as a social institution which is based on, and maintains, sexual divisions and male supremacy within a sexually divided society. Women are dependent upon men, and still perform, on average, 50 to 70 hours of unpaid housework per week. They do this for their husbands, for their children, and frequently for elderly relatives, but this work is obscured because women are assumed to be caring for others 'for love'.

The prevalence of the nuclear family within our society and the domestic ideology has profound consequences, according to Diana Leonard and Mary Anne Speakman, not only for married women but also for those women seeking alternatives to marriage (like remaining single or forming lesbian relationships) and for those, like widows and divorcees, who have alternatives forced upon them. When a society is founded on marriage and heterosexuality it can be very difficult to live differently.

Likewise, the authors argue, motherhood is difficult in our society and the social relationships within which it takes place are detrimental to both mothers and children, but it is also difficult for women not to be mothers. There is a profound conflict between what has been called 'the myth of motherhood' and women's experiences of motherhood. Childless women, single mothers and lesbian mothers find it particularly hard when women's role is primarily defined in maternal and marital terms.

Diana Leonard and Mary Anne Speakman emphasize the ways in which the family is interconnected with other institutions, the labour market especially, and this is the concern of my own essay in the volume, 'Women's Employment in Contemporary Britain'. This shows that despite the steady increase in women's involvement in the world of paid employment this century, women's patterns of employment are still quite different from men's. Most women have interrupted working histories, and many work part-time – over 1 million part-time jobs were created in the 1970s, almost all of these for women. Women's jobs are highly segregated within particular sectors of the economy, and black women, in particular, are concentrated in lower-level jobs. Full-time women's weekly earnings average 67 per cent of men's. Like Diana Leonard and Mary Anne Speakman I criticize a variety of sociological approaches to women's employment, for their failure to analyse the interconnections between the family and the labour market, for ignoring the role of ideology and the state, and for failing to conceptualize the operation of gender in the sphere of employment. I also discuss a number of issues which are problematic in the analysis of women's employment; divisions between women and men within the workforce, gender and skill, the relationship between the family and women's employment, the role of ideology, and the questions of gender, race and class. Finally, I consider briefly the question of equality at work and the strategies which feminists have used to achieve this.

The chapter entitled 'State Education Policy and Girls' Experiences of Schooling' by Madeleine Arnot considers the ways in which the education system has constructed and, to a certain extent, maintained specific concepts of femininity based largely on women's domestic role and their subordinate relation to men. The author traces the ideological origins of these concepts in state education policy in the nineteenth century, showing how the system education was organized around the two principles of gender and class differentiation. These principles continue to operate today, albeit in a slightly different form. Madeleine Arnot shows that the pattern of girls' educational experiences are different from those of boys, and that the 'class gap' between girls gets larger the higher the educational level which is reached. In addition to mapping out the relationships between the education system, the family, and the labour market, Madeleine Arnot discusses a variety of more specific ways in which gender inequalities can be reproduced: through childhood experiences, through the forms of school organisation, and through the organization and culture of the classroom. She tackles the contentious issue of whether mixed or single-sex schools are better for girls, which in turn raises the question of what a genuinely co-educational system would look like. Finally she points out that the education system is not always as successful in socializing children as sociologists have often assumed, and suggests that the contradictions between the school and family class cultures, and between race and gender, may provide an important impetus for girls trying to 'break out of the mould'.

The role of the state in reproducing gender inequalities is also the topic of the final chapter, 'Women, Health and Medicine', by Lesley Doyal and Mary Ann Elston. They trace the roots of the 'medical model' of illness to the nineteenth century and show that women's identity within medical discourse today is still defined in primarily maternal terms. Women today use medical services more than men, partly because they live longer and partly because of their reproductive capacities. The prevailing medical model, however, means that it is doctors who are in control rather than the women who are affected – it is the medical profession which has control over abortion and contraception, over the organization of childbirth, and over the analysis and treatment of mental illness. All too frequently social and moral judgements masquerade as medical ones. The authors also discuss women health workers. Women have a long history as healers, and they still do the bulk of health care work, both unpaid in the home and the community and as paid employees within the National Health Service. There is a strongly gendered form of hierarchy within the National Health Service, however, with relatively few women in the more prestigious consultant and senior management jobs. Finally the authors discuss the women's health movement, which arose from the activities of feminists in health care, and which attempts to integrate 'scientific' medicine with women's own experiences and to provide facilities for women in a different, and more democratic, way.

The essays in this volume raise a number of important issues. A first point is that they document the pervasiveness of gender divisions across a whole range of social institutions. This volume deals with the family, the labour process and trade unions, the education system and training schemes and the system of health care, but one could produce a far longer list which would include the mass media, the social security and tax systems, political parties, and the church, for instance. The question of why gender divisions are so pervasive in societies like Britain has been extensively discussed in recent years, particularly by feminists, and there is no clear agreement about the reasons for this. Most feminists (including all the contributors to this volume) reject biologically deterministic explanations which explain gender divisions in terms of biological difference between the sexes, although new forms of essentialism can be found in some recent feminist writings which assert that women are inherently more peace-loving, caring and nurturing, and men are inherently more aggressive and prone to war and to violence. If, however, one rejects biologically determinstic forms of explanation in favour of social constructionist theories (which see gender divisions as being constructed within society) or interactionist theories (which analyse gender divisions as a product of an interaction between the biological and social realms) this is by no means the end of the story. One must still explain the basis of gender divisions and provide some analysis of the reasons why these persist.

Earlier contributions to feminist theory tended to focus upon somewhat abstract structures in searching for explanatory variables: the operation of patriarchy (the institutionalized system of male domination and female subordination), or the presence of a sex-gender system, or the operation of particular sets of relations of production and reproduction (capitalist social relations in capitalist societies). More recently, however, feminist writers have tended to analyze gender relations more specifically, in particular historical periods, within specific discourses, and located within particular social institutions. The essays in this volume, all of which have fairly specific concerns, point to a number of variables which are critical to the analysis of gender divisions in Britain today. Diana Leonard and Mary Anne Speakman see marriage and the family as institutions which are crucial in underpinning gender divisions, and they show unequivocally how men in particular and society more generally benefit from women's unpaid work within the family. One implication of their analysis is that other institutions too benefit from this system of institutionalized exploitation of women. Other essays in the volume also underline some of the ways in which women's domestic labour affects their situation more generally. The essay on women and employment shows how women's participation in the labour market is affected by the sexual division of labour within the family, and particularly by their responsibility for dependent children; and the essay on health care points out that women continue to do a great deal of health care work, unpaid, in the family and the community.

A second variable which is central to the analysis of gender divisions and which is pinpointed in a number of the contributions is the role of ideology, in particular the ideology of femininity and familial ideology which continues to be critically important. The chapter on women and employment shows how the ideology of femininity enters into the construction of many women's jobs, and suggests that this takes a different form for women at different points in the life cycle and for black and white women. The chapters on girls' education and on health care show how important the ideology of femininity and what is variously described as familial or domestic ideology were in affecting the forms of provision in the nineteenth century and argue that similar ideologies are critical in defining how women are treated today. It was widely believed in the nineteenth century that boys and girls should be differently educated, and also that women of different social classes needed different types of schooling. The prevailing belief that schools should 'fit girls for life' meant that domestic economy had a central place in the system of education which developed in the nineteenth century. Discussing educational provision in the nineteenth and twentieth centuries Madeleine Arnot suggests that although education has changed considerably within the twentieth century with the extension of the period of universal state provision and the more recent development of comprehensive schools, the belief that girls will primarily be wives and mothers and only secondarily be in the labour market continues to prevail. Girls are thought to have 'dual careers' while boys just have 'careers'.

Similarly the medical model which in the nineteenth century asserted that women were physically weak because of their capacities to mother continues, in a modified form, today, according to Lesley Doyal and Mary Ann Elston. Women are believed to be biologically different and their sexuality is defined within medical discourse in primarily biological terms. Psychiatric illness among women is often seen to result from women's poor adaptation to their 'proper' role as wives and mothers, and women are frequently portrayed as being more neurotic than men. As the authors point out, although definitions of femininity have been liberalized since the nineteenth century and women are to a large extent now accepted as workers and as sexual beings, their identity is still constructed in mainly domestic terms.

A third variable which is critical in structuring women's position is the organization of the system of wage labour, and this is touched upon in one way or another by all of the essays in this volume. In some respects the changes in the patterns of women's employment have been some of the most marked changes to have occurred this century. Nowadays most women are in paid employment for most of their working lives, marriage is no longer a determinant of whether or not women are in the labour market (as it was in the earlier post war years), and any breaks in their patterns of employment are becoming shorter, especially among younger women. Nevertheless, these changes in the patterns of employment, which have undoubtedly given women some measure of independence and important social contacts outside the home, have only affected the sexual division of labour within the family to a very limited extent, and they have had little effect on the patterns of education and training for the majority of girls. They have been less significant in emancipating women than has sometimes been supposed.

The final variable which is touched on by most of the contributors to this volume is the state. Women have a particularly complicated relationship to the State which is itself a multi-faceted entity. It simultaneously propounds an ideology of equality of opportunity which does not make distinctions based upon sex (or race) and pursues policies (in the tax and social security systems, for instance) which embody the assumption that married women are men's dependents and should not, therefore, be treated as individuals in their own right. In some of its policies the household is treated as the basic unit, whilst in others the individual is fundamental. However, even in those areas where the official ideology is one of equality of opportunity or access for all individuals, the actual practices of state institutions frequently reproduce gender divisions, as the essays on the education and health care systems in this volume show quite clearly. The multi-faceted nature of the State is reflected in many feminist practices, and the State is variously seen both as an agency which ought to promote women's equality, or at least to eradicate discriminatory practices, and as an agency which is itself deeply implicated in reproducing gender divisions. It is for this reason that some feminist practices (self-help groups around health care, for instance) have often kept a distance from the State and have chosen to operate autonomously from it.

Different people analyzing women's situation in Britain today would place different emphases on these variables and analyze the relationships between them differently. The contributors to this volume (despite different emphases) tend to focus upon the interconnectedness of the variables, showing, for instance, how gender divisions within employment and in the system of education and training schemes and the sexual division of labour within the family reinforce each other. They show how these elements all too easily form a vicious circle from which it can be hard for women to escape. Such an integrated form of analysis, while underlining the pervasiveness of gender relations can also be problematic, since it paints an overly deterministic picture of women's situation and fails to recognize sufficiently the contradictions between the variables. There are conflicts and contradictions, for instance, between women's involvement in the paid labour force and their position in the family which have become more apparent in recent years, especially for middle-class women, and the inequalities between women and men in both spheres have increasingly been thought unacceptable. Likewise contradictions exist within state policy between the formal equality of the sexes, which is enshrined in the Equal Pay and Sex Discrimination Acts (at least so far as the public sphere is concerned) and the inequalities between the sexes which are systematically reproduced within many state policies. Feminists have often been acutely aware of many of these contradictions, but these have not always been adequately incorporated into more theoretical analyses.

One of the issues which has been a matter of some debate in recent years and which is touched on by several of the contributions to this volume is the question of the extent to which *all* women share a common experience of oppression. This has been highlighted by black feminists, in particular, who have suggested that the feminist analyses which have been developed recently are more appropriate to white women's experiences than to those of black women. The question also arises as to how far women of different social classes share common experiences. All the contributions touch on the question of race and ethnic differences, but these are not foregrounded sufficiently in the volume overall, and there is little analysis of racism. Class differences are mainly touched on in the chapter on girls' education. There are strong grounds for believing that black and white women and women of different classes, while sharing a common oppression as women, are affected rather differently by, for instance, opportunities in the labour market, or family relations, or education, or health care. Now that gender divisions between women and men have been so clearly delineated within feminist theory the issue of differences among women deserves far greater attention.

Veronica Beechey

Women in the Family: Companions or Caretakers?

Diana Leonard and Mary Anne Speakman

In this chapter we shall look in some detail at what is meant by the term 'the family' today – and at what goes on in contemporary families. Studying the family is important because it is not only a central part of most people's lives, but a particularly crucial area for women. Whether or not we agree with the adage that 'a woman's place is in the home', a woman's experience of family life – as a child and as an adult – greatly affects how she sees herself. Women's relationships as daughters, unmarried women or wives or widows, as mothers and grandmothers, with or without children or grandchildren, are crucial to their situation and experience. The family can provide women and men with many pleasurable and rewarding experiences; it can also be the source of much frustration, even pain – indeed it has been argued by some feminists that the family is a central, if not the greatest, source of women's oppression.

For reasons of space, we shall have to restrict ourselves to looking at present-day British families, with only a few references to the earlier part of this century and to the changes which accompanied the Industrial Revolution (1780–1840) and which developed in the nineteenth century. We shall also, unfortunately, be able to give relatively little attention to the interrelations between the family and other institutions in society, such as the labour market, the welfare state, the education system, and medicine – even though these have been the subject of considerable recent scholarly attention. Some of these interconnections are discussed in other chapters in this volume.

Our central theme here is that family life is an area of ambivalence for women. First, because the 'work' which goes on in families (for example, housework, childcare) is not seen as real work but rather as being done from and for love. It is seen as merely an element in the personal relationships of which the family is a centre. Working for love can bring happiness and satisfaction, but it constrains and limits women's lives in many ways. Family life is also an area of ambivalence because there is a tension between the idea that the family is a unit with shared aims and interests and the fact that the individual members of a family often have conflicting needs and desires. Relations of power exist within the family as within other areas of society, and, overall, women's interests come off badly.

A second theme running through the chapter is the question of the extent to which women's experience in the family has changed over the last few decades, and whether for the better or worse.

In the next two sections we shall take a critical look at what we mean by the

8

term 'family' and question some of the assumptions about family life that are found both in popular thought and academic research. Subsequent sections will discuss women's and men's relationships in marriage; not being married; the relations between generations; caring for children and for the elderly; and relationships between women and their mothers, sisters, daughters and friends.

The family and women's lives today

Newspaper headlines and the sorts of books reviewed in the quality Sunday *media* papers are constantly telling us that families are not what they used to be. An eminent American writer, Christopher Lasch, has suggested that 'the family has been slowly coming apart for more than a hundred years', but other scholars have shown that a century ago people were *already* deploring the demise of the home; so the fragmentation, if it is occurring, is certainly not new or sudden. But concern with the family is real, and current. Politicians, churchmen, head teachers and voluntary bodies all frequently voice their worries, give advice, and seek support for what many of them see as an ailing institution.

Thus, although the family is seen as the normal and natural, indeed the only possible way of life, it is also seen as frail and in need of constant support from the rest of society. It is seen to need both verbal, 'moral' support and legislative buttressing. Teachers should provide education for family life and speak to parents about their duties; law reformers, social workers, and politicians should ensure that any proposed changes in public policy do not undermine family relationships.

In the nineteenth century, the family became defined as a private sphere, separate and distinct physically and in its value system from other areas of social life. The Englishman's home had been his castle in the sixteenth and seventeenth centuries, in the sense that husband-fathers were responsible and spoke for their dependants, but this castle became geographically and to an extent economically separated from other areas of his life in the nineteenth century and was an arena into which the apparatuses of the State which developed as the nation grew (the law, the police and social workers) did not penetrate, providing things went well. However, if things did not go well, it was thought that failure in the family resulted in public ills, such as physically unfit recruits to fight in wars, weak workers, moral degenerates, juvenile delinquents and deserted wives and old people, who were a drain on the public purse. The State therefore started to provide a safety net of structures to support the family, but it also asserted a right to intervene within it–to provide education for motherhood, compulsory vaccination of children, and magistrates' courts with powers to extract maintenance from erring husbands, for instance–so as to help people to help themselves towards a particular way of life. Working-class families were seen as 'going wrong' more often than middle-class ones (not surprisingly, given their material circumstances and the fact that the standards of 'going well' were middle-class

), so this intervention mainly involved control of the working-class family.

As nineteenth-century values increasingly stressed the division between the private and public spheres, women became associated with the private sphere, with the home, and with the values attached to it. Men were expected to be competitive, outward-looking, calculating and unemotional, while women – the 'angels of the house' – were supposedly warm, caring, calm and stable, supporting other family members unquestioningly. Women and the home were the emotional lynch-pins for their menfolk: a secure haven from the pressures of the world.

The home thus became women's proper sphere in both senses of the word 'proper'. The family was where women properly belonged, and the home was the one place proper to women, that is, which belonged to them, where they exercised considerable control and influence, and which their husbands, the heads of the household, might choose either to leave to their managerial devices or to share with them in considerable equality. If women were to be found outside the home, it was not to be in the public arena in the full sense (i.e. it was not to be in politics or the Civil Service or management of factories or mending roads), it was to be in voluntary activities or jobs which were in certain respects extensions of their domestic caring roles (nursing, teaching, visiting the poor and helping to raise money for charity, jobs which were often unpaid). Again, these standards applied mainly to middle-class women. Rather different criteria were applied to working-class women: they *should* stay at home but if they had to earn money, they were quite likely to be employed to do rough, heavy production work or dirty domestic work like laundry and charring. Similar ideas of what is appropriate work hold today, particularly for black and immigrant women.

Much of the concern about the decline of the family really relates to the position of women, and is an expression of worries that attempts to change women's lives will disrupt a (supposedly) vital social institution. For instance, people who blame parents for juvenile delinquency are often really complaining about *mothers* not being at home when children come in from school.

'The family' is used not only as a synonym for 'women', of course. It has a variety of other meanings which need to be distinguished before going further. It can mean:

– all of a person's relatives: parents, grandparents, brothers and sisters, aunts, uncles and cousins, and their spouse and children ('all her side of the family came to the wedding');
– or just close relatives: parents, brothers and sisters ('he has no family left');
– or all those in a line of descent from a common ancestor ('it runs in the family');
– or having children ('they haven't started a family yet');
– or just an individual's spouse and children ('bring your family to stay for the weekend').

This diversity of related meanings is possible because 'the family' is not a thing, not something we can see and touch. 'The family' is an abstraction, an idea, a concept – or rather a number of related ideas and conceptions which we have begun to separate out here. It covers a group of people with particular sorts of relationship and legal ties, some of which are based on what we recognize as biological relationships, others on marriage. Members of this group are expected to interact frequently, and some of them live together or have lived together in the past. Various actual groups, ones we *can* see and touch, are then *called* 'families' because they are based on those particular sorts of relationships. But who and what are considered and treated as 'family' has changed over time (in the seventeenth century the family included servants and apprentices) and varies with the context, as has been suggested above.

So what is specific to family relationships today? How do they differ from, say, the relationships between employers and employees, or friends and neighbours, or teachers and pupils?

First, both sexes are always involved in family relationships. Family relationships also involve different generations.

In addition:

(a) There is an absence of calculation and exchange in regard to what family members do for each other, and in particular in regard to what women do for others. They do not have monetary-based relationships. What is done by one member for another is done for love, in both senses of the word (gratis and from affection).

There are also strong feelings of moral obligation and rights to give and receive help and to share income, goods and property in the family.

(b) Family relationships are long-term; they ideally last for a life-time.

They involve continuing social contact and often cohabitation.

The relationship is between particular individuals, related biologically or by marriage (a very special legal contract) or adoption (a legal relationship approximating to biological kinship). Family members cannot be substituted by any other individual.

(c) There is much more physical contact between family members than non-family members (touching, cuddling, tending); some of this may be:

(i) sexual: sexual relations are *prescribed* between certain family members; they are *proscribed* between others.

(ii) coercive: family relationships are more often physically coercive than any others; e.g. parents may chastise children, and husbands may chastise wives.

Other social relationships today have some, but not all, of these characteristics. For instance, friendships have some of the characteristics of family relationships; so do relationships between teachers and pupils. Certain relationships between employers and employees (notably male employers and female employees) may have some of the elements of family relationships, but many have almost none. On the other hand, not all relationships between people who fit the legal definition of family (biologically or maritally related) show hese features. Some relatives never meet, feel no sense of obligation and are financially calculating. But are they then 'really' part of a family (i.e. are they anything more than legally related)? Fully to qualify as 'family' requires, in other words, legal ties *and* interaction *and* feelings of affection.

The incidence of the nuclear family in Britain

Domestic lives in this country are *supposed* to be based on the nuclear family. Each of us should ideally live as part of a group composed of heterosexual, married couple and their dependent children–as part of a specific form of relationship between the sexes and the generations. The couple at the centre of the nuclear family household has ties with, but is relatively separate from, the rest of the kin, friendship and work relationships of the husband and wife. Their masculinity and femininity complement each other within the charmed circle of the four walls of the home.

This image comes at us from all directions–from such obvious sources as the Church, advertisements, television situation comedies, illustrations and stories in children's books, and in representations of the Royal Family which occur almost daily in the mass media.

All households that do *not* contain a man, his wife and 2.4 children are seen, for example, as *deviations* from the norm. Such households may be:

(a) young people sharing a flat before they get married (note that the accent is on the 'before', implying that this is merely a phase they pass through);
(b) homosexual or lesbian couples (a couple, unspecified, is heterosexual);
(c) single-parent families (the term suggests that there *should* be two parents);
(d) 'empty-nest' families (the children who make families complete having flown);
(e) second families (one's family, unspecified, is one's first and should really be one's only one).

The 1981 Census shows us that most people do indeed live as members of families. In Great Britain (England, Wales and Scotland) in 1981, only 3 per cent of the population lived in institutions (boarding schools, colleges, hospitals, barracks, hotels, hostels, monasteries or prisons). Of the vast majority living in private households, nearly 90 per cent lived with their spouse and/or children. Only 9 per cent lived alone (and these were predominantly widows), and only 2 per cent with people to whom they were not related.[1]

Even though, as is sometimes stressed, at any one point in time, only a minority of the population will be living as a member of what has been called the 'cereal packet family' (consisting of a man, with a full-time housewife and children under 16)[2], if we look at people's life-cycles as a whole, the significance of the family is clear. Even if an individual is not currently in a nuclear family, he or she probably was in the past and will be again in the future. Thus:

1   Nine out of ten men and women marry at least once. The partners are generally from the same class and ethnic background and live within five miles of each other when they meet, and the man is taller and around two years older than the women. (We choose who to marry, but within a structure and set of values given by society. How different is this from an arranged marriage?)
2   The average man and women spend 84 per cent and 75 per cent of their adult lives respectively in marriage

3   Nine out of ten married women have at least one child within the first ten years of marriage (75 per cent have two or more)
4   Eight out of ten men and women (i.e. married and unmarried) have one or more children and live with them for at least eighteen to twenty years, and possibly again in their old age.
5   Few people below retirement age are unmarried or live alone–though after retiring they often are and do so. Nearly one third of those over the age of 65 and half of those over 85 years, especially women, live by themselves or with unrelated people.
6   Nine out of ten people over retirement age live near to and see at least one of their children at least once a week. (Figures derived from Burkitt and Rose, 1981; Leonard, 1980; Rimmer, 1981.)

Kinship and marriage thus structure most people's domestic arrangements for most of their lives; most women are housewives, whether or not they are in paid employment, and are mothers all their adult lives. They are not, of course, mothers of *young* children for more than 10 to 15 years, but maternal obligations and concerns do not cease when children start secondary school.

In our society there is, indeed, an amazing degree of *uniformity* of family behaviour nowadays compared with, say, present-day third-world societies or our own society in the past. Almost everyone in Britain now marries and establishes their own household, whereas in the sixteenth or eighteenth centuries a substantial minority of the population never married or married very late. Individuals now live with their own parents until their (early) marriage, instead of moving to other households as apprentices, servants or lodgers, though they may spend a period away for training or in the forces. It is relatively rare for kin outside the nuclear family to live in the household; and rarer still for non-relatives. Almost all children born survive to adulthood, and almost everyone lives to see their grandchildren and increasingly their great-grandchildren.

If we compare Census snapshots, we can see certain recent changes. In the last twenty years, the proportion of households that contain 'cereal packet families' of man, woman and two children has actually declined, with a concomitant increase in households containing people living alone, especially among the elderly. There has also been a (smaller) decline in the number of grown-up children living with their parents, in the incidence of .
two or more families sharing the same household, and an increase in single parents with dependent children – because young people are marrying at an earlier age, because different generations are less willing to share accommodation, and because there has been an increase in divorce and in the acceptability of unmarried mothers keeping their children. One consequence has been that, despite the increase in the number of houses and flats since the Second World War, there has been no decrease in demand for housing. People now expect higher standards, which include privacy and independence.

What the Census shows to be rare today, but which would have been commonplace in households enumerated in 1891 or 1921, are boarders and lodgers, living-in servants, and couples with no children or only one child, *or* with four or more children. The two-child family has become much more common and it is also the size now most frequently *desired*. People are more often able to have children and to have the number they want when they want. Given this choice, most people want some but not many children.

The consequence of this change in the birth rate for women of child-bearing age has obviously been enourmous. As Richard Titmuss commented twenty years ago:

> It would seem that the typical working-class mother of the 1890s, married in her teens or early twenties and experiencing ten pregnancies, spent about fifteen years in a state of pregnancy and in nursing a child for the first year of its life. She was tied, for this period of time, to the wheel of childbearing. Today, for the typical mother, the time so spent would be about four years. (Titmuss, 1958,p.91)

Today only 15 per cent of couples with dependent children have three children, and only 4 per cent have four or more (Central Statistical Office, 1980, p.42). The experience of childhood has changed too: children are growing up in small families, generally having *a* brother or sister, but rarely more than one or two.

As the historian Tamara Haraven (1982) argues, lower mortality rates, increased affluence, access to family planning and treatment of infertility, the existence of a welfare safety net, improved communications and, until recently, secure employment, have led people to have a greater degree of choice about whether they marry or not, at what age to marry, whether or not to have children and how many, and whether or not to maintain links with kin. But the more choice people have had, the more we have chosen to follow, each and all, a similar path. This can make the situation of those whose ideas and experience are different quite difficult.

Although it is this uniformity of demographic experience which is most striking, we need to note that there are a number of ethnic and class differences that are important in determining women's experience. One is the substantial difference in the sex ratios in some immigrant groups. For instance Pakistani men outnumber Pakistani women by two to one. Another is variations in family size and patterns of legitimacy. Women born in the Indian subcontinent have rather larger families than those born in the UK or the West Indies, though the difference is decreasing. Many of the children of mothers born in the West Indies are born outside marriage, and the proportion is increasing (as is the proportion of 'illegitimate' births to women born in the UK.[3]) Finally, whereas women from manual backgrounds marry earlier than those from professional and managerial backgrounds – two-fifths of working-class women born between 1951 and 1955 were married by the time they were twenty – those who married unskilled workers had their first child much earlier than other mothers, partly because more of them were pregnant when they married, and partly because social classes I, II and III began to delay the start of childbearing during the 1960s and 1970s, while class IV and V did not.

The family is highly valued in all classes and ethnic groups in Britain. However, certain parts of the country (e.g. Wales) and certain groups (including Jews, South Asians and Cypriots) stress family relationships and recognize obligations to kin beyond the nuclear family more than others, while others (many Afro-Caribbean's for example) put less stress on marriage.

But if we accept that different groups draw the line around who is and who is not (close) family differently, and that individuals may not feel most strongly about the people to whom they are legally most closely related–i.e. that there is variation and choice involved–we have to face the question of how justifiable it is to talk about '*the* family' at all. Even if we find that most people *behave* alike, for example if we find that nine out of ten men and women actually do get married, does this mean that their *experience* is the same: does marriage mean the same to everybody? Are not domestic life and kin-relationships *the* area of life above all others where we are free to choose what we do? And are not all families different, each the product of the interaction of the particular individual personalities concerned?

We believe that we *can* generalise about family life, while recognising class, regional and subcultural variations, because there is a common overall structure and system of values in our society. Women and men do make choices about how to conduct their lives, but not within conditions of their own choosing. Individuals (and indeed whole subcultures) may struggle against 'accepted' ways of dong things and may try to organise their lives differently, but they are constantly constrained and regulated. This applies not only to how they behave, but also to how they think and feel. The ideology of what family life is like, and in particular what women's role in it should be, is very strong, and women are made to feel extremely guilty if they fail to live up to it. They therfore try very hard to be as they should be: to make their marriage, their parenting, their relations with kin, and their housewifery 'a success'. Consequently, people's actual behaviour and self-presentation in turn support the ideology of the family. People *do* get married and say that marriage is a good thing whatever their experience. And there are painful consequences in terms of censorship from workmates, neighbours and kin if one is seen to 'fail'. There are also painful material consequences in that state agencies, which support the family, can make your life very difficult if you do not conform; and painful economic consequences if you do not marry.

Recent critical perspectives on the family

Because of the strong emotions attached to the family, which are also deeply embedded in people's personality structures, it is particularly difficult to stand back and look at this social institution in a detailed and critical fashion. People's views are strongly influenced by their personal experiences–good and bad–as a child and as an adult, and their location in the family (as husband or wife, parent or child, brother or sister). And because each family is so long-lasting, complex and contradictory, any account seems to miss out *either* what makes each family different, *or* what makes all families alike.

Those who do research on the family encounter several problems deriving from the ideology of the nuclear family. One is that people do not see any need to study it–what it is and what goes on inside it is taken to be natural and obvious. The second problem is that the family is a private arena and it is hard to gain access and to observe what people actually do. Asking questions about family life is seen as prying, and if people do agree to talk with a researcher, they are quite likely to put up a front, saying they do and feel what they think they *ought* to do and feel. In consequence, we know a good deal less about what goes on inside the family than we know about what goes on in factories, schools or hospitals. This means that large areas of women's lives are relatively unexplored, although everyone tends to *think* they know about them. It is hardly surprising, therefore, that controversy surrounds the whole area.

The ideology of the nuclear family has been shared rather than questioned by most social scientists. The majority of sociologists, psychologists and specialists in social administration have assumed that if anything is the matter, it is that some families break up and some people never have a family to start with. The family itself they take to be natural and/or 'A Good Thing.' However, since the 1960s there have been a number of critical accounts put forward which suggest that all is not well, even within 'successful' families. It has been stressed that people who *have* families *also* have problems, because the nuclear family is based on inherent contradictions and is as much conflict-ridden and exploitative as it is loving and supportive.

A critique we shall be considering most here developed from women's pooled experience in consciousness-raising sessions in the Women's Liberation Movement and from the work of feminist social scientists. It countered the views that marriage has 'become companionate and egalitarian', by suggesting that all is not well for women in the modern Western family, and in heterosexual couple relationships more generally in our society.

The growth of companionate marriage
There is a general consensus within our society that family life has changed a lot since Victorian times, and generally for the better. The 'sweet friendship' which was the sixteenth-century Protestant ideal of marriage remains, but power relationships are thought to have declined. Patriarchal control (the rule of men over women and old over young) is said to have greatly diminished.

The main change stressed in this context has been the increasing friendship and equality of emotional involvement between husbands and wives, associated with an overall change in the nature of men's relationships with their families, and in the notion of masculinity. (Women's role and femininity have not been seen to have undergone so much change, perhaps not surprisingly given that most people have seen them as more 'natural'.) Michael Young and Peter Willmott in their studies at Bethnal Green in East London and later in *The Symmetrical Family*, John and Elizabeth Newson in their study of childrearing in Nottingham, and Ronald Fletcher in *Marriage and the Family in Britain*, are but a few of the many influential authors who have stressed and welcomed the decline of the authoritarian *paterfamilias* from the 1920s through the post-war period. Men, they have said, even in the Andy Capp land of the Northern working class, and certainly in the softer South and in the middle class, are no longer ashamed to be seen pushing prams, nor are they unwilling to help around the house from time to time–most happily give a hand with the washing-up. With rising wages and standards of living, husbands and wives have come to share their incomes and plan major purchases together. They are committed to having at least some shared leisure activities. Both husbands and wives now stress the importance of mutually satisfying sexual relations and fidelity.

Although the authors mentioned emphsize these as changes from an authoritarian to an egalitarian family form, quite how widespread either form has been at different times is in fact questionable. On the one hand, oral history now suggests that many fathers have long played an active and affectionate role in the family in all social classes; they have been solicitous of and helpful to their wives, and fondly engaged with their children. On the other hand some men today are only distantly concerned with their families, or are aggressively domineering and violent. The writers mentioned would probably accept this–their point is that a variety of forms of masculine involvement in marriage and parenthod have co-existed and continue to co-exist, but that the family-centred, companionship mode has become the dominant pattern in recent years and is still spreading.

The consensus is thus that something close to equality has been achieved within modern marriage. Husbands and wives today choose each other freely on the basis of romantic attraction and stay together from affection. They are (more or less) equal in status, have a (more or less) equal say in decisions, and each pursues (together and/or separately) their own tastes and interests. There are areas of domestic life in which husbands are much more likely to do things and to take the decisions, and other tasks and choices commonly undertaken by wives. What is stressed is that *over-all things balance out*; that husbands and wives are complementary.

Robert Blood and Norman Wolfe, who directed a famous piece of research on 731 families in Detroit in 1955 felt that their findings clearly showed that neither husbands nor wives had ultimate power in modern marriage, and that the particular outcomes–across couples and within any one couple–depended upon the different 'resources' brought to the marriage by the husband and the wife.

> Some husbands today are just as powerful as their grandfathers were–but they can no longer take for granted the *authority* held by older generations of men. No longer is the husband able to exercise power just because he is 'the man of the house'. Rather he must prove his right to power, or win power by virtue of his own skills and accomplishments in competition with his wife. (Blood and Wolfe, 1960,p.29)

Much the same conclusions were reached twenty years later by Michael Young and Peter Willmott in a study of London, which they published under the title of *The Symmetrical Family* (1973).

Sexuality within marriage was not much mentioned by writers about the family during the 1950s and 1960s, and indeed it was not much talked about outside marriage manuals and problem pages at the time. But this was certainly an area in which it was thought that past inequalities between men

Table 1 Allocation of power in decision-making areas (Source: Blood and Wolfe, 1960, p.21)

Who decides?	Decision (percentage of couples giving response)							
	Husband's job	*Car*	*Insurance*	*Holiday*	*House*	*Wife's employment*	*Doctor*	*Food*
Husband always	90	56	31	12	12	26	7	10
Husband more than wife	4	12	11	6	6	5	3	2
Both equally	3	25	41	68	58	18	45	32
Wife more than husband	0	2	4	4	10	9	11	11
Wife always	1	3	10	7	13	39	31	41
Not applicable	2	1	2	3	1	3	3	3

and women needed rectifying, and great progress was felt to have been achieved by the end 1960s. In the post-war period, popular literature put increasing stress on the importance of the sexual aspect of marriage. Good lovemaking was seen as cementing the tie between husband and wife and was an area in which women had a right to equality. Contraception was seen as having freed women from the fear of pregnancy. However, husbands were still expected to be more sexually experienced at marriage, and to have stronger sexual urges, so they were expected to educate their wives and to take charge in this area, being restrained and gentle though determined (since women enjoy being 'pursued and conquered'). Wives could then share in their husband's physical satisfaction. Indeed, it became incumbent on women to enjoy sex, and to have orgasms (hence a need to take them if they did not come). The other side of this coin was that wives would be the ones to use the contraceptives and would not henceforth gainsay their husbands. They would now have intercourse not out of duty but because it was fun and because it expressed their love for their husbands.

Feminist critiques of marriage
Having outlined the positive, prevailing view of marriage, we want now to contrast it with a feminist view, that of Lee Comer in *Wedlocked Women* (1974). Comer's book is a good example of Women's Liberation Movement writing on the family, combining personal accounts and insights with work from academic studies to produce a crisp and readable analysis. Her key arguments in the chapters on 'Monogamy' and 'Marriage and Economic Dependency' are that *both* the home and the world outside are centres of male

power and the two mutually support each other. Couples are not islands of equality in the sea of sexism. They can try to forge an egalitarian relationship against the odds of male supremacy in the world surrounding them, but this attempt is based on the man agreeing to forego certain privileges (i.e. he has the power to have them if he wants them, and can reassert them at any time). She sees romantic love and the ideology of 'the union of man and woman as one flesh' as serving to disguise the unpleasant power imbalances between men and women inside the home. Women identify with their husbands, sometimes to the extent of virtually thinking they *are part* of their husbands; that he and his interests *are* them and their interests.

Comer sees the main source of men's authority today as resting in their greater earning power (especially, obviously, when they are the sole breadwinner). The money a husband earns is seen as 'his money', and (especially among the middle classes) husbands are likely to handle the family's overall financial affairs. A wife at home works 'for love' and has no right to free spending money of her own. She has to ask her husband for money for clothes and entertainment, and often goes without from self-censorship. *The world's sympathy however is with the man for having dependants to support, rather than with the wife and children for being dependants.*

Comer also identifies men as having additional authority because,

(a) they are usually more educated or trained than their wives, and have jobs with higher status (as well as pay). Within these jobs, and in a multitude of everyday interactions, men are accustomed, and confident of their right and ability, to treat women as subordinates.

(b)Husbands are taken to be the heads of household and assumed to represent the family in the world outside.

(c) Where the family lives and its style and rhythm of life is determined by the husband's job, i.e. the family revolves around him, not vice versa.

(d) Husbands plead 'the demands of the job' (in the middle class) or what is appropriate to manly men (in the working class) to avoid domestic work.

(e) Husbands have the right to take the initiative sexually.

(f) Husbands have greater physical strength generally and can legitimately use a certain amount of violence, or threats of violence, to coerce obedience. (This is not class-specific: there is violence in middle-class families too.)

(g) Husbands are able often to define the areas within which the domestic struggle shall take place. The wife has to be in desperate straits before she quits.

Comer suggests that though the form in which male dominance in heterosexual couples is expressed may vary by class and race, the overall structure is very similar.

At times Comer seems to present a rather passive view of women, probably because she is focusing on the structural position of women–which she sees as *being* weak. But she does suggest that women use various strategies to fight back an improve their situation:

(a) Women use their verbal fluency in arguing, and their skill in interpersonal relations–emotional blackmail, 'silent hurts and resentments', 'not understanding him'–to get their way. This may, however, be over very minor areas (doing the washing-up, paying attention to the children, taking her out once in a while).

(b) Men love their wives and children and want their marriages to continue, so they will give (or give in!) to their wives. The alternatives to the family (loneliness, insecurity, social exclusion) are not very plesant for men either.

(c) Men lose face if their wives are not loyal, do not do the domestic work, cease to be concerned about their appearance, or behave disgracefully. (This last is especially true of subcultures where male pride is very bound up with their women's decorous behaviour–for example, those from Mediterranean countries, or Rastafarians. But most men in Britain seek to keep their wives 'sweet' *in part* for this reason.) A threat from a wife to 'show her husband up' publicly can be influential.

(d) Men need their wives' domestic work and sexual servicing. Wives who are, for example, dissatisfied with the housekeeping money they receive may serve cheese and biscuits for a week; or 'have a headache' every night.

(e) Women can accept the ideology of romance and sharing ('our money') and use it as a bargaining tool. They virtually have to, since without this their position is stark. (This probably accounts for many women's hostility to feminism 'telling it like it is'.)

(f) Women may resolve any conflicts within themselves by self-denial and totally identifying with their husband and children–spending only on food for others, clothes for others, things for the house for others–making the others feel guilty.

(g) Mothers claim the children, and may turn them against their father.

(h) Wives may undertake paid employment in addition to their domestic responsibilities and get access to money and outside companionship.

All these tactics, while often devastating in the immediate experience, are nonetheless evidently the manoeuvrings of a subordinate group, fighting back or making the best of their situation at an individual level. And most are very two-edged weapons.

In her account of marriage, Comer considers things squarely from the perspective of women and identifies herself with other women. Her view can be seen as biased, but most previous accounts of the family which have considered the consequences of, for example, new patterns of domestic life or motherhood or of women taking or not taking paid employment, have been written from the perspective of husbands, children, employers and the State–hardly, if at all, from the viewpoint of women. Women in sociological, literary and scientific accounts have been objects, described from men's point of view. Such writing as there has been about women has nearly always been *by* women, it is true, but they have been distanced, academic and 'impartial'. Women who have 'made it' into the professions where one gets to write have often not wanted to be identified *as women*. They have tried to act as if they were outside the gender divisions of society. They have tried to pretend, in

Betty Friedan's words, that there are 'men, women and me'. And they have presented 'the family' as having the same significance for women, men and 'society'.

A leading American sociologist, Jessie Bernard, describes her own development of a feminist approach late in her career while she was writing on *The Future of Marriage*. When first commissioned to write a book on this topic in 1968, she thought this would be 'one of the simplest assignments in my professional career'. But, as she wrote, she found she was compelled constantly to revise her ideas to keep up with changes in the world that were profoundly influencing marriage, such as the concept of no-fault divorce, the spread of contraception and greater tolerance of homosexuality.

She also revised her ideas because she encountered (and it came as a profound personal shock) disapproval of her supposedly academic objectivity, her lack of involvement, and her impersonality. This caused her to rethink her stance *vis-à-vis* research and her discipline: to realize, in respect of gender, how value judgements are implicit in the choice of research topics, in the questions which are asked and *not* asked, in the way findings are presented, and in what researchers *do* with (how concerned they are about) their findings.

She ended her review convinced that 'there really are two marriages in every marital union', His and Hers, and that marriage as seen from the women's side is usually presented and that is seen as *the* (only possible) perspective. She says that as she reread, with feelings, research reports on marriage, she wondered at her own past complacency and cavalier treatment of women's problems.

> I did not start out with a conviction that marriage was bad for wives. Nor did I expect this book to turn out to be a pamphlet on the destructiveness for women of marriage . . . a result all the more remarkable because most of the facts had been generally known, some of them for a long time. I had reported many of them myself a generation ago. This time round however, they looked different. The message of the radical young women had reached me. (Bernard, 1973, p.294)

Feminist accounts are not only frequently criticized for being one-sided and biased in representing and supporting the woman's viewpoint; they are also accused of over-statement, of showing only *an* aspect of the situation. It is said that they show the pain, manipulation and power relations of family life, the boredom of housework, the frustrations of life with small children or elderly relatives – but never the love, support and creativity and 'The Joy of Cooking'. In addition, it is charged that they stress marriage and motherhood as institutions, not as a series of individual choices; and yet, critics argue, women *have* choices and they are not dupes. Women (and men) seek and support the very monogamy, motherhood and domestic life these (young, middle-class) women trample on.

Though there is some truth in these allegations, they are often based on stereotypes rather than on actually reading what feminist writers say. For even to *mention* the darker side of family life can make people blind to the rest of the message, so resistant are we to seeing *our* marriages, *our* relations with *our* fathers, mothers, spouses and children in any except the best light. The implications are so dreadful, we do not want to think them through. Yet, at the same time, people, and women in particular, may respond almost with a shock, recognizing how directly feminist accounts speak to (covert) parts of their experience. We may experience an intense feeling of relief: it is not our personal *failing*, not our fault. It is a shared experience; a result of power relations in the structure of society. (This is one of the meanings of the slogan: 'the personal is political'.)

Feminist accounts also do not say that women are dupes. Quite the contrary. They stress that women choose what to do, and that their choices are reasonable. But they stress that women's choices are made within a situation which is not of women's own choosing – within a sexist (and class-based, racist and age-based) society. One way of making the best of such a situation is to go along with it: to play the feminine role (appropriate to one's class, race and age) to the hilt. Another is to try to change it. Both responses have their problems. The feminist approach counters the view that women are in large measure to blame for their situation: i.e. that 'women are their own worst enemies', by seeking to explain why some women support the *status quo*.

Rethinking marriage: domestic work

The division of labour and power within the family

Earlier, we briefly mentioned a study of marriage in Detroit in the 1950s. This gave its respondents a list of eight domestic tasks and decisions, and asked them who did which tasks in their household and who made what sorts of decisions.[4] As we said, the authors of the study, Blood and Wolfe, concluded that their findings showed that marriage nowadays is an equal partnership. They believed the tasks and decisions they selected were typical of all the decisions made within the household, and could be used to construct a 'mean power score' for husbands and wives which would enable researchers to compare the relative power of husbands and wives in rural and urban families, in different socio-economic groups, and among blacks and whites.

There are several criticisms which can be made of this sort of work. One is that such studies of the family only question one partner (often the wife). If husbands are also spoken to they may well have a different view of what 'usually happens'. An even more important criticism, however, is that the 'resources' the authors see spouses 'bringing to their marriage' are in fact a *constitutive part* of the family, not a variable *explaining* differences in power between the spouses. That is to say, which 'resources' a 'spouse' has is largely determined by sexual divisions inside and outside marriage, and marriage is by definition a union of the two sexes. Decisions made by individual couples need to be seen as taken within a overall social structure based on sexual divisions (men's power over women) of which marriage itself is an integral part: a contributory institution.

A final criticism of surveys like Blood and Wolfe's, is the question of how typical and how important are the tasks and the decisions which they used as their measures. A whole multitude of tasks are done in households day by day. If we chose a different set (as other researchers have done), we can end up with an apparently quite different 'division of labour' between husbands and wives. And are things about which decisions are made comparable? Some of the ones Blood and Wolfe used (e.g. how much to spend on groceries each week) were quite minor but were made frequently, others were made rarely but affected the whole life of the family (e.g. whether the husband should accept a new job).

It has therefore been suggested by feminists that, contrary to the findings of studies like Blood and Wolfe's, things do not balance out within the family: that women work longer and harder than men and get lesser rewards. That is to say, the bulk of housework is done by women, often in addition to paid employment; women are given little credit and regard and a smaller share of the family 'cake' than men; and they have less say in major matters affecting the family, despite the importance of what they do for family well-being.

In addition, whether an individual has or does not have a 'resource' to contribute must be evaluated in terms of whether it implies a one-sided or a reciprocal dependency within the relationship. Although there may be considerable mutual dependency between husbands and wives (i.e. they may need each other more or less equally) to have children, for *legitimate* sexual expression, and to achieve adult, worthy status with the community, women are in many ways one-sidedly dependent on men.

Their lives are more bound up with having children, and most wives are dependent on their husbands for the essentials for survival (food, shelter and clothing), for luxuries, for their social standing, and for actually *having* sex. (Men have recourse to prostitutes and more possibilities for adultery).

Marriage, in other words, is not the result of a random selection of individual choices, with 'resources' contributed within each pair by 'spouses' who just happen to be men or women. *Marriage is a social institution, regulated by law and custom, based on and maintaining sexual divisions and male supremacy within a sexually divided society.* The significance of who does what and who makes what decisions must be set and interpreted within this framework.

These points have been made frequently by feminists in the last few years, and in a variety of ways. Pat Mainardi used humour, producing an account of the dialogue she had been having with her husband for a number of years.

'I don't mind sharing the housework, but I don't do it very well. We should each do the thing we're best at.'
Meaning: Unfortunately I'm no good at things like washing dishes or cooking. What I do best is a little light carpentry, changing light bulbs, moving furniture (how often do you move furniture?).
Also Meaning: Historically the lower classes (black men and us) have had hundreds of years' experience doing menial jobs. It would be a waste of manpower to train someone else to do them now.
Also Meaning: I don't like the dull stupid boring jobs, so you should do them.

'I don't mind sharing the work, but you'll have to show me how to do it.
Meaning: I ask a lot of questions and you'll have to show me everything every time I do it because I don't remember so good. Also don't try to sit down and read'

while I'm doing my jobs because I'm going to annoy hell out of you until it's
easier to do them yourself. (Mainardi, 1970)

Other writers have made the point by constructing 'budgets' of how much
time people *actually* spend doing what during a 24-hour period, as contrasted
with what they *say* they do overall, and comparing men and women. Such
time-budgets have been collected by government agencies and market
researchers in many countries (notably the USA, France and Scandinavia) at
intervals throughout this century according to carefully specified and
uniform categories, and it has therefore been possible to compare changes over
time, in different countries and between rural and urban households. These
show that the average number of hours spent on housework per household has
remained pretty well constant at around 50—70 hours a week throughout the
last fifty years, and that men everywhere continue to do much less than
women.

The egalitarian marriage ethic suggests that (accepting that most men have
paid employment) when men *are* at home (for example, at weekends) they do
50 per cent of the domestic work done at that time. In fact most do not. Most do
very little except repairs. And since they are not at home most of the time, they
obviously do far less housework overall than women.

A Canadian study (Meissner *et al.* 1975), for example, compared families
where there were children under ten years old and those where there were not,
and where the wife was a full-time housewife, and where she was employed
outside the home part and full-time, to see the effect this had on the amount of
housework done and the distribution of work between husbands and wives.
The researchers found that in couples without a child under ten and when the
wife was not employed, husbands did an estimated 3.2 hours of regular
housework a week, increasing it by an insignificant 6 minutes when their
wives went out to work. For couples with a young child, things were only
slightly different. The 5 hours of regular housework of such husbands
increased by one hour a week when their wives worked for pay. This applied to
both old and young husbands, and to those with high levels of education.

As the demands accumulated—with part-time, full-time and over-time
employment and one, two or three children—women cut down more and
more on the time they had for sleep and meals, for television, and for
gardening and visiting, especially on weekdays. (These findings are in
agreement with a number of other studies, e.g. Walker and Woods, 1976. They
are not once-off results.)

Such time-budgets not only clarify the different amounts of housework
contributed by men and women, they also underline the enormous amounts of
time and effort (still) spent on domestic work in all countries; more than is put
into paid employment, and an amount which has not declined this century,
unlike the industrial working week.

One of the consequences of the development of the ideology of public and
private spheres in the nineteenth century, was that 'work' became what was
done outside the home. So when writers on companionate marriage suggested
that men were getting involved with their children, they had in mind not so
much physical servicing as the development of emotional relationships:

caring in the sense of caring *about* rather than caring *for* (or tending). Women too continued to be seen as at home primarily to provide emotional support and love; to be its warm centre, looking after people; conciliating between members, socializing children and ministering to the sick — in a rarified, inactive way. It detracted not a little from the Angel in the House's supposed calm serenity to show that she might well spend her time on her knees cleaning toilets, mopping up vomit, throwing out rubbish, and in a state of perpetual motion.

The 1970s brought the start of research that treated housework *as a form of work*, though initially it was difficult to get it taken seriously. Pat Mainardi ends her 'marital dialogue' with her husband coming in, and, discovering she is writing about housework, saying 'My God, how trivial can you get?'. And when Ann Oakley wanted to study women's attitudes to housework in the same way as industrial sociologists had studied other people's attitudes to their occupations, she found that her

> request to register a thesis entitled 'Work Attitudes and Work Satisfaction of Housewives' at the University of London in 1969 met with frank disbelief or patronizing jocularity. The only person I could find who was willing to supervise such a work spent the next three years trying to convince me that women's sexual satisfaction and adjustment were at the heart of the problem. Similarly, I am now mildly amused, though I was at the time outraged, by the fact that two major British publishers turned down the book I produced on the grounds that everything that needed to be said about housework had already been said, and was I really serious in being serious about such a boring subject? (Oakley, 1980, p.11)

However, scholarly work is now well advanced on unearthing the history of housework, looking at the influence of technological innovation and architectural and social changes. This has shown how the physical exertion and time required by certain work around the home has been greatly reduced by utilities (e.g. indoor plumbing, electricity, and rubbish collection) and small machines (e.g. vacuum cleaners, washing machines and electric irons), and by the availability of commodities (purchased pre-processed or semi-processed goods) and services (such as take-away good and dry cleaning) — yet the overall time commitment of housewives has not declined. Rather, housework time per household has been reallocated to different individuals and different tasks.

First, there are no longer as many women's hands to do the work. Domestic work used to be done mainly by daughters and female servants; but servants declined in numbers sharply around 1900 and had almost disappeared by the late 1930s (certainly full-time, living-in servants had departed), and families are smaller and daughters are in school. Nowadays virtually all 'women's work' is done by the wife/mother.

Second, although many things previously produced at home are now mass produced, the quantities of goods to be purchased and hence the work involved in shopping, and then maintaining them, have greatly increased. Much housework today is what has been called 'consumption work'. On the other hand, certain 'labour-saving devices' (e.g. yoghurt makers, food processors, deep freezers, home laundries) are in fact labour-*extending*, since they involve tasks being taken back and done in the home, largely by the housewife, which were formerly done outside, or by tradespeople employed to do particular tasks in the home; and the appliances themselves may need elaborate cleaning, storage and maintenance.

The third reason for housewives still doing as many hours' work as before is that standards have risen, especially those of cleanliness and childcare.

Finally, as tasks have changed, so women have taken them over from men. For example, in the USA, husbands used to help with the washing-up, but with the advent of dishwashers, wives have become responsible for loading and unloading them (Bose, 1979).

This constancy in the time spent on housework by wives alongside the change in tasks and personnel has been possible because of differences in the evaluation of men's and women's time. There is a much less clear distinction between 'work' and 'leisure' for women than there is for men. For a man, whose main work is elsewhere, his family has become to a considerable extent 'a leisure activity', whereas for most women it is an important (if not their sole) workplace. How men and women perceive family leisure obviously varies, therefore, and it also varies between different couples depending on their type of marital relationship.

For some women their leisure is largely domestic, spent in the home with female kin and neighbours, with an occasional 'night out with the girls' or going with their mother, sister or girlfriend to bingo or the local theatre. Their husbands' leisure is largely extra-domestic, spent with a male group or friend. If the wife has paid employment in such a marriage, she may effectively have no leisure at all because of the pressure of commitments. In other marriages which stress husband and wife doing things jointly, a certain amount of domestic work, childcare, and family events may be consciously shared with the woman by the man as part of their partnership—so that some of her domestic work is quasi-leisure, and some of his leisure, quasi-domestic work. A husband may also take over certain of his wife's chores to give her individual leisure, recognizing it as part of her rights within the marriage. But even in joint marriages, the man is seen as helping his wife. It is she who is responsible for domestic work and he can choose to withdraw his assistance if he wants to. Her responsibility involves being 'on call' 24 hours a day. It relies on her having no 'time off'.

A further difference between wage work and housework is that the wage worker does a particular agreed task (often negotiated by a trade union) in the time he or she sells the employer, but domestic work and childcare are open-ended. A wife does whatever task is needed for whatever length of time is necessary. She is a Jill of all trades, unceasingly available. Since perfection in household management and the servicing of family members can never be achieved, her work is never done.

How clean should 'clean' floors be? Some of Ann Oakley's informants washed their kitchen floors every day—but they were still not satisfied because there were times when they were not clean. Or again, how much attention does a small child need? How comfortable can you make your spouse? How much effort can a wife save her husband?

> A good woman does not have to be told what her husband and children think or need; she knows—often before they do. It's her job to know them better than they know themselves, at least in certain ways. One effect of a woman's engaging her thoughts in the lives, minds and bodies of men and children is to free them from the responsibility of thinking about and meeting certain of their own needs, and thus to give them time, time to work and time to grow up. (Harding, 1975, pp.290—1)

Those working for people they love should not stint. The very idea of rational calculation is an anathema. But the housewife is bound, in body and in mind, to the extent that those she cares for are released.

The indefinite pressures on women's time and energies, and their priding themselves on 'coping', mean they feel there is always something left to do. This leads to their habitually doing two if not three things at once: cleaning the floor, minding the baby and listening to the radio; watching television, mending or knitting and keeping an ear open for the children upstairs in bed. Men experience this much more rarely—they concentrate on one thing at a time—and are notoriously remiss if asked to do something extra. This 'secondary use of time', as time-budget studies describe it, leads to certain tasks being made infinitely more difficult (e.g. doing the shopping accompanied by a 15-month-old toddler). It also greatly contributes to the fragmentation of women's time, to their being unable to concentrate because of being constantly interrupted, and feeling harassed and never having the right to be alone—even in bed: 'Often the only time you can really be alone in the home is when you lock yourself in the lavatory.'

Husbands not only have more leisure time than wives, they have a different quality of leisure. They have solid periods of time, whereas wives 'snatch five minutes to sit down' here and there, or when not needed to do something specific—they are still available. Men do fewer secondary activities during their leisure (e.g. they don't work while watching television), and they are more able to spend their leisure outside the home. Most importantly, they do not have endlessly to think of others and the effects on others whom they love of what they do. And yet it is housewives who are told 'their time is their own'.

Thus, although it appears at first sight that women control their time in the home, the obligation to serve others means that their 'control' is but a freedom to choose how to subordinate themselves most effectively. This applies in other areas too. For instance, women handle much of the spending for the family, and do most of the shopping, so it has been argued that they control what the family consumes. But if we take the example of food, we find that the husband's likes and dislikes and the children's food needs (in that order, and with the wording carefully chosen) determine what is bought and how it is cooked. Women attach minimal importance to their own preferences and simply find having the responsibility day in and day out onerous. That is to say, women 'control' money and food within the family, but this does not mean they feel free to spend money on themselves to indulge their own tastes, or (after the first few years of catering) get satisfaction from being creative in shopping and cooking. Rather, it provides an occasion for them to give privilege to the tastes and needs of other family members.

The fact that women have control of the purchase and processing of food also means that they consume qualitatively and quantitatively different meals from their husbands. Although economists talk of households consuming what 'they' purchase, families do not eat what is actually sold in shops. Goods are purchased, brought home, stored, processed (cooked), served and utensils cleared away afterwards. The person who does all the work does not 'consume' the same meal as those to whom she serves it. You cannot wait and be waited on simultaneously. Serving the meal also allows the cook further chances to put others first — taking the smallest chop or helping, or going without if she hasn't cooked enough.

Some may argue that it is not unreasonable for women to continue to provide the bulk of domestic work and caring in the home: there is less housework to be done, women are better at it (either innately or because they have learned the skills), so if women are at home full-time or for more time each day than men, then they should do it. They may also suggest that Parkinson's Law holds: that the reason why the amount of housework has not declined is because women allow it to expand to fit the time available.

Others would say that women don't want to spend so much time 'cooped up in the home' and that housework should be shared so that women can in turn share the responsibility and the sense of personal worth that comes in our society from earning the family income. Also that it is not women, or not only women, who require the constant raising of standards of cleaning and tidying and decorating and entertaining the children: these can be and are imposed upon them because women's time and energy are not valued in the same way as men's.

Whichever view you support, the net result is not in dispute: housework has become restricted to a fairly small set of oft-repeated tasks and one woman does it alone in each home. Consequently the boredom and isolation of housewives has become marked as they pursue higher and higher standards and feel more and more personally responsible for the well-being of all family members.

Women's satisfaction with being housewives
Housewives are by and large not happy with their work. Ann Oakley concluded from her study:

> The major finding is that dissatisfaction with housework predominates. Seventy per cent of the women interviewed came out as 'dissatisfied' in an overall assessment of feeling expressed about housework during the course of a long in-depth interview. This figure lays to rest the idea that only a tiny minority are discontented. (Oakley, 1974, p.182).

When comparing her sample of housewives with studies of factory workers, she found more complaints about monotony, the fragmentation of the tasks, and the excessive pace among housewives; and the latter were particularly resentful of the low status of their work and of feeling economically dependent. Although most women said they liked the autonomy of 'being their own boss' in the home, she found that, in fact, since most women set themselves standards and routines which they felt they must keep to (whatever the source of these standards), this autonomy vanished. The 'rules' felt external to the individual who set them, and came to regulate the pace of the daily routine. However, these rules were not pointless: they were an important way in which housewives found such 'job satisfaction' as they did. They expressed feelings of personal responsibility for the work done, they helped to make sense of a multitude of bits and pieces, and they set a limit on potentially endless tasks.

The stresses and personality effects caused by the nature of housework and caring for others have seldom been taken seriously. The drinking cook is always considered to be a joke and the complaints of housewives in the present century have been treated as frivolous. Yet as Jessie Bernard says in one of the more famous comments in *The Future of Marriage*, 'being a housewife makes women sick' (p.48). After a few years of marriage, women often 'dwindle' into wives: they become helpless, lose ground in personality development, lack confidence and lose interest in sex. They 'feel like cabbages'. An American study on the incidence of psychological stress in adults found that:

> ... working women were overwhelmingly better off than housewives. Far fewer than expected of the working women and more than expected of the housewives, for example, had actually had a nervous breakdown. Fewer than expected of the working women and more than expected of the housewives suffered from nervousness, inertia, insomnia, trembling hands, nightmares, perspiring hands, fainting, headaches, dizziness, and heart palpitations. The housewife syndrome is far from a figment of anyone's imagination. (Bernard, 1973, p.47)

A roughly comparable study in Britain (in Camberwell and the Hebrides) found a very high incidence of depression in married women in urban areas (Brown and Harris, 1978). Fifteen per cent of the women (aged 18—65) in South London had a definite psychiatric disorder, and a further 20 per cent had a borderline condition, i.e. *one woman in three*, was clinically depressed. (Unfortunately the survey gives no comparative information on men.) The authors, George Brown and Tyrill Harris, add to Bernard's points the realization that working-class women are more exposed to risk than middle-class women because they experience more severe life events and difficulties, especially when they have children — connected with housing, finance, not having confiding relationships with husbands or boyfriends, and to do with their children's welfare. Hence, when they experience a severe loss or disappointment that involves their view of their own self-identity, they are four times as likely to fall ill.

Brown and Harris exposed a vast area of loneliness and isolation *in the midst of the family*, which undermines the myth of the family as successfully adapted to modern conditions, at least so far as women are concerned. They also showed the callousness of those who pay attention to the positive benefits of employment and nursery provision only from the point of view of employers or children, and not from the point of view of women, since both would substantially improve many women's health and happiness.

The consequences are well known. As Diana Harpwood puts it in *Tea and Tranquillisers, The Diary of a Happy Housewife*, 'I start the day the Valium way at seven-twenty a.m., when my departing husband brings me a mug of tea and Diazepan tablet. A Valium a day keeps psychiatrists at bay.'

The variety of wives' work and employment
The work women do as wives is not, of course, confined to housework — i.e. to the conventional list of tasks covering cooking, washing, shopping and cleaning. These are merely the tasks all wives (and daughters) do in the home. They are what is common to *all* households. In addition, some wives help their husbands in their occupations. The wives of publicans serve in the bar and make the sandwiches, the wives of theatre directors fill in for any member of the staff who falls sick (prompting, helping out behind the scenes), the wives of heads of state and ambassadors entertain and the wives of university lecturers proofread and make indexes! Many wives also help in their husbands' leisure: making sandwiches at the cricket club and getting grass stains out of flannel trousers; or keeping their husbands' diaries and sorting out constituents' problems if they are in politics.

Wives also contribute to the family economy by undertaking paid work. This is a fairly recent pattern outside the lower working class. There have been a series of changes from the sixteenth to the nineteenth century in attitudes to single and married women being employed outside the home, but in all social classes by the early part of this century it was assumed desirable that married women should not have paid employment. For a wife to have a go out to work was considered shameful, indeed unnatural, and even for her to undertake paid work within her own home (e.g. by taking in laundry, wet-nursing babies, or being a landlady) or to work in other people's homes (as a washer-woman, needlewoman or children's nurse) lowered the family status.

Within the space of two generations however (1931–1971) there has been a change in expectations, so it is now accepted that married women probably will work, possibly part-time, except when they are needed full-time to care for members of the family who are sick or infirm, when there are young children, or when they can help their husbands with their employment. The pattern of married women's involvement in the labour market–when they work, whether full or part-time or casually, and where and at what sort of jobs–thus remains very sensitive to home demands, whereas married men's does not. And time-budgets show that women undertake paid work *on top* of domestic responsibilities. The latter are not shared evenly when both spouses have paid employment.

In some couples it is openly expressed that the wife 'works' if, and only if, her husband 'allows' her to. Although husbands in Britain ceased to be the legal owners of any money their wives earned in 1882, it is worth noting that there have been marriage bars in a number of occupations–only in the 1944 Education Act was the marriage bar in teaching abolished. Some women in Britian today still keep their paid work (e.g. domestic cleaning) secret from their husbands–the latter having refused to countenance it. Most wives today, however, make their own decision about whether or not to take a job; but this has to be seen against the background that, *if* wives decide to take employment or to return to education and training, it is on condition that it minimally inconveniences their husbands. The extra hours must be found from *their* free time, and any extra costs involved (e.g. childcare, more convenience foods) must be met out of *their* earnings. The assessment of how much income they are contributing to the household will be calculated as what they earn less these replacement expenses.

Despite these contraints, many married women clearly are 'choosing' to return to paid employment when they can, or not to 'drop out' at all if they have careers. Great concern has been expressed about the consequences of this for 'the family' (so the women concerned not only work very hard, they also feel guilty). Concern has mainly been about the effects on children, but there have also been worries about the effects on the marital relationship. Certain psychiatrists, for example, have suggested that men's authority, hence feelings of responsibility, self-image and even potency, will be undermined if their wives' employment threatens their role as breadwinner and head of household; and it has also been proposed that women will experience role-conflict if they have to be 'instrumental' at work and 'expressive' at home.

How far marriages are actually affected by women's employment is uncertain. There is no evidence to suggest that an employed wife 'repudiates her femininity' by not complying fully with the domestic role and thereby 'causes' greater conflict in her marriage, though when wives are employed greater conflict is often *expressed*, and more women who divorce have paid work, and more highly paid women divorce more often. We need to ask, however, whether it is conflict that leads women to seek employment, or whether, *having employment*, they can afford to express dissatisfactions. Likewise, it is not clear whether having a source of income enables or encourages women to contemplate divorce, or whether women whose marriages are bad take employment when they see divorce on the horizon, but if they can't get a job, have to 'make a go' of their marriage.

There is certainly evidence to suggest that husband–wife relations are more egalitarian when the wife is employed and that this changes when the wife ceases employment with the birth of children. The wife's position as an equal is progressively undermined by successive births. Ironically, as having more children increasingly restricts the options open to the wife, she may choose to have another child as the *only* viable action to assert herself, thereby further extending her powerlessness, and completing the vicious circle.

There is also evidence that the effects of wives' employment varies with social class. The say in decision-making of employed wives in working-class couples has been found to be significantly greater than that of employed wives married to middle-class men, where wives' earnings are generally much lower relative to their husbands' and less essential to the family's economic survival. There is also more resistance to the wives of middle-class men, especially businessmen, undertaking employment, particular if the jobs available are of low status. For example, on a Wales estate studied by Gaynor Cohen (1978) the wives of young business executives were not allowed to take the only jobs that were available locally with convenient hours – as school dinner ladies. The money they would have earned would have been minimal compared to their husbands' incomes, and the loss of status was unthinkable. When an employed wife's contribution to the maintenance and improvement of the family's overall standard of living (income and status) is *seen as essential*, or is *substantial*, however, she may enjoy a relationship of some equality with her husband.

The latter situation among the middle classes has been studied particularly by Robert and Rhona Rapoport. Following a survey of *Women in Top Jobs* with Michael Fogarty, they undertook intensive research on sixteen couples where both husband and wife had senior jobs and an active involvement in family life, describing five couples in detail in *Dual Career Families* (1971). These couples, interviewed in the late 1960s, had not deliberately set out to have an innovative form of family, and although they had received some supportive admiration, this had been more than counter-balanced by social sanctioning of their behaviour by relatives, friends, colleagues and neighbours, who suggested they were harming their children or putting their marriages at risk. The Rapoports' book itself was criticized for promoting an improvement in the situation of middle-class women at the expense of working-class women. Reviewers suggested that it was demeaning to use people (women) other than family members to do domestic work, childcare and personal servicing (even if paid), and greedy for two people in a family to have prestigious, well-paid careers. (This is not of course a criticism levelled when adult children living at home have careers. Two incomes to the household *then* seems acceptable.)

Ten years on, in a 're-examination' of their earlier study (1976), the Rapoports report a much greater acceptance of variations in sex roles and family structures. People attempting dual-career patterns are now criticized much less. However, such couples still have to wrestle with the same material difficulties – finding jobs in the same place, career demands that take no account of private lives, presumptions by the husband's employer that the wife of the employee will act in support of his career by not having one of her own, absence of support agencies offering domestic services, and inadequate childcare facilities. New resolutions are being evolved, however – such as separate residences and spending only weekends together, work sharing (each spouse works part-time), job sharing (the spouses share one job between them), developing more independent children, and in the management of overload (see Rapoport and Rapoport, 1978).

Clearly, however, the solutions the Rapoports propose are not necessarily appropriate for non-professional couples. Problems of childcare arrangements and domestic support are experienced by all two-job couples, but the issue of 'choice' is not one that has faced the majority. In most two-job couples, the wage brought in by the wife is a necessity – government surveys show three times as many families would be below the poverty line if the wives were not in employment – and there is little to spare to purchase replacements for her domestic contribution.

For a relatively small proportion of couples (just over half a million in Britain in 1974), the wife is the sole or primary earner. These are typically older women with retired or permanently sick husbands and no dependent children, though about twenty thousand working wives have student husbands (Hamill, 1976). In 1971 there were also around one hundred thousand unemployed men whose wives were earning. However, men under retirement age who are out of work are *much less* likely to have employed wives than are employed husbands, partly because of the disincentive effect of men's social security benefits for dependants and partly because of concern for appropriate gender roles.

After talking with unemployed men and their families in the early 1970s, Denis Marsden reported that couples' reactions to unemployment initially depended on the previous pattern of the marriage. Couples who had had close marriages (joint roles) welcomed the extra time together, at least initially, though the men did not take on more of the housework 'partly because there is not enough to occupy two adults [and] partly because their wives still embraced the role'. Couples with segregated roles, however, who had not voluntarily spent time together before the man's unemployment, found that his unaccustomed presence generated pressures:

> 'He gets on your nerves . . . I haven't the time' . . . 'I muck the place up, and that's what she gets mad about' . . . 'It's the money really that gets you down, and being on top of each other all day.' (Marsden and Duff, 1975, p.167)

Some husbands therefore reverted to leaving the house each day – for a hut in the garden or an allotment, going to a social club to drink or hanging around on street corners. Many took to the informal economy (doing odd painting and decorating or window-cleaning or poaching), in part at least to get out of the house.

Colin Bell and Lorna McKee, who interviewed unemployed men and their families in Kidderminster in 1982 and 1983, point out however that involvement in the black economy can have dire effects on the family. One consequence of unemployment is that the private lives of benefit-recipients and their dependents become open to public scrutiny and observation – not only from social security investigators, though they are a reality for unemployed people in a way it is hard for the permanently employed to appreciate, but also from neighbours, occasionally kin, and even the local unemployed (since people quickly make classifications into the 'respectable' unemployed, such as themselves, and 'scroungers'). Hobbies or routine household chores or neighbourly exchanges can become perceived as 'work' or as fiddling, and denounced.

Both these studies, and others which have looked at the effects of redundancy, agree that unemployed husbands certainly do not take over the housework from their wives, enabling the women to try for jobs (except occasionally in households where there are no children, (Morris 1983)). Quite the reverse. Men's unemployment often actually increases their wives' work load, through the need to 'shop around' and 'make do and mend' on a much reduced budget, and through the need for wives to be present in the home, e.g. to cook a meal at midday, and for women friends not to be around when the husband is at home, thereby restricting women's day-time freedom of movement and association. A husband's unemployment also generally precludes a wife's employment because this would overturn appropriate gender relations:

> Mr Vickers, looking back on his spell of unemployment after he had found work, admitted that he could never have allowed his wife to go out to work while he did the housework. 'You see, I'd have lost my, sort of, manly status, if you like. That's what he's done, isn't it, the bloke who sends his wife out to work. Fine, OK, if it's the only way of providing a reasonable standard of living, and the option is for both of them to both sit at home on national assistance and both be even more miserable. But at the same time you would certainly feel – well I would – I would certainly feel as though I'd lost a bit of my manly status'. (Marsden and Duff, 1975, p.170)

> The loss of the male economic provider role struck deep chords amongst both wives and husbands and a passionate defence of men's right to provide was invariably raised. The views often read as extreme or atypical but they were in fact widespread and did not relate easily to either occupational grade, age or other beliefs about gender roles. Very fundamental emotions concerning self-esteem, self-image, pride, views of masculinity, respectability and authority resounded in the expressions of both men and women. (McKee and Bell, 1984, p.19)

If a man has lost his manly status at work, should a wife deny it him at home too? Whatever the costs to her? The other side of the coin, of which many women are conscious, is that if the husband moves in to 'help' in the home, he gains rights in those few areas where his wife previously had some autonomy and sense of pride – as we shall see shortly in relation to childcare. Hence, the gains and losses of employment for married women are not simple.

Rethinking marriage: affection, sexual relations and violence

We have concentrated so far mainly on the work women do in the home and said little about the emotional and physical contact husbands and wives have with each other and with their children. We shall discuss these now, before turning to look at the consequences of not being married and marital breakdown.

Affection and companionship in marriage

Problems that husbands and wives encounter in maintaining a relationship of 'mutual help and comfort' are obviously not unrelated to the division of labour that exists between them. Wives service husbands and husbands benefit from their wives' labour; wives depend on their husbands' income and husbands support their wives (and often see their wives as in their debt). This is a difficult basis for an egalitarian relationship. Problems also arise because the sexual division of labour results in men's and women's lives being very different. They do and experience different things and may end up with little to talk about, even though the different things they do are seen as contributions to a common enterprise and they feel a loyalty to each other. This is obviously most true where roles are segregated. As the blush of early marriage fades, the desire to talk across the interests of the sexes may decline, and each will seek friends or relatives of their own sex as companions. Such difficulties are often exacerbated by emotional differences. Women expect to express feelings and to talk about worries and personal problems, whereas men are expected to show self-restraint and reserve.

Some commentators have argued that this makes the sexes complementary. The private sphere, and women in it, have been assigned the qualities of intimacy, affection and solace, and men turn from the public sphere, where these qualities are lacking, to their homes and to mothers, wives and lovers for missing parts of their personalities. Women perceive and value this as men showing their love. Others, however, have seen these as infantile needs in adult men which 'have been sentimentalized and romanticized long enough as "love"; it is time to recognize them as arrested development' (Rich, 1980, p.221). Rich believes women give too much of themselves to men, and they should reserve more of their nurturance for themselves—and for other women. She sees the nuclear family, and particularly companionate marriage and joint marital roles, as a very mixed blessing for women. They have separated women from other women, and focused their love on a single man.

Linda Imray and Audrey Middleton, while living as participant observers in localities in Yorkshire, noted that in any case men do not always turn to their families to meet their emotional needs. There is a lack of intimacy in many marriages and men can give or withhold emotional involvement as a means of controlling their wives.

> Animated, loquacious men in the social club on weekday evenings when the company is mostly male, turn into bored, silent companions of wives on Saturday evenings when it is customary for some men to 'give the wife a night out'. Couples sit around the edges of the club, many of them silent, many of the women looking uncomfortable in the company of a husband who is patently not enjoying himself. If several couples get together and the women start talking, the men tend to be silent, censorious and controlling, all the time looking with envy at the all-male group standing in the bar area. We would suggest . . . that many men turn primarily to the public sphere, to all-male groups, for emotional support. (Imray and Middleton, 1981, p.30)

It is also argued that the fact that women are expected to service other people emotionally rather than to think of themselves and be independent and assertive is harmful to women in a number of ways. One is that, as Simone de Beauvoir put it, women accept such a role 'to avoid the strain involved in undertaking an authentic existence'; or in Colette Dowling's phrase, 'because lounging back into a tub of tepid water is easier'. 'Because tending flower beds and organizing shopping and being a good — and provided-for — "partner" is less anxiety-provoking than being out there in the adult world fending for oneself' (Dowling, 1982, p.17).

Many women end up, Dowling says, in a neurotic double bind, hating and fearing both dependence and independence simultaneously. Women feel frustrated and angry at being nurturant and dependent, yet even the most outwardly successful tend to search for love and to become reliant on and to subordinate themselves to someone else, seeking help and protection from a world which is difficult, challenging and hostile—*especially* for women.

Thus, although some marriages are extremely happy and supportive, many are not. The pleasures, stresses and strains that we have just described get played out also in the marital bed.

Sexual relations in marriage

We mentioned earlier that mutual enjoyment of the sexual aspect of marriage has been increasingly stressed as an expression of the partners' love for each other. But we also noted that husbands were expected to 'educate' their wives in love-making and to take the initiative at least in the majority of instances. Men and women receive very different social conditioning for their heterosexual roles in the family, and this relates not just to whether they can mend fuses or cook, but also to their actions and responses in sexual intercourse.

This has been well dramatized in satires. For example, Jennifer MacLeod showed the difference between what is still expected of a wife and of a husband in their interpersonal relations, by inventing a magazine for young men, *Modern Bridegroom*, and suggesting that husbands be given the same sort of advice as that customarily received by brides:

> *How to hold a wife: a bridegroom's guide*
> Oh lucky you! You are finally bridegroom to the woman of your dreams! But don't think for a minute that you can now rest and be assured automatically of marital happiness forever. You will have to work at it. While she may only have eyes for you now, remember that she is surrounded everyday by attractive young men who are all too willing to tempt her away from you. And as the years go by, you will lose some of the handsome masculinity of your youth: you will have to make up in skill and understanding what you will lack in the bloom of youth ...
>   Now men's passion, of course, often does not equal that of women. But you have a wonderful surprise in store for you, if you concentrate your efforts on your wife's pleasure and don't worry selfishly about your own. For sooner or later you will discover the ecstacy of truly mature penile coital orgasm ...
>   If you do your job well—for husbandhood is the true career for all manly men, worthy of all your talents—you will keep your wife happy and hold her for the rest of her days. Remember that marriage, for a man, should be Life's Great Adventure. So relax—relax—relax—and enjoy. (MacLeod, 1970; quoted in Bart, 1971, p.737).

Husbands are expected to initiate sexual relations, so they take place when men want them to. Men control the progress of coitus and can so regulate things as to ensure their own satisfaction. (Intercourse ends when the man has an orgasm.) Husbands have also, ultimately, the right to use coercion (there being no rape within marriage) indeed heterosexuality is all too often intertwined with violence. Wives, on the other hand, are not allowed to make demands—that is seen as threatening and producing impotence—but they should always respond to male advances, 'voluntarily surrender', and, if necessary, fake orgasms. For a wife to initiate or to veto intercourse is unacceptable, it puts a strain on the marriage. Moreover, should it come to it, the courts will reinforce sexual rights by granting men (but not women) divorce for lack of sexual access.

Although for some women most of the time, and for most women some of the time, sex within marriage is a wonderful experience, for others it may become a perfunctory, or even a threatening experience. One woman responded to the questionnaire distributed by the American researcher, Shere Hite, 'My entire marriage revolves around making love to my husband. It makes me feel loved and wanted' (Hite, 1976, p.425). But a woman in her thirties, married six years and with three small children told an English interviewer, Lesley Holly:

> At first when we first met it was really good. Suddenly it got really bad. I was expecting Mark and I was sick and I didn't want sex at all. Afterwards the doctor said sex was all right after two weeks. He was pulling me about after a week. I was terrified of getting pregnant again. I could easily have left it for six months. When we did do it after two weeks I just hated it. I really felt like nothing. I lay on my back and I just cried. I couldn't believe that he could treat me like that. He didn't say anything. Really it's been wrong since then. I put it off. I sleep on the edge of the bed. Hanging on the edge. But eventually I have to, just to get it over with. It must be me - nobody else complains - well, the trouble is that it's the rest of your life. (Holly, 1980, pp.5-6)

We lack any well-conducted study that involves sympathetic understanding of women's sexuality in marriage, so it is hard to say how typical such different accounts are: how many women are at one extreme or the other and how many somewhere in between. It is, in fact, unusual for women to talk openly and seriously with each other about their experience of sexual intercourse with their husbands - though they treat the subject lightly and joke about it among themselves often enough. The reasons include loyalty to their husbands, and the taken-for-granted attitude in society that everybody needs and enjoys sex; and that any problems are individual, not social, in nature.

We also lack information on married men's recourse to prostitutes and on the incidence of adultery, often facetiously referred to as one of the chief supports of marriage. Eileen McLeod's study in Birmingham (1983) suggests, however, that there are about 800 women working as prostitutes in that city alone (not to mention male homosexual prostitutes) with a total of around 14,000 client contacts per week. Geoffrey Gorer in *Sex and Marriage in England Today* (1971) suggests that around 10 per cent of his informants (aged 16-45) had had extra-marital (post-marital) experience - but these included twice as many husbands as wives. A study currently underway, with a large but non-random sample, suggests that, by the age of 40, 40 per cent of women and 60 per cent of men in long-term relationships (married or cohabiting) have had an adulterous relationship - causing great joy and a feeling of being fully alive, but generally ending unhappily (Lawson, 1982). The finding from both studies that men have more adulterous relationships is probably valid, even though they vary so wildly in their estimates of incidence. It reflects men's right to initiate and control sexual relationships, their greater opportunities to meet possible partners, and social reinforcement for such behaviour. It also reflects the fact that men's field of eligibles does not decline with age in the way women's does.

Another source of strain in sexual relations for women lies in the continuing fear of pregnancy for many. In her study of women's experiences in the post-war period, *Only Halfway to Paradise*, Elizabeth Wilson points out that although new methods of contraception enable many women (1 in 3) to have intercourse freed from virtually any worries about unwanted pregnancy (whatever their worries about the effects of the Pill or coil), the form of contraception used in many marriages, the sheath (1 in 5) or withdrawal (1 in 20) is male-controlled. (These are also the most common methods used in premarital relationships.) And many couples (1 in 4) use no contraceptives.

Thus, although companionship and sexuality are shared by men and women in marriage and they are dependent on each other for them, there is again a power relationship between them and consequently husbands and wives have very different *experiences*.

Domestic violence
Nowhere is this power dimension (and difference of experience) more obvious than in relation to violence between spouses. If women are assaulted, it is likely to be by a man they know, and within their own homes, whereas men are most often assaulted, also by men, but by men they do not know, in public places. The home is a safe place for a man, but for many women it is not.

The most comprehensive recent research on the incidence of violent crime was undertaken by Rebecca and Russell Dobash in Edinburgh and a district of Glasgow in the mid-1970s. They examined a year's police records and noted all the reports of violence prepared for the courts. They found *assault on wives to be the second most common form of violent crime* (25 per cent of crimes noted by the police), but given the unwillingness of police to charge husbands and cohabitees, they feel wife abuse is probably *the* most common form of violence. Seventy-two per cent of assaults on women were by husbands (and they also got assaulted by sons). Women do not assault men on anything like the same scale – assault on husbands accounted for just 0.4 per cent of reported crimes, and the incidence of non-family violence by women was also minute.[5]

Table 2   Types of assault occurring between family members, Edinburgh and Glasgow, 1974

Person attacked	No.	Percentage
Wife	791	75.8
Husband	12	1.1
Child	112	10.7
Parent	73	7.0
Sibling	50	4.8
Mutual	6	0.6
Total	1 044	100.0

The question most often asked, once the existence and scale of wife-battering is accepted, is why do women stay with violent husbands?–a question which itself involves a certain amount of 'blaming the victim'. Recent research suggests the answer is (a) in part because some men are contrite and loving in between episodes of violence; (b) in part because women are ashamed to admit it is happening, or do not know where to seek help, or have no financial resources to enable them to leave; and finally (c) in part because they may actually find themselves returned to the home by the various 'helping agencies'–police, marriage guidance counsellors, doctors, social workers and housing departments–they go to.

'one well-travelled progression by individual abused women is from experiencing physical and sexual violence to being prescribed tranquillizers and anti-depressants, and then being admitted to mental hospital or attempting suicide. Experience has shown that the further women move along this progression, the more difficult it is to reverse the negative impact of the 'help' they receive.' (Hanmer, 1983, p.42)

One psychiatrist who treats battered women identifies a 'specific stress syndrome' produced by the endless torture of living with an assailant. Its symptoms include,

. . . agitation and anxiety bordering on panic were almost always present. Events even remotely connected with violence–sirens, thunder, a door slamming–elicited intense fear . . . Nightmares were universal, with undisguised themes of violence and danger.

In contrast to their dreams, in which they actively attempted to protect themselves, the waking lives of these women were characterised by overwhelming passivity and inability to act. They were drained, fatigued, and numb, without the energy to do more than minimal household chores and child care. They had a passive sense of hopelessness and despair about themselves and their lives. They saw themselves as incompetent, unworthy, and unlovable and were ridden with guilt and shame. They thought they deserved the abuse, saw no options, and felt powerless to make changes.

Like rape victims, battered women rarely experience their anger directly . . . Aggression was most consistently directed against themselves. (Hilberman, 1980 p.1337).

Not being married

If marriage is such a mixed blessing for women, why do so many women get married and stay married? Before considering the possible answers to this, we need to consider the alternatives available.

Remaining single

Until the separation of employment from the home took place in the eighteenth and nineteenth centuries, the majority of single women worked for their fathers and brothers or as servants, and were maintained by their relatives or masters and mistresses until they married. Who they married, and when, was largely controlled by their families–as indeed, might be their 'choice' of a religious vocation. Marriage was generally seen as an advance in status made by a mature woman when she became the mistress of her husband's household.

Marriage is still today the usual way in which young people establish their independence from their families of origin; most do not leave home until then, and while they are still at home they owe a certain measure of obedience and deference to their parents. Marriage is still generally a status more highly valued by both sexes. All the words used to describe unmarried women carry some disrespect or implied lower status or are for the young only (e.g. 'Miss'). And both men and women who are not married by their thirties find themselves accused of selfishness or of lacking social, personal or sexual competence.

Despite this moral opprobrium, a considerable number of women do not marry – because they do not find an acceptable partner or from choice. However, sociologists, and historians too, have accepted the ideology that being single is just a phase and have ignored those who are unmarried in middle life. Thus, despite the fact that never married women (25 and over) have comprised between 20 or more per cent and (currently) 8 to 9 per cent of the female population in Britain, we know little about their lives.

With the growth of wage labour, it was possible for working-class women in most parts of the country to find work that enabled them to survive economically apart from marriage and living with parents from the early nineteenth century onwards. From the mid-nineteenth to the early twentieth centuries, concern over the 'surplus' of women, due to differential child mortality, male emigration and war losses, and concern that those who did not marry should have a fulfilling occupation, led the first feminists to campaign for the opening of middle-class occupations and the professions to women. From the first half of the twentieth century it has become acceptable for middle-class women to be employed until they marry or have children. So for the last two generations it has been possible for women from all social classes to be self-supporting.

Women on their own however, in addition to experiencing a lower income than single men, have greater difficulties in finding somewhere to live. Unmarried men have access to clubs, barracks, hotels, Oxbridge colleges, lawyers' chambers, monasteries and lodgings which are not open to women or to which women have much more restricted access. And women used to experience considerable difficulties in obtaining mortgages to buy their own homes. Many single women have therefore looked for jobs which include housing (e.g. as servants, shop girls or in nurses' hostels) or lodged with widows or female kin.

Nevertheless, despite these negative aspects, many of those who are single relish the experience of 'the single status as an essentially honorable estate, possessing its own characteristics, social dynamics, and niche in the social order', as Margaret Adams found in a study of single people (Adams, 1976, p.32). They count personal independence as the status's most valuable feature, stressing their self-sufficiency and hard-won economic solvency.

The single people she interviewed also stressed their freedom to come and go as they pleased and to indulge their own wishes, to express points of view or to buy things, without being accountable to anyone else. They recognized clearly that close interpersonal relations, especially those of couples, impose social restrictions, and felt that intellectual satisfactions and the company of kin and friends were viable alternatives to constant sexual relationships and their accompanying involvements. Adams suggests that single people see their jobs as 'an important and unchanging point in their lives and a major source of self-esteem and personal development' (and that this applies not only to professional middle-class careers but to other jobs as well). Certainly full commitment to employment or to any other endeavour does not fit easily with marriage for women. (Colin Bell found that of the high achievers enshrined in *The Dictionary of National Biography*, only 10 per cent of the men who died this century were unmarried, but no less than 42 per cent of the women (Bell, 1972).)

The single cannot be open in their criticism of marriage however – this is as welcome as Mick McGahey at the CBI – but they can get away with expressing their views through irony. Stevie Smith, for instance, who herself never married but lived with her 'Lion Aunt', wrote in her novel *The Holiday*:

> I like to see how the married ladies get along, and I sit and listen and watch, and I see how much they think about their husbands, even if they hate 'em like hell there is this thought, this attention.
>
> How can you keep it up, Maria? I ask the women friends, I think you are absolutely marvellous to keep on thinking about them and listening to them and having the children and keeping the house going on turning round the men. I have never had such a thing heigh-ho.
>
> And they are at first immensely pleased about this that I have been saying, but then they begin to wish not to stress how martyr-like wonderful it is, and they begin to say how much one is missing if one does not have it; so I have had trouble with my married women friends, and with those who are living free-like and unmarried with their darling chosen one, I have had trouble for two reasons, because sometimes I like the chosen-one too much, but mostly and the most trouble, because I do not like him enough, and because I think it is so wonderful of the women to be so unselfish and so kind. But I can see that they have to do it, if they are going to have a darling husband and a darling home of their own and darling children, they have to do it, there is no other way, and if you do not then you will live lonely and grow up to old solitude. Amen.

Choosing women

Some women, including many in the modern women's movement, would argue that restrictions arise for women not only, or not so much, from couple relationships, which can be supportive and enriching, as from couple relationships *with men*, given the way heterosexuality is constructed in society. They suggest that one way in which women have protested against being accorded an inferior position in society is through lesbianism, not just as a sexual preference, but as a style of life. Thus Lillian Faderman (1982) in *Surpassing the Love of Men* suggests she accepts, not Sigmund Freud's analysis that it is envy of men's penises that causes some women to reject sexual relations with men, but his contemporary Alfred Adler's view that is anger at men's power, advantages and freedom.

In earlier eras, when lesbians accepted other people's definitions of them, they often felt compelled to agree that they were men trapped in women's bodies or that they had had traumatic childhood experiences or that they were 'truly twisted'. When they did not agree they kept silent. With the rise of feminism, when lesbians in large numbers finally defined themselves, their definitions were more like those of Adler and Beauvoir [in *The Second Sex*] than of the theorists, as were their explanations of lesbian genesis. Jill Johnston *(Lesbian Nation)*, for example, explains of her own choice that she was raised by her mother and grandmother, and the woman-centred life of her childhood gave her an 'uninhibited chauvinism' about her identity as a female; she had no 'super-ego daddy' in her. As an adult, she found that heterosexuality meant that she would have to sacrifice her female chauvinism to male chauvinism. Lesbianism, on the other hand, meant that she could continue to see femaleness (and herself) as prime, and not be forced to view as secondary what she had always happily viewed as primary. (Faderman, 1982, pp. 286–7)

The women of Barbara Ponse's sociological study, *Identities in the Lesbian World*, typically remark, 'I always had a choice about being a lesbian. It didn't happen to me . . .'. I've had relationships with men and think the negativity of those relationships for me was not because I didn't enjoy sex with men but because I didn't like the other expectations that went along with it, the kind of role playing that happens in relationships with men. The kind of thing where his work should become before mine . . . I wasn't prepared to accept that.' (p.287).

In a study of lesbians contacted through clubs, the gay press and at conferences in London in the 1970s, Betsy Ettorre discerned two groups. One group agreed with the conventional view that they were inherently different, 'born lesbian', even 'sick', but did not regret their condition, accepting and enjoying it as part of their lives. The other, newly-emerged group's members actively refuted the suggestion that there was anything wrong with *them*, saying it was society that was in a mess, the first group saw lesbianism as primarily a question of sexuality: a sexual identity based on whom one was attracted to and slept with; the latter group saw it as a statement of total commitment to women within a male-dominated society: part of empathizing with women and always putting them first.

Ettorre suggests that whatever the motivations of the members of the two groups, they both objectively constitute a challenge to 'straight' society if they are open and positive ('out') about their lesbianism. They assert a different sexual practice – that it is not necessary to be sexy in a male-defined way, or a wife and mother, or under a man's protection to survive as a woman and to have stable relationships. Such lesbians are economically independent and sexually fulfilled without the marriage contract. They thus show there is a viable alternative to heterosexuality and its values, and deny the alleged primacy of men in women's orientations.

The second group identified by Ettorre, by bringing lesbianism out of the ghetto and the closet into which society has consigned unapproved activities, also made clear that lesbian couples do not necessarily, or indeed generally, reproduce heterosexual couple roles – with a butch and a femme. They show that a variety of relationships can be forged within the alternative way of life which they feel is available to *all* women. They see themselves as women who have chosen a particular, collective, response to the oppression of women in general throughout society. Hence there is for them a clear connection between their lesbian struggle and the general women's struggle.

Others have developed Ettorre's line of argument further since the time of her study. They have stressed that the lesbian community and particular lesbian relationships are not a refuge from male abuses – not a case of weak women finding shelter in each other's arms – but rather 'an electric and empowering charge between women' (Rich, 1980, p.658). They believe the existence of lesbian communities and a lesbian culture is a source of knowledge and power for all women – and that (in consequence) it has been constantly crushed by male-dominated societies. Economic and theological pressures, jokes and taboos, the whole weight of childhood socialization, the media, the silences about lesbianism, and outright physical coercion all exist to turn women to heterosexuality. They see heterosexuality as an institution (i.e. not just as a sexual orientation, but as the turning of women's whole lives towards men and their identification with particular men – their fathers, husbands and sons), as the 'bulkhead of male dominance'.

Changing heterosexual relationships
Other women are less pessimistic about heterosexuality, or want anyway to continue sexual or close personal relationships with men. They have therefore tried to change the nature of the relationships between men and women, especially in couples, by both partners continuing in employment (as in the dual-career marriages discussed above) and by changing the ways in which the couple live and the relationships they have with other people.

In the Bloomsbury Group to which Virginia Woolf belonged, for instance, 'The institution of marriage itself was accorded no special priority over other relationships' (Morgan, 1974, p.11); it was as much a close network of kin and friends who provided emotional security and stimulation as individual spouses. Servants supported the day-to-day style of living. Members of the group had close work and intellectual interests; they shared homes; all lived near each other in Bloomsbury (hence the name); met regularly as friends and in informal groups and societies; spent weekends together at their various country homes; wrote each other letters constantly and compiled each other's biographies. They excluded from the group certain people's wives, husbands or lovers who might have been included, and included others who might have been excluded, accepting various affairs and three-way relationships. In particular, the Group included close relationships between men and women which were not sexual attachments, and relationships between men and men, and occasionally women and women, which were.

More recent and more conscious attempts at group living arrangements came with the communes of the 1960s, but these did not seem to change the relationships between men and women living in them to any great extent, according to a survey by Philip Abrams and Andrew McCulloch (1976). This study was based on published and unpublished writings on communes, on observations made of sixty-seven communes, and replies to a postal questionnaire from 700 members of the commune movement. Abrams and

McCulloch concluded that, although most communes explicitly sought to be alternatives to the monogamous single-family household – to establish new forms of intimate and caring relationships and new possibilities for self-realization, and to try out new modes of domesticity – most did not significantly reduce inequalities between men and women.

They suggest that the reasons for this were two-fold. First, although the aim of the communes was to create situations within which each individual could be 'more' himself or herself, the nature of male–female relationships was not altered all that much. The sexual dual standard remained and most childcare tasks were done, and child–adult bonds of affection maintained, by women. This meant that men were simply able to use their existing advantaged position to produce new forms of exploitation of women. Indeed they could do this with lighter consciences since 'at least it's not marriage', equality was the stated ethic, and there were no legal difficulties if they chose to depart. Women, especially those with children, were not significantly freed, and indeed lost certain forms of traditional support: the legal rights of marriage and recourse to the ideology of romantic love. Second, outside pressures (e.g. from schools and children's peer groups) for children to have stability and 'normal' parents (i.e. not to be 'children of the commune') were particularly difficult to counter. Because it was easier for men to exert their freedom within the commune (they tended to get up and leave the commune if they did not like the way things were going) it was the women who were mothers who responded to these pressures. They fulfilled the externally imposed role, maintaining traditional male–female–child relationships.

However, more recent studies by Bernice Eiduson and J.W. Alexander in the USA, and by June Statham in Britain, suggest that some communes and co-operative living ventures including women–only communal households with outside relationships, have *recently*, with the advent of the Women's Liberation Movement, succeeded in achieving a far greater degree of equality, both in terms of childcare and other areas. Although the mother–child bond still usually remains paramount, the father and other members of the commune or co-operative are taking an increasingly significant share in the responsibilities involved in bringing up children, making motherhood a less all-demanding and less totally female role, and trying to change hetero-sexuality to a less male-dominated form.

So far we have considered alternatives to marriage – remaining single, choosing women, changing heterosexual relationships – which have clear choices involved. We now turn to two others – divorce and widowhood – which are more often thrust upon those concerned.

Divorce

The writers on companionate marriage in the 1960s and 1970s had to account for the uncomfortable fact – of which they were constantly reminded by those lamenting the decline of the family – that there had been a considerable increase in the incidence of divorce, which trebled from 1966 to 1976. If marriage was now so good, so egalitarian and so successful, why were the number of breakdowns escalating?

Two answers were current, relating to two opposed standpoints on the need for divorce law reform. On the one side were those who argued for divorce reform so as to help people locked in bad marriages (especially those with an insane or cruel spouse) or forced to cohabit because of a past 'mistake' (i.e. because they or their spouse had a previous marriage which could not be dissolved), or whose children had the stigma of illegitimacy attached to them; while on the other side were those who argued that to make divorce any easier would further encourage the breakdown of the family. The former accepted that the new democratic family would inevitably be associated with a certain amount of divorce. Like American commentators before them (the USA having had a high divorce and remarriage rate for many years), they interpreted divorce as showing not the decline of marriage, but its increased importance. They saw a high rate of divorce as evidence of people's unwillingness to settle for bad or indifferent relationships. Those who opposed divorce law reform, on the other hand, held that people should accept the duties and responsibilities of married life, and that much divorce was due to the feckless pursuit of romance and sexual variety.

The pattern of divorce has undeniably been changing. Following a very low rate in the early years of this century, there was a massive increase and peak in the late 1940s, which was attributed to the failure of hastily contracted war-time marriages and the strains imposed on existing marriages by war and its aftermath. Then the divorce rate fell steadily for years, starting to increase again only in the 1960s. This sharp up-turn was regarded by most official commentators in the early 1970s as more apparent than real, however, and as no serious cause for concern. Almost all the increase, it was held, was attributable to either the regularizing of existing 'common law' unions following changes in the law (since the remarriage rate rose along with the divorce rate) or to demographic changes.

Changes in the provision of legal aid made divorce financially possible for the poor as well as the rich from 1960, and changes in the procedure and grounds for divorce came in 1969 in England and Wales, 1976 in Scotland, and 1979 in Northern Ireland. From a concept of divorce based on 'marital fault' – that is, marriages dissolved if one partner committed adultery, was cruel, or deserted the other, and where only the innocent party could sue for divorce – there was a general move to 'irretrievable breakdown' as the basis for dissolution of marriage, with either partner able to get a divorce after five years' separation even against the wishes of their (ex-) spouse[6]. This enabled many who had wanted to end their marriages previously to go ahead and do so. In addition, a reduction in the adversarial nature of the process, and especially in the associated publicity, made divorce more socially acceptable. Where divorce is by mutual consent (and 89 per cent in Britain are currently uncontested), or after five years's separation, there are now no public hearings of charges of adultery, with reports from private detectives who have lurked outside hotel bedrooms, or salacious accounts of 'unreasonable conduct', or 'cruelty' for the press to record and use to titillate its readers. If there is mutual agreement and no young children, a couple can now get a decree nisi in eight weeks (provided they have been married more than three years) and without needing a lawyer.[7]

The increase in divorce in the 1960s was also partly explicable in terms of demographic changes. A higher proportion of the population was getting married, and people were getting married younger. (The average age at first marriage fell by three years for men and women between 1931 and 1971 – to 24.6 and 22.6 years respectively.) In addition both sexes were living longer. Thus more people were married for more years; hence there was an increase in the population 'at risk' of divorce. In the past, there had also been many short-lived marriages and much remarriage (especially by men) and few marriages lasted very many years. The new pattern simply reflected the fact that, as the historian Lawrence Stone laconically put it, 'divorce is the twentieth-century substitute for death'.

As we write (in 1985) it is generally accepted, however, that the further major increase in divorce since the early 1970s shows not just a regularizing of existing co-habitation and the effects of demographic change, but also 'a genuine change in social mores' (Central Statistical Office, 1981b); 'a fast-growing tendency to see divorce as the appropriate remedy for marital failure' (Chester and Streather, 1971). And it is women who are taking the initiative. (From near parity in the 1950s, by the 1980s the position had been reached of 70 per cent of divorce petitions being filed by women.) Some argue that things have gone too far. Others think we should stop seeing an increased resort to divorce as necessarily bad, as a social problem to be explained and excused. Divorce may be the best course of action for a particular person in the long term. Some hold that it is good for girls to recognize that their marriages may not last, since it will encourage them to take their own employment seriously and to maintain their autonomy. Others point to the immediate problems and casualties resulting from marital breakdown in a society that is still based on the primacy of biological parenthood, husbands and wives as central companions, and family households, each with a male breadwinner with an income big enough to support one (but only one) family.

If remarriage is to be seen as the successful resolution to the problems of divorce (and this is not necessarily our point of view), women certainly fare less well than men; and older women much less well than older men. A study carried out for the Office of Population Censuses and Surveys, taking 1,000 couples who divorced in 1973 and looking to see which of them had remarried during the following five years, found that 56 per cent of men and 48 per cent of women had remarried, but of those aged over 40, only about 33 per cent of divorced women had remarried compared with about 50 per cent of divorced men. (Leete and Anthony, 1979).

Furthermore, even if people do remarry, and do so relatively swiftly, this does not mean that all emotional problems are solved, as supporters of the 'high rates of divorce and remarriage merely shows people have high standards' school tends to presume. Second families are different from first ones – in ways which fairy-tales have stressed are not wholly advantageous to the children from the first marriages, nor to second wives and step-mothers. And those fairy-tales themselves, with their stories of witches and disinheritance and attempted murder constitute stumbling blocks for all concerned (as discussed by Brenda Maddox (1975)).

Third, although divorce for those without property or children *may* now be relatively unfraught, battles certainly continue for virtually everyone else, i.e. for the great majority. Divorce in the past provided some emotional redress for the injured party: a wronged wife could 'take her husband to the cleaners', a wronged husband could 'cut her off without a penny' – the principle was clear. 'But now no one is to blame, battles over property division is *the* most controversial area of family law, and battles over child custody make miseries of their own. The obligation to maintain a less than innocent spouse can extend to death – and beyond' (Maddox, 1982). Sixty-seven per cent of civil legal aid in England and Wales is now spent on matrimonial cases, thanks to such disputation.

The divorce law of 1973 laid upon the two spouses equal responsibility to maintain each other. That it is predominantly men who are still obliged to pay their ex-spouses is because of the nature of marriage: it is almost invariably women who give up employment to care for children, women who have lower earning capacities, and women (especially elderly women) who are less likely to remarry. The new 1984 legislation seeks to move away from this, to maintenance for a limited period or a 'clean break', because of what vocal pressure groups and MPs regard as the intolerable burdens on men and their second families.

Because they are the main caretakers, women get custody of children in nine cases out of ten – unless they are lesbians, when they are unlikely to get custody in contested cases (see Harne, 1984). This giving of custody to women has led Christine Delphy to argue that we should see divorce not as the ending of a marriage, but its continuation in a somewhat different form. Ex-wives continue to provide childcare unpaid for ex-husbands who have rights of access, in exchange for certain help with its costs (Delphy, 1976).

In the USA where the divorce rate has long been high and there is even less post-divorce financial provision for wives, there are currently women's groups that offer solidarity and support to other women to help them through the process of divorce and to ensure help and training for 'displaced home-makers'. Such special support groups would be welcomed in Britain too. Women in middle age have a greatly reduced likelihood of remarriage and their chances of getting a job with any sort of career ladder or pension are slim. The economic and social, not to say sexual, prospects of a fifty-year-old divorced woman who has been a housewife for twenty-five years can be grim.

Widowhood

Although currently less in the public eye than divorce, widowhood affects far more women. (In 1979, 2.6 per cent of women in England and Wales were divorced and not remarried, while 11.5 per cent were widows.) Still more will be affected in the future. The proportion of the total population over retirement age has been rising throughout the century. A boy born in 1901 had a life expectancy of 48 and a girl, 52; those born in 1977 could expect to live to nearly 70 and 76 respectively. Since women generally marry men older than they are themselves, three times as many women as men experience the grief of losing a spouse and adjusting to living on alone. The majority of elderly men (i.e. over 65) live with their wives (73 per cent) but this is true for only a minority of elderly women (36 per cent).

In the seventeenth century, women often experienced widowhood in their thirties and forties, and some could take over management of their husband's estate or business while raising their children. Those with property found themselves sought-after marriage partners for younger non-inheriting men – though many had to depend on charity.

Today, by contrast, women usually experience widowhood in late middle or early old age rather than in early middle age, and they generally no longer have young children when they are bereaved. Improved health care ensures that most widows are still able-bodied and can expect to live on for many years. However, they can seldom take on their husbands affairs, thanks to the separation of home and work and the development of non-family forms of property ownership, and if pension provisions are inadequate, they are likely to spend many years in poverty. They are also not likely to remarry, given the sex ratio in the relevant age groups and changed norms about proper age relations between husbands and wives.

Many widows feel the loss of closeness and affection keenly – as the journalist Mary Stott movingly described in her autobiography *Forgetting's No Excuse:*

> My own basic problem was not money or security or health, it was simply learning, after thirty years, to live alone. The practical things were a bit troublesome, but few were impossible. What was so hard was breaking the habit of having someone to talk to – about the day's papers, what went on at work, the meals, the garden, the state of the nation, anything that came to mind . . . It wasn't, with me, that there was really no one to talk to . . . there was no one I could talk to as of right. When you are suddenly bereft of your 'speech-friend' (as William Morris called it) you fear that by engaging in conversation with anyone else you are asking a favour . . . I began to have some insight into loneliness, the creeping paralysis of the social responses. All those letters from widows spelling out for me their sense of isolation, of being excluded from society, made me well aware of what the poor beggars were clutching at, and that I too might clutch too hard, might expect too much of my friends, might strain their kindness . . .

She says she went through various phases after her husband's death – numbness and just getting through the days, energy on behalf of the Three Million other widows in this country but also personal loneliness, pointlessness and half hopes of death, to a slow return after two years to laughter, and the establishment of a new life.

> . . . A person began to emerge who might not have been able, or wished, to emerge had our joint life continued . . . I owed my partner so much that it was no conscious sacrifice to refrain from any action, any writing, that would even fractionally embarrass, hurt or damage him. But now I am alone I am free. Sometimes I am very lonely, and more painfully so when there is some small triumph or success and no one to rejoice with me, than in trouble or disappointment. But freedom has its compensations – freedom to come and go; freedom to do the things one refrained from before; freedom to explore new

patterns of life; freedom, if one has a mind to it, to become an elderly eccentric. (Stott, 1973, Chapter 11).

Mary Stott experienced in marriage 'an integrated life with another human being', someone to live with, to talk to 'as of right', who made her feel a whole person. Whatever its constraints, and whatever the new lease of life she has now, she would have wanted this partnership to continue. Hers was undoubtedly a 'good marriage'. But she was traumatized by its loss. So is it a good idea to have a social structure that encourages people to put all their (emotional) eggs in one basket? She has good and bad things to report about finally living on her own, but perhaps gives too little recognition to the fact that it is the massiveness of the marital majority, and the closed nature of couple relationships, that create many of the problems for those who are not half of a pair: for those who are, as she feels it, 'less than half a person'.

Perhaps it is the presumption that everything from portions in supermarkets to incomes adequate to purchase homes come in couples and that those on their own are not only alone but lonely that produces problems for single people. It is the presumption that each household will have a full-time housewife and a breadwinner that justifies school hours being out of step with employment hours, and 'pin money' wages for all women and a 'family wage' for all men. Part of the answer to the question of why women marry is therefore that alternatives are not without their problems and are certainly represented as more unattractive than they are sometimes found to be. The other part is that many women find much happiness, and their adult status, as wives.

Rethinking motherhood: childcare

In previous sections, we have examined the ways in which relations between husbands and wives are organized and experienced. In this section, we turn to a discussion of parents and children, concentrating on motherhood, but also looking, briefly, at fatherhood.

The presumption that it is women who should be charged with childrearing, that they are 'naturally' suited to raising children, is one that has received much critical attention from feminist writers. Several have used the phrase 'the myth of motherhood' to challenge the assumption that there is a biological connection between gestation, childbirth and breastfeeding, and the care of children for the rest of their dependent years. Oakley (1976) argues that this myth basically revolves around three inter-related assumptions:

(i)   that children need their mothers;
(ii)   that all women need to be mothers (especially to give birth);
(iii) that mothers need their children;

All these assertions are dubious. Children develop quite 'normally' without the *constant* presence and undivided attention of *a* (biological or permanent single substitute) mother. Children need stability and good care from a few adults, but they positively benefit from nursery experience and a contented (possibly 'working' provided she is not overworked) mother (see Rutter, 1972; Hoffman, 1974). Many women lead fulfilled lives without having given birth (even in a culture which depicts them as barren and unfeminine), and many manage to have abortions or to 'give away' their babies without dire after-effects.

It must be stressed that when feminists say motherhood is not natural but rather is socially constructed, they are not attacking mothering, but the requirement that all women be mothers and the circumstances under which one becomes a mother in our society. It is the idea that women should be mothers, that 'good' mothering is partly measured by the number of hours a woman spends with her children as well as by the quality of mothering in the time they are together, and the social organization and consequences of motherhood in our society that are being challenged. In fact, some feminist writers would argue that to devalue motherhood itself would be an extremely dangerous thing to do, and could have 'potentially disastrous effects on the status of women in a society where their position is tied to their childbearing function' (Russo, 1976, p.148).

Over the last one hundred and fifty years, many changes have taken place in the position of children in society. Childhood has become more and more a separate, protected phase in the lifecycle. This has had great effects on women's lives.

Children were excluded by law from full-time employment in many occupations in the 1840s, and progressively from other full-time and then part-time, and even casual employment in this century. Thus even in the poorer sections of the working classes, children are now financially dependent on their parents until their mid-teens, and sometimes later.

From the early nineteenth century, the middle classes increasingly separated their children from adult life – ostensibly to preserve the children's innocence, and this later spread to other social classes. Where possible, children lived in separate parts of the house (nurseries), were looked after by special servants, and occupied with special games and activities, wearing special clothes, and protected from participation in, or even knowledge about, such areas of life as gambling, drinking and sex. From the 1870s it was compulsory for children to attend school, or to be educated at home by governesses – until 11 or 12, then 14, and now 16 years of age. Some stay on in education until their late teens or twenties.

As a consequence of this extension of childhood, although women may have fewer children than in the past, their time as a mother in fact extends over as long (or longer) a time-span, and the quality of care they are expected to give during that time has also risen. During some or all of the time when they have dependent children women will probably also be in employment, since most households nowadays need two incomes to maintain an adequate standard of living. Women may also find themselves asked or expected to help with caring for grandchildren.

For all women, whether or not they do eventually have children of their own, the probability of giving birth and bringing up children is part of their lives from early childhood and is a central focus of their socialization experiences. The types of toys that young girls are given, the household tasks they are trained to carry out, the lessons they learn at school, and the sorts of occupation they are encouraged to enter, are all geared towards preparing them for an adult life as wives, housekeepers and especially mothers.

This idea is so central to the socialization process, to the way in which women see themselves, and to the generalized view of women in our society, that women who do not have their own children or who do not enjoy motherhooid are viewed as odd or abnormal. Women who are unable to bear children often see themselves as failures; and women who make a conscious decision to remain childless, especially if they are married, are often seen as peculiar, unfeminine, selfish, or just plain awkward. Married childless women are forced into a position of constantly having to explain or justify their situation to all and sundry: to their own family circle, work colleagues, the church, the Family Planning clinic, etc. In contrast, the decision to have a child is rarely questioned: it is seen as 'natural'. One writer has called the process by which motherhood is seen as women's *raison d'etre* the 'motherhood mandate' (Russo, 1976).

However, the female role and identity is not defined solely in terms of motherhood, but in terms of *marriage and motherhood*. A woman who conceives, gives birth to and raises children outside marriage is also seen as deviant, though perhaps less so nowadays than for the last hundred years and not equally in all ethnic groups or all parts of the country. Nevertheless, motherhood and 'marriage' still go together like the proverbial horse and carriage, and a woman's reproductive capabilities are especially closely linked to her sexual identity within a heterosexual relationship. The married mother is a woman whose virtues have been extolled over the centuries, the respectable and acceptable image of woman in middle life. This image has been supported by various ideologies, often drawing on biology as their basis, and we shall look at these shortly.

Since the late 1960s, however, the position of women as mothers has been the subject of critical debate by many feminist writers, at least in part because these writers were trying to come to terms with their own reproductive capabilities: with their desires to have children or to remain childless; or their involuntary childlessness or unwanted pregnancy. They wished to under-stand how having children affected their identity and situation as women, and to improve their opportunities for equal access to education and employment if they had children or dependent kin without causing them damage. They wanted, in many cases, to have the same right as men *not* to make choices. In addition, they were convinced that knowledge of the *reality* of the experience of pregnancy and motherhood had to be shared – that the soft-focused advertisement and the Madonna image should be challenged.

Micheline Wandor for instance contributed to a book called *Why Children* (Dowrick and Grundberg (eds), 1980) in which eighteen women discussed how they had reached decisions to have or not to have children. She said she felt she had married and had two children because

> in the face of a cold and hostile world of work, love, marriage, building home and family were exciting and potentially fulfilling prospects.

But she felt that the effect has been that

I went from one family to another – with only the three years of university in between. I wish I could have avoided that. Compared to many other women (and compared to almost all men) I missed out on those vital few years of coping with an adult life among adults, earning my living as a non-mother. Since I didn't start earning and writing seriously until I was nearly thirty, I reckon I have lost about eight years. It's no good being told that the experiences I have had 'compensate' for those years. Of course at some level my life and work now must be affected by the insights and experiences I had during that time – but it is very hard to work out what the real relationship is. Motherhood is so intense and *private*, so individually experienced, so extraordinary, that I have no real grasp of how it affects the rest of my view of the world – except at occasional moments when symptoms erupt: I get impatient at the 'childish' way a friend is behaving and 'tell her off', or someone sneezes and I offer them a tissue from the store of things I keep in my bag 'just in case'. During the years when my children were small, my handbags seemed to get bigger and bigger.

However, despite my 'lost' years, I have never once wished I had not had my children. To wish that would be like wishing they were not alive, and that carries the weight of a kind of blasphemy. I have very often wished I could have suspended their material beings, magically rolled them up and carried them in my head, whole and complex as they concretely are – and then given re-birth to them six or seven years later than I actually did. That way I could have had the best of both words – had my work and my children, and we would all have lived happily ever after . . . I forgot: happily ever after is a BF (before feminism) concept.

The American poet, Adrienne Rich, in explaining why she wrote her book *Of Woman Born*, said:

I only knew that I had lived through something which was considered central to the lives of women, fulfilling even in its sorrows, a key to the meaning of life; and that I could remember little except anxiety, physical weariness, anger, self-blame, boredom, and division within myself: a division made more acute by the moments of passionate love, delight in my children's spirited bodies and minds, amazement at how they went on loving me in spite of my failures to love them wholly and selflessly. (Rich, 1977, p.15).

Such authors contest the image of mothers as calm and serene, giving unconditional, continual, selfless love. Nor do they accept the way in which mothers are always held responsible for their children's ills and suffering. They suggest any problem could equally be due to the child's personality in interaction with the mother's, or be caused by poverty or other problems quite outside the woman's control. In addition they refuse to accept motherhood as the overt sign of femininity, as constituting the fulfillment of adult womanhood.

Both Rich and Wandor stress the many positive aspects to being a mother. Rich found the physical pleasure of holding and feeding her children, the beauty of a young child's body, the heightened sensitivity of bearing her first child and the learning of new skills such as patience immensely rewarding, and Wandor talks about the pleasures of sharing experiences and doing things with her adolescent sons, and the support they give her when she's low. But they also both found they experienced other, negative feelings – exhaustion and the sense of years slipping away; conflict between their own needs and those of their children; a feeling of having no identity outside motherhood; resentment at the lack of contact with other adults and being unable to continue work they enjoyed alongside motherhood; and guilt at feeling less than totally satisfied with their lot. Rich suggests that such negative feelings are exacerbated by the isolation of mothering from other areas of life and of mothers from each other, each bringing up their children in separate homes, with little opportunity to share their experiences honestly.

Rich argues that the relationships between a mother and child, which should be a source and experience of love, is mutilated and manipulated. This results from motherhood being an 'institution' in which women's reproductive powers are regulated by men via the legal and technical control of contraception, fertility, abortion, obstectrics, gynaecology and paediatrics. That is to say, she holds a *biologically essentialist* position. She believes that biology, and specifically the ability to give birth, has endowed women with a particular nature, which she sees as having been alienated from women by a male-dominated society. Male control limits the potential of female biology so that it is not experienced by women as a resource or as a source of female power.

Rich suggests this happens because men are envious of women's reproductive capacities and want to keep these under control. When women attempt to assume control over reproduction, they are defined as deviant – for instance, when they bear an illegitimate child, have an abortion, or use artificial insemination.

She suggests motherhood as currently institutionalized allows only certain views and expectations – it demands instinct rather than intelligence, selflessness rather than self-realization, an unquestioning attitude from women. It thus under-employs female consciousness and reduces the potential of women's experience of motherhood. One of the aims of feminism should, she believes, be to help women to get back in touch with their biological potential by promoting a re-evaluation of femininity and female biology as equal to masculinity and male biology.

This is but one variant of a number of views which suggest that the 'underlying biology' of motherhood (or women's nature more generally) has been 'deformed', 'mismanaged', or 'devalued' by society. Rich sees male advantage as the root of this warping and devaluation, whereas others see it as the product of 'an immature, acquisitive and materialistic society' which has got its values out of balance – masculine characteristics like aggression being given much more weight than feminine caring ones (Mia Kellmer Pringle, 1980, p.5).

We cannot accept explanations based on 'inherent' masculine/feminine characteristics and universal values, because the anthropological and historical evidence shows just how varied the relationships between the sexes and generations can be. Nor can we support the idea of 'underlying biology' distorted by society, because we believe biology, environment and behaviour are in constant and continual interaction – one is not a modification of the constant base provided by the other. However we would want to retain from Rich's account her stress on the significance to women of their experience in pregnancy and breastfeeding as important influences on how women perceive themselves, and would agree with her that the social relations which structure women's experience as mothers today are detrimental to mothers *and* children.

In this connection, it is perhaps salutary to reverse the usual phrasing of the question and ask not only how and why women come to mother, but how and why men do not. This makes clear that what is at issue is not just 'nature' or socialization experiences, but social control and power. 'Men (as a group) don't rear children because they don't *want* to rear children' (Polatnick, 1973, p.60). By relegating childcare to women, men are free to engage in activities outside the home that carry more power and status. Because parenting is an enormously demanding, time-consuming and unpaid occupation outside the world of public power, it accrues lower status, less power and less control of resources.

The conditions of childcare in the home
Despite sentimental songs about 'Mother' and the idealized image of mother-and-child, motherhood is generally paid only lip-service: it is not given practical consideration or value. The actual conditions under which parents raise their children make it difficult, if not impossible, for mothers to achieve the ideal of the serene and competent mother figure, or even to feel generally happy and in control.

One reason for this is because childcare is often exhausting and time-consuming, and the demands of a child to be given help with homework or to be taken to the park may conflict with women's other responsibilities, or leisure, e.g. the need to do the washing or peel the potatoes, or to sit down and relax. Table 3 comes from Ann Oakley's study of forty London housewives, all of whom had at least one child under five, and shows the number of hours per week spent in housework, depending on the number of children in the family.

Table 3 Weekly* housework hours and number of children. (Source, Oakley, 1974, p.93)

| Number of children | Weekly hours spent in housework | | | | | | | |
	40–49	50–59	60–69	70–79	80–89	90–99	100+	Total
One	1	2	5	5	1	1	1	16
Two	0	1	1	5	4	0	1	12
Three or more	0	0	0	2	8	2	0	12
Total number of women	1	3	6	12	13	3	2	40

*'Weekly' means a seven-day week.

Secondly, the design of housing, in tower blocks or on large housing estates for instance, and its distance from play areas, doctors' surgeries, schools and shops also creates far from ideal 'working conditions' for mothers. Steps, curbs and busy roads can make going out a real problem if there is a pram or pushchair to negotiate up and down. Shops and other buildings will often not allow a pushchair inside and children's clothing and toy departments seem rarely to be on the ground floor. Despite the assertion of the joys of childhood, children are welcome almost nowhere, and in some places, such as pubs, actively prohibited. A woman breastfeeding her child in public is usually taboo and it is difficult for a father to attend to his baby – there are very rarely changing rooms in men's loos, for instance. Shops and doctors' surgeries do not provide crèches and yet people look askance at children who are tempted by brightly coloured packets of sweets by the supermarket check-outs, or who refuse to sit still during a lengthy wait.

Thirdly, children impose strains on family finances, especially when there is only one earning parent and/or a single parent. Expenses occur when there is a new baby, when there are clothes, feeding equipment, and a pram to be bought from scratch – and the maternity grant of £25 has remained at that level since 1969 (with inflation, this meant that in 1980 its relative worth was £6.29); and when food, clothes, shoes, and school uniform have to be bought for fast-growing children, and money found for school outings, babysitters' fees, dinner money, pocket money, holidays, etc. One researcher found that the strains on the family budget are particularly great when there are teenagers, who cost even more to keep than adults (Wynn, 1970). But the main cost, of course, is the earnings foregone when a caretaker has to drop out of full-time employment, leading to many working-class families sinking below the poverty line.

Campaigners like the Child Poverty Action Group have long argued for an increase in Family Allowance that would *begin* to distribute the cost of raising the next generation among the population as a whole, instead of it resting substantially on those who have children, but they have had relatively little success. They are often faced with the rather punitive attitude that 'if people choose to have children, they must face the costs'. The same response greets those who try to establish creches at workplaces, leisure centres, conferences and summer schools. What is expressed is not a desire to help parents, but rather one of making them pay, with money and time, for the pleasure of having children.

A final source of difficulty and feelings of lack of control for mothers can come, paradoxically, from the childcare professionals who seek to advise and support them. The assumption that bearing and rearing children comes naturally to women makes many new mothers feel anxious when they in fact find it difficult and worrying at times. Doctors, health visitors etc. to whom they turn for much needed advice often do not give the answers the mothers seek, but rather answers to the questions the professionals think the mothers should be asking. They tell mothers what they think they should do, disregarding the mothers' opinions. They may also blame a mother, suggesting she does not love her child, if she does not do what they say even if there good reasons why she does not (e.g. it conflicts with other goals of family life, or makes too big a demand on limited resources).

Father and children

The bulk of feminist work on parenthood has been about women/mothers, but there has been by no means complete silence about men and their role as fathers. Over the last decade or so, and concurrent with the growth of the Women's Liberation Movement, there has also been a growth in the number of popular childcare books that discuss fathers, in research on men's experience of pregnancy and children, and in organizations concerned with fathers' rights to children after divorce. There have also been moves to give fathers of illegitimate children rights of legal custody and access, and concern with sexual abuse of children by fathers.

We noted above that the move towards companionate marriage is thought to have resulted in a greater participation by men in the family and especially involvement with their children, and vice-versa (men seen helping with the children is taken as evidence of egalitarian marriage). Yet when we look at what involvement and 'helping' actually mean in practice, we find that by no means all childcare tasks are shared equally by men and women, either in terms of time spent, or the actual tasks performed.

In companionate marriage, engagement in paid employment to provide material resources for their children is still the central aspect of the male parenting role, but there is less concern with having children to provide heirs to inherit property, or to be workers in a family firm, to give care in old age, or as proof of virility. Fathers are now more concerned with children as valued objects, beings to enjoy and help develop as individuals. Hence the new fatherhood has a focus on forming pleasurable personal relations with children. This has ambivalent effects on women.

In a study of forty families, first reported in 'Are husbands good housewives?', Ann Oakley (1972) found that fathers participated only in certain aspects of childcare:

> . . . these men seem to avoid all but the sheerly pleasurable aspects of childcare. The physical side like the bulk of the housework is, in most cases, avoided . . .

And she went on to say,

> . . . this enlargement of the father's role is an unfortunate one for women who stand to gain nothing from it but temporary peace to do household chores . . . while they themselves stand to lose some of the very rewards child-rearing has to offer.

Furthermore men still have the choice of 'opting out' (Holly, 1982). Fathers are more likely to see parenting as something you *can do* (and therefore don't necessarily, or always, *have* to do), whereas mothers see being a parent as someone you *are*. Fathering is experienced as a matter of choice, mothering is part of the self.

Altering the sexual division of labour and power *within* the family can thus actually be disadvantageous to women when the gender-related power relations *outside* the family remain unchanged. Women have so little power outside, and shared parenting can have the result of removing what little power they have as primary parents. The activities with children that produce most emotional satisfaction are taken over by fathers, leaving women only the tedious and routine activities and responsibility. Under the guise of equality and liberation, the broadening of the dimensions of fathers' roles can have subtle, but serious, consequences for women.

For instance, men are increasingly seeking custody of their children on divorce, and there are various organizations, such as the Campaign for Justice on Divorce, and Families Need Fathers which argue that the law is tipped too much towards women. They claim there should be a clean financial break and that either parent should have an equal right to children when marriages split up.[8]

However, as we stressed earlier, the fact that it is generally men who pay 'maintenance' to women after divorce is because it is generally women who give up employment to care for children, and men who earn more. Men's rights to employment *and* children only become an issue at divorce, whereas women routinely have to make a choice or exhaust themselves trying to have both. While family law still sustains overall a patriarchal family system (Brophy and Smart, 1981), it would be unjust to take away such legal rights and customary preferential practice as mothers now receive, so as to share them equally with men, when women have so little power elsewhere.

Concern to extend the parameters of fathers' rights is often disguised by claims about the 'best interests of the child'. This is particularly evident in the discussions about the rights of illegitimate children that took place during the late 1970s. The Law Commission's Working Paper (1979) on illegitimacy overtly sought to abolish the stigma of illegitimacy and to give illegitimate children the same rights as legitimate ones.[9] But in fact the main concern was with the rights of men. As the Rights of Women Illegitimacy Campaign Group points out, the aim of the Working Paper – giving men automatic rights of custody, access and guardianship to the child born of a woman with whom they have had sexual intercourse – actually means extending fathers' rights, and hence men's control, over women they had never married (ROW, 1979, p.2).

When men share custody of children or have rights of access to them, they have a legal right to know, and can control, where the mother lives, and can monitor and take issue with many aspects of her day-to-day life, including her sexual behaviour. This is particularly difficult for her if she left her husband or boyfriend because of his violence. She cannot keep her whereabouts secret, and has actually to meet the man who has attacked her and/or to hand over her child as a 'hostage' to him at regular intervals.

There is also cause for certain caution in regard to fathers' relationships with children, particularly their daughters, given the rates of child sexual abuse which are now being brought to light.

It is impossible, of course, to know the true incidence of this, the best-kept of family secrets, because, like rape, it is a greatly under-reported and hidden crime. Some studies suggest, however, that it is more common than other physical abuses of children, and USA surveys suggest that one woman in four is abused, once or repeatedly over months and years, before the age of eighteen, by some male adult in a position of trust or authority over her (by a father, stepfather, uncle, mother's lover, older brother, lodger, a friend's father, teacher, local shop keeper etc.). One in ten women is abused by a man in her immediate family – generally her father.

Feminists prefer to speak of child abuse rather than incest, since the latter can refer to the sexual activity of consenting adults, whereas what they see as at issue is the abuse – ranging from indecent exposure through masturbation to rape – of children, overwhelmingly female children, by adults, almost exclusively male adults. The cases which get into the papers are accounts of violent assaults by strangers, not girls' fears of Uncle or Daddy or the man next door.

> The stereotype of the child molester is that of a perverted, insecure, possibly alcoholic, over-sexed or under-sexed, emotionally deprived, possibly homo-sexual male with 'poor impulse control'. It is also suggested that sexual abuse occurs only in poor and over-crowded families. Research and our own experience at the London Rape Crisis Centre, however, have shown us that, on the contrary, most sexual abuse of children, whether on boys or girls, is committed by heterosexual males with 'normal' personalities who come from all races and classes.
>
> The nature of male power in families means that there is always a possibility of sexual abuse on any child because men and society regard families as places in which men do what they choose. Abusers see "their" women and children as belonging to them – not primarily as individuals with feelings and needs and rights but there to service/fulfil their emotional, sexual and domestic needs. The girls it happens to are not any different to those who are not abused – rather some of us escape because the men who are our fathers/guardians/friends choose not to abuse their power. (Hamblin and Bowen, 1981, pp.148-9).

The literature on the subject often makes every attempt to explain and excuse the behaviour of the male offender by blaming it on the victim, or the mothers and wives of the offenders. The effects of sexual abuse, particularly on female victims, are usually minimized. However, as one woman wrote anonymously in response to a request for information:

> It happened to me as a child and nobody knows what hell I went through because nobody cared but it has ruined me. Nobody knows, I'd no one to turn to. It has ruined my marriage. I'll never get it off my mind. Nobody knows what I went through. (Quoted in Jeffreys, 1982, p.59).

Single parents and lesbian mothers
The fact that having children within marriage is seen as the only acceptable way has consequences for both women and men who raise their children on their own.

As a result of widowhood and increases in divorce, separation and illegitimacy, in 1971 there were 570,000, and in 1980 920,000 one-parent families in Britain, accounting for approximately one in eight families. Most of these families are headed by women (eight women to every man), and on average three-quarters live as separate households – though this ranges from

88 per cent of widows to only 48 per cent of unmarried mothers (who often move back or continue to live with their own parents in three-generational households). They are most frequent in central districts of large towns and low in the suburbs, frequent among Afro-Caribbeans and low among Chinese and Asians.

Most of the concern arising from the increase in single-parent families has centred around the possible emotional damage suffered by children outside the intact two-parent family, especially when this situation has arisen from divorce. There is no doubt that warring parents can have traumatic effects on the children involved at the time (but this can occur not only if they divorce but also in 'normal' family life). However, the evidence on long-term effects of family tension and divorce is far from conclusive, especially as much of the research in this area has not controlled for other factors.

Adjustment to the loss of one parent is certainly difficult but studies by the National Children's Bureau have shown there is no evidence that there will necessarily be long-term effects on children's social and emotional behaviour or academic achievement (Ferri and Robinson, 1976). Rather, it is the low incomes, poor housing, etc., of single-parent families, especially women-headed families, that create difficulties. A further, not often remarked factor, is that many single mothers have the additional burden of a child with a disability. The birth of a handicapped child is often the event that 'sparks off' the breakdown of a marriage and it is usually the father who leaves (Hunt, 1973).

If we consider the income of 'motherless' and 'fatherless' families, the most obvious difference is the dependence of the latter on State benefits rather than parental earnings. In part this is because it is more difficult for lone fathers to get state benefits to remain at home. Pressures are also put on fathers to

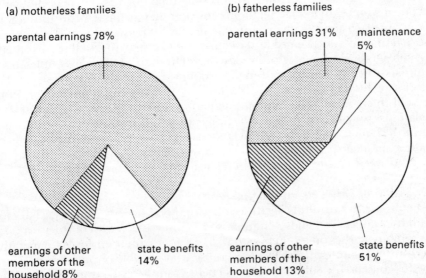

(a) motherless families

parental earnings 78%

earnings of other members of the household 8%

state benefits 14%

(b) fatherless families

parental earnings 31% maintenance 5%

earnings of other members of the household 13%

state benefits 51%

Figure 1 Sources of income in single-parent families.

continue in employment. But it is also because it is difficult for lone mothers *not* to rely on benefits. If they take paid work, they generally get low wages. A lone mother is often faced with the invidious choice of either raising her children at the low standard of living provided through the Supplementary Benefits system, or seeing very little of her children because she has to work long hours to achieve a reasonable wage. However, if she does rely on State benefits, she will lose benefit in her own right if she begins to cohabit, which will hinder the possibility of her forming a new heterosexual relationship. These factors impose real constraints on the control of her life and that of her children.

Lone fathers often face problems in finding support from the neighbourhood; for example, it takes a lot of courage for a father to attend a 'mother' and toddler club. O'Brien (1980) describes the feelings of marginality and stigma encountered by lone fathers in dealing with outside agencies. She cites, for example, the case of one lone father who, although he had looked after his son single-handed for over two years, still found that teachers phoned his ex-wife first if there were any problems at school. Another difference is that men, even more than women, find problems in taking time off employment when a child is sick, or to visit the school on sports day. On the other hand, lone fathers usually find it easier to obtain full-time nursery places as it is assumed that they will be in full-time employment. Indeed it is also assumed that men *should* work full-time, and they may find themselves regarded as work-shy if they give employment up to care for their children.

The rise in the number of children born outside marriage who are kept by their mothers indicates that some women are now *choosing* to have children on their own, exercising this choice either before conception or afterwards. There is one group of women in particular for whom this choice represents a very significant step forward in forming their identity, that is, lesbians. Women who begin lesbian relationships after they are married are unlikely to be granted custody of their children if they subsequently divorce as their sexual practices are deemed by the courts to make them unsuitable as mothers. So some lesbian women who decide to have children, alone or in couples, have turned to artificial insemination, from donor sperm, either administered by a doctor or by themselves. This is a means of separating reproduction from sexual intercourse, or becoming pregnant without having to form a sexual relationship with a man, and deliberately preventing any man from knowing he is the father. Such a choice can be seen as a very explicit political statement of lesbian identity and represents for those concerned a real alternative to the conventional family situation (see Hanscombe and Forster, 1982).

Provision of childcare outside the home
The problems of finding facilities offering good quality care, especially for children under five, and even more so for those under two or three, impose enormous stresses on mothers who wish, or more commonly need financially, to continue employment. But even those who are able or prepared to take a period out of the labour market benefit from a break from the constant demands of young children. Significantly, even the parents of handicapped

children get little help, and cannot claim Attendance Allowance (i.e. state benefits to help offset the costs of getting someone in to help take care of a child which needs 24-hour supervision) until the child is two years old.

Most concern has been expressed about the provision of facilities for pre-school children (i.e. under fives)[10], and a distinction is drawn here between 'care' and 'education'. Care facilities may be provided privately (employers' nurseries, childminders), by voluntary groups (e.g. playgroups), or by Social Services Departments. Education facilities are provided almost entirely by local Education authorities. There is far less full-day than part-time care, and less full-time than part-time nursery and primary school provision. It is estimated that around 60 per cent of under-fives receive no provision of any type whatever.

To understand the variation in provision, we need to look at the reason for providing, or not providing, the different facilities. Essentially, most childcare experts and government departments agree that some, limited, part-time provision is beneficial to a child, especially if it is *educational* (as in nursery schools) or contains a play element and involves mothers in its organization (which is the philosophy behind playgroups). However, full-day *care* is frowned upon, thought to be potentially harmful to children and to weaken maternal responsibility – the 'best' source of pre-school childcare is thought to be mothers. Thus, local authority day-nursery places are currently reserved only for children in 'special need' or 'at risk', though when mothers' labour has been required on a large scale, such as during the Second World War, nurseries have been made available on a much wider scale. Childminders provide care in a familial setting which is more acceptable than an institutional environment, even though the quality of care is hard to monitor and has been the subject of much concern (e.g. Petrie and Mayall, 1977).

It is worth noting that the official statistics do not cover all pre-school provision. Many children are, in fact, cared for privately, in their own or someone else's home, usually by relatives or by nannies, au pairs and unregistered childminders. In addition, some government statistics actually exclude children in households containing more than one family with children under five, which may be another situation where care is provided by others than the mother – a viable, alternative living arrangement for some people.

Several studies have shown that the extent of provision falls far short of demand. One study, carried out by Margaret Bone for the Office of Population Censuses and Surveys in 1974, demonstrated that some form of nursery place was wanted for 90 per cent of three- and four-year-olds, and for 46 per cent of children under three. Such research has also shown that women from ethnic minority and lower income groups find the most difficulty in obtaining satisfactory care, work at the Thomas Coram Research Centre found, for example, a much higher turnover of childminders among these groups.

Even when the children are at school, the problems continue. The hours between the end of a school day and the end of a full-time working day, school holidays, and days when a child is ill, all have to be covered, presenting different problems but ones that are just as intractable as finding care for children under five. Furthermore, all the health and advisory services to which parents need access operate on the assumption that mothers are not employed, even though nearly half of them are, and are open only during the day.

The lack of facilities restricts the amount of choice available to women with children, which in turn affects the way they organize their family life and its quality. For example, the low self-esteem and a loss of sense of adult identity, often resulting in depression, which can occur with full-time confinement in the home, often comes when children compel this confinement. The depression in turn affects the quality of all the internal relationships within the family. The debates around the supposed ill effects of maternal employment on children nearly always fail to give attention to the problems that can arise from full-time mothering within the (supposedly ideal) nuclear family, as well as ignoring the positive benefits that employment can give to the women themselves.

Not having children

Married women, especially, face an expectation that they will have children – to make their family a 'real' one, and to give their lives meaning. This view is a powerful one, sanctified in the Church's view that one of the purposes of marriage is procreation, and in the psychoanalytic argument that this is the way women make sense of their bodies. More practically, it is presented constantly by, for instance, marriage manuals and women's magazines, as the natural outcome of a loving, successful relationship.

Because of this presumption that having children brings women their greatest fulfilment, and completes a marriage, many women who are unable to bear children experience a deep sense of personal failure and a feeling that they have let down their husbands, and their own parents. In 'the misery of an infertile marriage', Juliet Miller recognized the source of her feelings as being societal expectations, but this does not lessen the strength of her experience.

> I am thirty-one, married and childless. For three-and-a-half years we have been trying to start a family. We have done the rounds of infertility clinics, doctors and hospitals, and suffered the indignities of cold showers, temperature charts and endless examinations. It now seems most unlikely that we shall succeed in our desire. As I attempt to face this fact I am beginning to look back on a period marked solely by an obsessive drive towards motherhood and to question my own and society's attitude to infertility . . .
>
> I can now see that what has made the last few years so difficult is that I accepted, along with society, that childlessness within marriage is not only abnormal but socially unacceptable . . .
>
> During the last three years I have sometimes longed to be told that I could never have a child. Not because this is what I want, but because accepting the fact would allow me to live again. Yet hospital, family and friends conspire to protect me against this. They see my attempts at acceptance as 'giving up'. Whereas I see it as the only possible step towards the future. (Miller, 1979, pp. 159–60).

The aspect of childlessness that is most often ignored is the grief experienced because of the loss of a baby during a woman's pregnancy. Although stillbirth, perinatal death or the loss of an older child is recognized as a traumatic and devastating experience, spontaneous miscarriage and ectopic pregnancy[11] are seldom seen as also causing grief for the women involved. The fact that miscarriage most frequently occurs in the early weeks, when pregnancy does not show and may not have been made public, means that it is most often a private affair – many women who have miscarried are surprised to find how many other women they know have also aborted spontaneously. The grief and sense of bereavement is not given public legitimacy and most women have to come to terms with their loss privately with little support or understanding.

> I cried so much that I didn't think I had any more tears left. Even now, when I think about it, the tears want to come. I wasn't in very much physical pain, maybe it would have been better if I had been. Then I would have had something else to concentrate on besides that terrible feeling of emptiness sinking over me . . . I felt sorry for *me* when it came to it. One day I had a baby growing inside me and the next day I didn't . . . It's hard to describe the sense of devastation and loss I felt . . . *This* baby . . . was not to be. (Melba Wilson, in Dowrick and Grundberg, 1980, p.114)

For another group of women, not having children is a conscious choice, and yet not one arrived at easily but only after much soul-searching. Because of the power of the motherhood mandate, and the way in which social arrangements hinge on the family with children, it can be frightening and painful for a woman to think of herself as remaining childless. The decision means coming to terms with socialization experiences that stress that women who do not raise children are selfish and self-centred; it means facing the sadness of parents who will never have grandchildren; of seeing 'BARREN, EMPTY, in neon lights' (Shulman, 1979, p.7).

The decision to have, or not to have, children is not a once-off occasion; a decision to be childless made in the early twenties is not irreversible; once a woman has worked at her career, she may decide later on to have a child. Yet the possibility of deferring childbearing is not, for women, one that can be put off for ever. The decline in their fertility and the higher probability of conceiving a baby with Down's Syndrome, or incurring other pregnancy complications which increase with age are matters of very real concern after the age of 35, whereas men have few fears. (Little research has been done on the impact of fathers' age on the likelihood of handicap, infertility, etc. – the assumption is that the 'fault' is with the woman, not the man.)

Deciding not to have children does not mean that a woman necessarily wants nothing to do with other people's children, but the isolation of children within traditional nuclear families and parents' jealously guarded 'ownership' of their children, means that participating in childcare is not easy for the childless woman (Wallsgrove, 1985). Even women in communes and co-operatives have found it difficult to participate as fully as they would wish in the care of commune children, and they risk losing all contact if the mother moves away. For men, of course, it is even more difficult to find the opportunities to form relationships with children other than their own. Physical contact is especially taboo, particularly with older children.

But for some women, the choice to be childless is a necessary step towards confirming an identity that should be just as viable as the maternal one for those who want it. It represents, for them, the right to control and enjoy their own bodies and lives.

> I'm forty-four . . . I have no children. I'm not sure how, or when, or how many times, I made that choice. I do know now that the choice is irreversible unless I were willing to take some considerable risks, not all of them mine, and unless I were willing to become, with a great wrench, a very different person. But by now I also know that I wouldn't want a child, and never did, really. This realization is neither the result of hindsight nor sour grapes, but rather the result of working hard to untangle a particularly messy set of feelings. I am trying to be that anomalous creature, a woman who, just so, has never had a child. I choose, at last, to be who I am. Writing this is part of making that choice . . .
>
> I want to say, clearly and at last, that as far as I am concerned, children are the last thing we need be on about. I want to be with my peers, my friends, to try to think in new tracks, if we can find them, to do things I've never done, to imagine new worlds, to create durable bonds with no biological imperatives to cement them, to be a woman in unheard-of-ways, to play, goddamit, to learn to work together (the way we're going now, that alone is enough of a challenge to absorb the life of several generations) . . .
>
> The idea of having a child can be profoundly seductive, and treacherous. Along with all the accompanying mystifying clap-trap, it can lodge in our heads, in our imaginations, and take up a hell of a lot of psychic room. It can obscure the possibilities of other modes of generation, which we need far more . . . When in history have women belonged enitrely to themselves? What might we not come up with if all our conceptual and imaginative energies were directed at the challenge in front of us, the urgency of which no amount of having babies will change. (Shuman, 1979, pp.7, 23).

Whatever the personal reasons, the positive aspects of being childless or child-free (freedom, the ability to follow a career and explore other sorts of relationships) are too often ignored and the alternatives to motherhood derided.

Rethinking kinship: the care of the elderly

Close to one in five (20 per cent) of the population is now over retirement age–about 9½ million people (this proportion was 16 per cent in 1971, 9 per cent in 1931 and 6 per cent in 1901). In 1978, 58 per cent of people over 60 and 76 per cent of people over 85 were women. Thanks to better health and retirement while still fit, most elderly and retired people, and women in particular, are not, as they are sometimes presented, dependants and a drain on national resources, but rather givers of help to their families and the wider community. The Meals on Wheels service, for example, is run very largely by women over retirement age (Bristol study, cited by Land, 1981). Women are particularly important givers of time and special affection to grandchildren (and increasingly great-granchildren).[12]

But some elderly people do need a lot of care and we are still far from a situation where the welfare state has relieved families of responsibility for those who are no longer earning and/or who are infirm. Public provision is not adequate to allow older people to view retirement with security and pleasure – for quite a number of women there is no pension to rely on, and they are forced onto Supplementary Benefits which they see as 'charity'. Many children therefore wish to give financial help to their parents, and other relatives also help out.

However, not only has the age balance of the population shifted, but those elderly today were young adults at a time when marriage rates were low and family size dropping fast; some of their children were killed in the Second World War, or emigrated. Consequently, quite a number of this sizeable section of the population have no family – no spouse, brothers, sisters or children surviving or living nearby. (An average family size of four children over the generations gives an individual many more close relations than a family size of two, which is more common today.) And in other cases there is only one child to take full responsibility. So for society as a whole there is an increasing 'problem of the elderly'.

A whole series of studies have shown that, contrary to popular belief, younger people (and not only grown children but also neighbours) feel concern and responsibility for elderly people. They provide a great deal of domestic assistance and 'pop in to see them' regularly. There is certainly no evidence that where elderly people have kin, the kin – and especially the person's children – neglect the old people or seek to avoid responsibility and lightly put old people (or severely handicapped younger people) into institutions. A disproportionate number of those in residential accommodation are childless. Most old people see relatives weekly if not daily and their own children even more frequently – 83 per cent of parents over seventy-five are visited by their children at least once a week and receive a lot of help from them on bereavement.

Elderly people do not want the help they receive to take the form of living with their children while they are still able to care for themselves. They like to keep their own home, their own friends, their independence and privacy. They want to live near their relations and not segregated out in old people's homes.[13] Nor do they want to be cared for by younger people if this makes them a burden. Prior to cuts in public spending in the early 1980s, welfare provision for the elderly – pensions, housing, meals on wheels, domicilary nursing, home helps, and better general health – had made this preferred life-style possible for more and more women (and men). Their situation is rapidly worsening and their choices are reduced.

What most authors on old age note, but do not adequately stress, is that the bulk of the physical care given to old people is given not by their 'children', but by their *daughters* and *daughters-in-law*, and not by their 'neighbours' but by their *female* neighbours. Men often care for their wives if they become disabled; but care for the elderly, handicapped or sick otherwise falls to men only if there are no women whatsoever available. This care is sometimes as heavy a lead on women as childcare.

Audrey Hunt found, in a national study of home help provision, that one in five housewives[14] aged between thirty-five and forty-nine had a disabled person or someone over sixty-five in the household, and among those aged fifty to sixty-four, one in four had an elderly or infirm person present (1970, p.424). *Half of all housewives can expect to look after such a person at some time in middle life.* Not all these elderly people will be infirm, but many of them will be–or they would not have given up their own homes or sought help. In another study (1978), Hunt found that nearly one fifth of women who had given up paid employment between the ages of forty and fifty had done so to care for someone other than a husband–and this is likely to increase as more people live longer, and to fall on fewer and fewer shoulders (one daughter per family). Moroney (1976, reporting a national study in 1970) found that 36 per cent of the handicapped and 50 per cent of very handicapped elderly people were living with their children. Married women *also*, of course, are likely to have to care for their husbands (who are likely to get sick or frail first–as they are older, initially, and die younger).

The ideologies pertaining to women and motherhood can be seen in a broader sense here, as ideologies of caring. Women's roles in caring as mothers are extended to other forms of caring, as for the elderly, sick and handicapped. However, the prescriptive way in which these ideologies are put into practice–through definitions of 'good' or 'correct' mothering, and the monitoring of the quality of care by professionals–are not yet developed with respect to caring for the elderly, though medical social workers can exert great pressure on daughters to take elderly relatives out of hospital. This means that women probably have more freedom in determining exactly how they carry out their care of the elderly than their care of children, but it also means that care is even less recognized as a standard part of their lives.

The motherhood model of caring may not however be appropriate to tending for dependent adults because it produces tension in the relationship between the carer and cared for. Although some old people may be prepared to revert to infancy, others resent the loss of independence implied (Ungerson, 1983).

The traditional caring roles associated with women means that they are expected to provide much of the regular support and care needed by the elderly and chronically sick living in the community as well as in the family. Little account is taken of these women's needs, still less their wishes, for employment outside the home. And, of course, the comment about the proportion who give up jobs to give care should not lead us to forget that most women work *and* care; women are not absolved from domestic responsibility just because they are in the labour market–unlike men.

Rethinking kinship: daughters and sisters–friendship and support

In earlier sections we have briefly mentioned that, apart from the relatively short period of courtship and early marriage, many men and women spend most of their work, leisure and domestic lives in the company of their own sex. There are, in effect, in much of Britain, two worlds which rarely mingle, either at work, at leisure, *or even in the home.* For women, female relatives, neighbours and friends are important practical supporters and confidents. Even those with close joint marriages spend most of their days apart from their husbands and often with their 'sisters'.

Studies of kinship and local communities suggest that both middle-class and working-class people look to their kin, especially their parents/children, as their preferred sources of long-term reciprocal exchanges over the life cycle (help when they themselves have small children or when they need care in old age), and that such relationships are especially important and useful at times of crisis, when kin will travel long distances or go to great trouble to help one another. These researches also show that people keep in touch with their kin—again especially their parents, but also their grandparents and their own brothers and sisters—not only instrumentally and from a sense of obligation, but also sociably, for a sense of belonging, for assured moral support, and for companionship. These ties are especially important to women since they are more tied to the home and need more help in domestic work and domestic crises, and because the relatively few leisure activities outside the home participated in by women are generally attended with kin or a neighbour. Women seldom venture out alone: without husband, kin or neighbours they are stuck.

Most studies of kinship share with studies of marriage and parenthood, however, a stress on emotionality rather than work. Although recognizing that women play key roles in maintaining links—that they are 'pivotal kin'; that they are the ones who send out Christmas and birthday cards, who remember wedding anniversaries and who chivvy sons to 'come and see your father—he does enjoy it so', or who ask their husbands 'have you rung your mother?', who do the shopping for elderly neighbours or visit the sick - writers have not seen this as 'caring *work*'.

The expenditure of women's time and energy, both routinely and at moments of crisis, has been overlooked for the same reasons that homework has been overlooked. The importance of women in the community doing a variety of unpaid (domestic and voluntary) *labour* is only slowly becoming visible.

A second shortcoming of most studies of kinship has been that they rarely mention conflicts in such relationships. But the fact that people see quite a lot of, and help, their kin and neighbours does not mean there are not stresses and strains. Kin provide support and warmth, but they also place constraints and limitations upon individuals. Those who live in tightly knit circles, where people (and especially women) do not move far afield, and where everybody (and especially women) know everyone else's business and feel free to comment and criticize an individual if he or she steps outside a narrow range of acceptable behaviour, have to guard their behaviour.

Ann Whitehead, who lived in and studied a village in Herefordshire for some years, criticized the work of many past male researchers who, she felt, had been 'captured' by their male informants. They had accepted at face value the local men's hostile view of the 'secret world of mothers and daughters', which they saw as excluding men and united against them. Whitehead

suggests this occurred partly because men's and women's lives are so segregated that unless a research team studying a community includes both men and
women observers, they will only with great difficulty be able to collect information on women's lives. She herself found that women do *not* always side
together; indeed women as a group may constrain an individual woman's
behaviour or the behaviour of a younger age-group of women.

Thus mothers restrain their daughters and women restrain adolescent girls
generally. This is particularly marked among ethnic groups where the norms
of the immigrant generation are different from those of their British-born
daughters. Mothers do not always, indeed do not often, take their daughters'
side in disputes with their husbands. There is a strong rule about non-
interference in other couples' domestic affairs, which leads to even an
appearance of one-sidedness being quite counter-productive; and older
women will refuse to help younger ones towards even a limited degree of
freedom if they disapprove of their behaviour. They will not babysit if they
suspect the younger ones plan to go 'gallavanting' (i.e. out without their
husbands) or if they want to get a job so as to be economically independent.
This may appear punitive but Ann Whitehead says:

> It has been suggested to me that this does not have to be seen as the act of a
> woman who resents freedom which she does not have, but that the older women
> may be more aware of the quite serious consequences for women if they do not
> toe the line. That women cannot support themselves financially is only one
> aspect of a number of psychological and physical consequences (battered wives,
> the incidence of mental breakdown) which might lead to accommodating
> ideologies. (Whitehead, 1976, p.198)

The tensions, as well as the affections, experienced between mothers and
grown-up daughters, and between sisters, have recently been considered in
various books (e.g. Judith Arcana's *Our Mothers' Daughters*) as women have
sought to understand how their jealous competition for male approval, their
resentment of control (past and present) and the restrictions they have
mutually placed on each other – because of the structure of the family in
patriarchal society – has interfered with their desire to be close. Some women
hate their mothers as intensely as others love theirs. Most love *and* resent,
having a close but less than frank relationship.

Certainly much less social support is given to women's ties with female kin
than their ties with their husbands. A woman's primary obligation is to her
husband, then to her children, and only then to love and help her parents,
sisters and friends. Yet the latter ties often exist and can even undermine the
ideological primacy of the conjugal bond. Women's solidarity is a potential
source of strength, and is particularly important in the event of an unhappy
marriage, as Maila Stivens found when talking with women in a suburb of
Sydney, Australia.

> The women's main source of help, care and 'moral support' came from kin ties
> mediated by and through women, in spite of the prevailing ideological pressures
> against female solidarity. One instance of these pressures is the constant
> denigratory jokes about mother-in-law, usually the wife's mother. Doctors,
> psychologists, and other 'professionals' too, promote the idea that women who

retain strong ties with female kin like their mothers or sisters are dependent and infantile. (Stivens, 1978, p.161).

We have thus far suggested that kinship ties outside the nuclear family are important to women, but that accounts of these relationships have ignored the time and energy that women put into them and the conflicts that exist alongside the solidarity. A further point is that too often attachments and conflicts, when recognized, have been attributed to individual personality complementarity or differences rather than being seen as *structural*. And gender-structured differences in particular have been ignored. This applies overwhelmingly to *the* relationship in which conflict is anticipated: the one Maila Stivens mentioned above – the relationship with a mother-in-law.

Constant jokes establish an expectation that an individual's relationship with his or her mother-in-law is not going to be easy. When conflict does materialize, it is usually attributed to the older woman being impossible to deal with, being jealous and spiteful. Yet anthropologists studying other cultures have as one of their basic axions that accusations of witchcraft, for example, are not questions of 'personality' but, rather arise between people in particularly stressful *structural* relationships vis-à-vis one another; and that the working through of such accusations allows the resolution of the intolerable situation. It is easy to see structurally why there should be conflict of interest, and hence tensions, between families of origin and of marriage in our society. Though our culture lacks formal ways to work this situation through, seeing a mother-in-law as intolerable, spiteful, nosey or possessive, justifies severely curtailing contact, or breaking off the relationship altogether. The blame is thus placed, not on the structure of generations but on the older woman. In addition, since the jokes are about 'in-laws', the fact that the sources of strain are different between husband and wife's mother (where there is fear of female solidarity) and wife and husband's mother (where there is rivalry for the husband/son) gets glossed over.

Such gender differences in kin relationships have generally been ignored by sociologists; and feminists who might have pointed them out have generally ignored kinship relationships between women. In contrast, friendships between women were in a sense rediscovered by feminism. The line which runs 'I find other women so boring; I much prefer talking to men', and seeing women's company as distinctly second best – going out with a girl friend being what you do when you haven't a man to be with – has been strongly criticized within the Women's Liberation Movement as a key element in dividing women from one another. The virtues of being and working with other women, the mutual strength and pleasure this provides, and the absence of the tensions and power relations endemic to relations between men and women, have been extolled (if at times overstated), and feminist historians have begun to discover the intimate relationships between women in the past (Vicinus, 1985).

Conclusion

We said at the start that there were two central themes to this chapter: first, that the family is an area of ambivalence for women; and second, the question of whether the situation of women in the family has got better or worse in the last fifty years.

The material we have presented shows that women derive many positive and valued experiences from their relationships with their mothers and fathers, husbands, daughters and sons, sisters and brothers, and from the work they do in the home. On the other hand, these relationships and this work constrain and overwork women, and may at times (as with domestic violence and sexual abuse) be very unpleasant indeed.

Stepping back a bit from the family, we see also that the family is so important to women because they are restricted in their participation in *other* areas of life – in the public sphere. This public arena affords *men* many positive experiences (in sport, voluntary associations and politics, many hobbies, the pub and street life). The exclusion of women from the public sphere is both cause and effect of their restriction to the home and family and the fact that domestic and caring work is consigned to them.

The restrictions placed on women's lives by their role in the family, which we have suggested can be seen as constituting inequalities and power relations (subordination), have led to demands for change. We have looked at some of the changes that have actually already occurred, both those that are said to indicate the decline of the family and those less remarked but arguably more important to the situation of women. The former include increases in divorce, illegitimacy, single parenthood, and wives' employment. The latter include changes in the nature of housework, the decline of servants, the lengthening of the period of childhood and raised standards of childcare, the ageing of the population, the decrease in the birth rate, men's increased participation in relations with children, and the recognition of the existence of domestic violence. In each case we have tried to establish critically the extent of the change and how it affects women, recognizing that each change affects both the family as a unit and each family member differently.

We have also looked at changes that have been proposed for the family in the future, or that people have actually tried to effect in their lives – dual-career families, communes, single parenthood, lesbian couples. Society *as we know it* 'needs' the family, since the family is part of society as we know it. But the family can change and society can change, and perhaps it needs to, since the family today is far from perfect. However much people may try to look on the bright side, at romance, affection and sharing, the darker sides of the family – emotional manipulation, restriction, physical coercion, perfunctory sexual relations, women's subordination, the trauma of widowhood, the isolation of the single, and the stigma of homosexuality – are integral to it because it is based on power relations, exclusive bonds, and institutionalized heterosexuality.

We think it is clear, however, that change cannot come about swiftly and easily. Even those who most want change could not support a call to 'smash the family'. Given the overall disadvantaged position of women in the society, in the short and medium term women would be generally worse off without marriage. There have to be changes in women's obligations to do domestic work and childcare *and* in women's position in the labour market before women cease to need the protection of legal rights to share men's 'family wages'.

Part of the struggle for change must take place at the level of ideas, in challenging ideologies. This implies recognizing that knowledge about the family, like other areas of knowledge, is political. Those who see the family as in decline, those who see it as 'a modern success story', social reformers, feminists, and antifeminists, all argue a case. Each collects new data and presses new analyses to support the interpretation (understanding) of family relationships he or she considers valid, and in contradistinction to those perspectives and actions he or she considers to be wrong. Feminist accounts such as we have given much space to here, are *seen* as political because they challenge previously orthodox 'obvious' views, but other views are also value-laden. Feminist accounts of the family imply new ways of seeing things and call for the collection of information from a new perspective, women's perspective, with a view to changing things so that they can be better for women.

They also call for women to share their knowledge of the family, in all its multiplexity. For, as Jessie Bernard argued, it is not that women are powerless in marriage, it is not that they *never* make important decisions, never enjoy sex, always do the childcare; nor is it that 'keeping women in their place' has not always been a universal problem for men. It is, rather, that institutionalized patterns and internalized norms have given men superior power, especially within the family, and its privatized nature means that each women fights back, and generally loses, alone. Shared knowledge, shared actions and solidarity, are needed if things are not only to be improved, but also not to be allowed to get worse.

Notes

1 The Office of Population Censuses and Surveys enumerates the population every ten years by counting people *in their homes*. The forms record where everyone slept on a certain night and their relationships with the people who slept in the same building (with whom they share domestic life, and to whom they are related). For the Census:

a household is either one person living alone or a group of people (who may or may not be related) living at the same address and sharing their housekeeping, i.e. eating most meals together.

a family is defined by the existence of marriage and/or parent-child relationships.

Thus, for the Census enumerator, if three generations live together, or if the wife's sister lives in, they count as two families in one household.

Although there is no age limit on the definition of a child, marital status is relevant. A household containing a widow of 80 and her never-married daughter aged 55 is classified as a single-parent family (because the Census definition of a child is 'a never-married person living with one or both of his or her parents'). But if the daughter were married, widowed or divorced, she would not be a 'child in the family', so the household would be classified as 'not containing a family'.

Note that since the statistics refer to what respondents give as their legal status, a cohabiting couple who declare they are not legally married are classified as two single unrelated people. We shall treat long-term cohabitation as equivalent to marriage in most of this chapter.

2 If, however, instead of taking *people* as our units, we take *households*, we find only three out of four households contain married couples and/or parents and children (families on the Census definition), and of these less than half contain a married couple with dependent children. And of these, less than half (i.e. one-sixth of all households) have an employed father and full-time housewife/mother. Thus, despite our image of this as the 'typical household', only a small minority of houses flats etc. contain such a group at any one moment.

3 Being pregnant at the time of marriage declined dramatically during the 1970s, thanks to contraception and abortion. Premarital sexual activity itself increased.

4 The lists consisted of:

household tasks
mowing the lawn
keeping track of money and bills
doing the washing up after the evening meal
shopping for groceries
repairs around the house
clearing snow from the front path
tidying up the front room when visitors are coming
getting the husband's breakfast on work days

decisions
where to go on holiday
what car to buy
what job the husband should take
what house or flat to take
whether the wife should have a job or not
how much money the family can afford to spend on food each week
which doctor to call when someone is sick
whether or not to buy life insurance.

5 Children are the next most common victims of family assault and although we lack good statistics, estimates from social workers suggest assailants are as likely to be men as women. Given the greater number of hours women spend with children, it appears therefore that the *rate* of male violence to children is greater than that of women to children.

6 In Scotland and Northern Ireland, although there has been a general move to 'irretrievable breakdown' and the concept of 'no fault', adultery *per se* still remains grounds for divorce.

7 In Northern Ireland, there is still a requirement that the couple attend court and give oral testimony. There is also a statutory provision for reconciliation to have been attempted, and a mandatory Social Services report is required on the welfare of children under 16. Divorce is thus more difficult here than in the rest of the UK.

8 In Northern Ireland, fathers' rights over children under the 1886 Law on Guardianship are still extensive. Fathers can determine the child's domicile, schooling, religion and medical treatment.

9 It needs to be stressed, though, that illegitimate children are more equal to legitimate children now than they were previously. Not only has the stigma of

illegitimacy decreased, but illegitimate children now have the same rights of inheritance from intestate parents as legitimate children (under the Family Law Reform Act, 1969, and Inheritance (Provision for Family and Dependants) Act, 1975).

10 Note that there is nothing 'magical' about the age of five, when children in Britain start compulsory schooling. In other Western countries (e.g. France or Sweden), school starts at six or seven years and nursery provision is available on a much wider scale than in the UK, usually from the age of three. In Britain, before the First World War, at least half of three- and four-year-olds attended elementary school.

11 An ectopic pregnancy is one in which the embryo starts to grow outside the uterus, usually in the Fallopian tube. This condition requires surgical intervention and almost always removal of the tube and foetus.

12 The increased incidence of divorce seems to be having harmful effects on relations between one set of grandparents and grandchildren. Some people argue that grandparents should have formal rights of access, too.

13 Only 2 per cent of people over sixty-five live in residential accommodation, though 10 per cent will pass through such 'homes' during their life-time. This figure, however, excludes hospitals, which may account for another 2 per cent.

14 Hunt defines 'housewife' as the person in a household, other than a domestic servant, who is responsible for most of the domestic duties; i.e. it can include single women, and men, and those with as well as those without employment.

References and Further Reading

ABRAMS, P. and McCULLOCH, A. (1976) 'Men, women and communes', in BARKER, D.L. and ALLEN, S. (eds) *Sexual Divisions in Society: process and change*, Tavistock pp. 246–75.

ADAMS, M. (1976) *Single Blessedness: observations on the single status in married society*, Heinemann.

ARCANA, J. (1979) *Our Mothers' Daughters*, Women's Press.

BELL, C. (1972) 'Marital status', in BARKER, P. (ed.) *A Sociological Portrait*, Penguin.

BERNARD, J. (1973) *The Future of Marriage: His and Hers*, Souvenir Press.

BLOOD, R.D. and WOLFE, N.M. (1960) *Husbands and Wives: The Dynamics of Married living*, Collier-Macmillan.

BONE, M. (1977) *Pre-school Children and the Need for Day Care*, OPCS, Social Survey Division, HMSO.

BOSE, C. (1982) 'Technology and changes in the division of labour in the American Home' in WHITELEGG, E.L. *et al.* (eds) *The Changing Experience of Women*, Martin Robertson.

BOTT, E. (1971) 'Urban families: conjugal roles and social networks', in ANDERSON, M. (ed.) *The Sociology of the Family*, Penguin.

BROPHY, J. and SMART, C. (1981) 'From disregard to disrepute: the position of women in family law', *Feminist Review*, 9, pp. 3–16.

BOWLBY, J. (1953) *Child Care and the Growth of Love*, Penguin (1967 edition).

BROWN, G.W. and HARRIS, T. (1978) *Social Origins of Depression*, Tavistock.

BURKITT, B. and ROSE, R. (1981) 'Why be a wife?' *Sociological Review*, 29 (1).

CENTRAL STATISTICAL OFFICE (1980/81a/82) *Social Trends*, HMSO, Nos. 10/11/12.

CENTRAL STATISTICAL OFFICE (1981b) *Population Trends*, HMSO.

CHESTER, R. and STREATHER, J. (1971) 'Taking stock of divorce', *New Society*, pp. 153–4.

CHODOROW, N. (1978) *The Reproduction of Mothering*, University of California Press.

COHEN, G. (1978) 'Women's solidarity and the preservation of privilege' in CAPLAN, p. and BUJRA, M. (eds), *Women United, Women Divided*, Tavistock.

COMER, L. (1974) *Wedlocked Women*, Feminist Books.

DELPHY, C. (1976) 'Continuities and discontinuities in marriage and divorce', in BARKER, D.L. and ALLEN, S. (eds) *Sexual Divisions and Society: Process and Change*, Tavistock.

DEROW, E. (1981) 'The work of parents: time use, childcare and costs', Policy Studies Institute, mimeo.

DOBASH, R.E. and DOBASH, R. (1979) *Violence Against Wives*, Free Press; Open Books, 1980.

DOWLING, C. (1982) *The Cinderella Complex: women's hidden fear of independence*, Fontana.

DOWRICK, S. and GRUNDBERG, S. (eds) (1980) *Why Children?*, Women's Press.

DUNNELL, K. (1979) *Family Formation 1976*, OPCS, HMSO.

EIDUSON, B.T. and ALEXANDER, J.W. (1978) 'The role of children in alternative family styles', *Journal of Social Issues*, 34 (2), pp. 149—67.

ETTORRE, E.M. *Lesbians, Women and Society*, Routledge.

FADERMAN, L. (1982) *Surpassing the Love of Men: Romantic Friendship and Love between Women from the Renaissance to the Present*, Junction Books.

FERRI, E. and ROBINSON, H. (1976) *Coping Alone*, NFER Publishing Company.

FLETCHER, R. (1973) *The Family and Marriage in Britain*, Penguin, 3rd edition.

GORER, G. (1971) *Sex and Marriage in England Today*, Nelson.

HAMBLIN, A. and BOWEN, R. (1985) 'Sexual Abuse of Children', in RHODES, D. and McNEILL, S. (eds) *Women Against Violence Against Women*, Only women Press.

HAMILL, L. (1976) 'Wives as sole and joint breadwinners', paper from the Economic Advisers' Office, DHSS, mimeo.

HANMER, J. (1983) *'Violence against women'*, Unit 15 of U221, *The Changing Experience of Women*, Open University Press.

HANSCOMBE, G.E. and FORSTER, J. (1982) *Rocking the Cradle—Lesbian Mothers, a Challenge in Family Living*, Sheba Feminist Publishers.

HARAVEN, T. (1982) *Family Time and Historical Time*, Cambridge University Press.

HARNE, L. (1984) 'Lesbian custody and the new myth of fatherhood',*Trouble and Strife*, no. 3.

HARDING, S. (1975) 'Women and words in a Spanish village', in REITER, R. R. (ed.) *Toward an Anthropology of Women*, Monthly Review Press.

HARPWOOD, D. (1981) *Tea and Tranquillisers: The Diary of a Happy Housewife*, Virago.

HILBERMAN, E. (1980) 'Overview: the "wife-beater's wife" reconsidered', *American Journal of Psychiatry*, 137, 11 November, pp. 1336-47.

HITE, S. (1976) *The Hite Report: A Nationwide Survey of Female Sexuality*, Collier-MacMillan.

HOFFMAN, L.W. (1974) 'Effects of maternal employment on the child—a review of the research', *Developmental Psychology*, 10 (2), pp. 204-28.

HOLLY, L. (1980) 'Conversation with five women about sex in marriage', unpublished manuscript.

HOLLY, L. (1982) 'A new image for fathers—or new gloss on the old man?', *Spare Rib*, 122, Sept., pp. 52-55.

HUNT, A. (1970) *The Home Help Service in England and Wales*, Government Social Survey, HMSO.

HUNT, A. (1973) *Families and their Needs*, HMSO.

HUNT, A. (1978) *The Elderly at Home*, Government Social Survey, HMSO.

IMRAY, L. and MIDDLETON, A. (1982) 'Public and private: marking the boundaries', paper presented to the BSA Conference, mimeo.

JEFFREYS, S. (1982) 'The sexual abuse of children in the home', in SARAH, E. (eds.) *On the Problem of Men*, Women's Press.

KELLMER PRINGLE, M. *et al.* (1980) *A Fairer Future for Children*, Macmillan.

LAND, H. (1981) *Parity Begins at Home*, EOC/SSRC Joint Panel on Equal Opportunities.

LASCH, C. (1977) *Haven in a Heartless World: The Family Beseiged*, Basic Books.

LAW COMMISSION (1979) 'Family law: illegitimacy', *Working Paper No. 74*, HMSO.

LAWSON, A. (1982) Article by Polly Toynbee on research by Annette Lawson, *Guardian* Women, 22 November 1982.

LEETE, R. and ANTHONY, S. (1979) 'Divorce and remarriage: a record linkage study', *Population Trends 16*, Summer, HMSO.

LEONARD, D. (1980) *Sex and Generation – a study of courtship and weddings*, Tavistock.

MACLEOD, J. (1970) 'How to hold a wife: the bridegroom's guide', *Village Voice*, February: quoted in BART, P. (1971) 'Sexism and Social Science', *Journal of Marriage and the Family*, November.

McLEOD, E. (1982) *Working Women Prostitution Now*, Croom Helm.

MADDOX, B. (1975) *The Half-Parent: living with other people's children*, Andre Deutsch.

MADDOX, B. (1982) 'Money and divorce: who pays for no-fault divorce?', *The Economist* April 24.

MAINARDI, P. (1970) 'The politics of housework', in MORGAN, R. (ed.), *Sisterhood is Powerful*, Vintage Books.

MARSDEN, D. and DUFF, E. (1975) *Workless: some unemployed men and their families*, Penguin.

McKEE, L. and BELL, C. (1984) 'His unemployment: her problem. The domestic and marital consequences of male unemployment', BSA conference paper.

MEISSNER, M. HUMPHREYS, E. W., MEIS, S.M. and SHEV, W.J. (1975) 'No exit for wives: sexual division of labour and the accumulation of household demands', *Canadian Review of Sociology and Anthropology*, 12 (4), pp. 424–39.

MILLER, J. (1979) 'The misery of an infertile marriage', *Sunday Times* (28 January 1978) quoted in Bristol Women's Studies Group (eds) *Half the Sky*, Virago, pp. 159–60.

MORGAN, D.H.J. (1974) 'Bloomsbury and the definition of the family: an exploration', mimeo.

MORONEY, R.M. (1976) *The Family and the State*, Longman.

MORRIS, L. (1983) 'Renegotiation of Domestic Division of Labour in the Context of Male Redundancy', paper to BSA annual conference.

NEWSON, J. and NEWSON, E. (1965) *Patterns of Infant Care in an Urban Community*, Penguin.

NEWSON, J. and NEWSON, E. (1970) *Four Years Old in an Urban Community*, Penguin.

NEWSON, J. and NEWSON, E. (1976) *Seven Years Old in the Home Environment*. Allen & Unwin.

OAKLEY, A. (1972) 'Are husbands good housewives?', *New Society*, 17 Feb.

OAKLEY, A. 1974) *The Sociology of Housework*, Martin Robertson.

OAKLEY, A. (1976) *Housewife*, Penguin.

OAKLEY, A. (1980) 'Prologue: reflections on the study of household labor', in BERK, S.F. (ed.) *Women and Household Labor*, Sage Publications.

OAKLEY, A. (1981) *Subject Women*, Martin Robertson.

O'BRIEN, M. (1980) 'Some recent trends in fatherhood research', in *Early Childhood*, II (3), pp. 12–13.

OFFICE OF POPULATION CENSUSES AND SURVEYS (1981) 'Family and household statistics from the 1981 Census', in CSO (1981) *Population Trends*, HMSO, p. 16.

OFFICE OF POPULATION CENSUSES AND SURVEYS (1981) *Marriage and Divorce Statistics, England and Wales, 1979*, HMSO.

PETRIE, P. and MAYALL, B. (1977) *Minder, Mother and Child*, University of London, Institute of Education.

POLATNICK, M. (1973) 'Why men don't rear children–a power analysis', *Berkeley Journal of Sociology*, XVIII, pp. 45–86.

PONSE, B. (1978) *Identities in the Lesbian World: The Social Construction of Self*, Greenwood Press.

PRESTON, B. (1974) 'The surplus of women', *New Society*, 28 March, pp. 761–3.

RAPOPORT, Rh. and RAPOPORT, R. (1971) *Dual Career Families*, Penguin.

RAPOPORT, Rh. and RAPOPORT, R. (1976) *Dual Career Families Revisited*, Martin Robertson.

RAPOPORT, Rh. and RAPOPORT, R. (1978) *Working Couples*, Routledge & Kegan Paul.

RICH, A. (1977) *Of Women Born: Motherhood as Experience and Institution*, Virago.

RICH, A. (1980) 'Compulsory heterosexuality and lesbian existence', *Signs*, Summer 1980, 5 (4). Reprinted as a pamphlet by Only Women Press, 1980.

RIGHTS OF WOMEN (1979) 'Illegitimacy campaign group information pack', ROW.

RIMMER, L. (1981) *Families in Focus: Marriage, Divorce and Family Patterns*, Study Commission on the Family.

RUSSO, N.F. (1976) 'The motherhood mandate', *Journal of Social Issues*, 32 (3), pp. 143–53.

RUTTER, M. (1972) *Maternal Deprivation Reassessed*, Penguin.

SHULMAN, S. (1979) 'Lesbian feminists and the great baby con', *Spinster*. (Shortly to be republished in Gothic, Only women Press.)

SMITH, S. (1979) *The Holiday*, Virago.

STATHAM, J. (1981) 'Childcare in communities', *Undercurrents*, 46, pp. 14–17.

STIVENS, M. (1978) 'Women and their kin', in CAPLAN, P. and BUJRA, J.M. (eds) *Women United, Women Divided*, Tavistock.

STOTT, M. (1973) *Forgetting's No Excuse*, Faber & Faber.

TITMUSS, R.M. (1958) 'The position of women', in *Essays on the 'Welfare State'*, Unwin University Books.

UNGERSON, C. (1983) 'Women and caring: skills, tasks and taboos', in E. Gamarnikow *et al.* (eds),. *The Public and the Private*, Heinemann.

VICINUS M. (1985) *Independent Women, Work and Community for Single Women 1850-1920*, Virago.

WALKER, K. and WOODS, M. (1976) *Time Use: a measure of household production of goods and services*, American Home Economics Association.

WALLSGROVE, R. (1985) 'Motherhood revisited', *Trouble and Strife*, no. 6.

WHITEHEAD, A. (1976) 'Sex antagonisms in Herefordshire', in LEONARD BARKER D. and ALLEN, S. (eds) *Dependence and Exploitation in Work and Marriage*, Longman.

WILSON, E. (1980) *Only Halfway to Paradise*, Tavistock.

WYNN, M. (1970) *Family Policy: A Study of the Economic Cost of Rearing Children and the Social and Political Consequences*, Penguin.

YOUNG M. and WILLMOTT, P. (1962) *Family and Kinship in East London*, Penguin.

YOUNG, M. and WILLMOTT, P. (1973) *The Symmetrical Family*, Routledge & Kegan Paul.

2 Women and Employment in Contemporary Britain

Veronica Beechey

This chapter is concerned with women's paid work. It has become increasingly clear in recent years that women's experience of paid work is to a large extent different from men's, yet the ways in which it is different and the reasons for this are very much open to debate. In this chapter I shall present a good deal of empirical evidence about women's work, looking at how women's participation in the labour market has changed over time, which women do paid work and at what points in their lives, and the kinds of paid work which women do. I shall then discuss a variety of different explanations of women's position in the labour market, including conventional sociological approaches, dual labour market theories and Marxist and feminist perspectives on women's employment. I shall discuss a number of issues which are problematic in the analysis of women's paid work, including the question of divisions between women and men, gender and skill, the relationship between the family and women's employment, the role of ideology, and the question of gender, race and class. Finally, I shall briefly discuss the question of equality at work.

Conceptions of Work

Before embarking on the more substantive discussion of women's employment, it is worth reflecting for a moment on the conception of work which prevails within common sense thinking and considering how far this is appropriate for analyzing women's work. For in commonsense thinking we tend to have a masculine conception of work. We think of only paid work as being work and exclude other kinds of work (e.g. housework, DIY and voluntary work) from our definition. We tend also to have a conception of paid work derived from an analysis of manual work in manufacturing industry, which was perhaps more appropriate to nineteenth century conditions than to the present day. Workplaces are generally thought of as strictly demarcated from the home and from family life. Similarly, we think of workers as people who leave home in the morning to travel to these workplaces and who work for a certain number of hours (usually all day but sometimes all night) in a world of work that has nothing to do with the home. We also usually think of people as being 'in work' or 'out of work' and as working full time from the time they leave school or college until they retire at

60 or 65 (or certainly as wishing to follow this pattern if there are jobs available). These conceptions of work and workers would seem to be an accurate characterization of some kinds of paid work. However, they are not very satisfactory as a characterization of women's paid work.

There are four important respects in which women's working experience is different from the masculine norm. First, most women (white women especially) have interrupted working histories. They mostly give up paid employment for a time after having a child, and return to work afterwards, often part-time. Second, many women (particularly white women) work part-time, very often when they have children or other dependants whom they have to care for. Third, women work in a wide variety of workplaces. Some women do work in factories (in the textiles industry and in food and drink production, for instance), and most factories employ some women as clerical workers and cleaners. However, many women work in other kinds of workplace, for example, in hospitals, shops and offices. Finally, a good deal of women's work involves caring for, or servicing, other people. Women work as teachers, nurses, social workers and home helps – all jobs which involve caring. Other kinds of women's work involve servicing people – both in manual occupations like cleaning and catering, and in non-manual forms of work like secretarial work. These important aspects of a lot of women's work are often ignored by conventional analyses of work, and the prevalence of a masculine conception of work, particularly within academic studies, has often obscured important aspects of women's work, or has led to its being treated as marginal.

The reasons why women's working experiences are often different from men's are complex, and the different theoretical perspectives discussed later in the chapter offer rather different explanations. In part the differences have to do with the domestic division of labour, and in particular the role which our society assigns to women in bringing up children. In part they have to do with the ways in which young women are differently treated in the education system and training schemes. But they are also a product of the ways in which the labour market has evolved, and result too from more general ideological conceptions about what constitutes appropriate work for women which are embodied in many state policies and held by employers, trade unions, and indeed by many women themselves. These play an important role in limiting the opportunities open to women in the labour market, and affecting their experiences of paid work.

The first part of this chapter discusses empirical evidence about women's employment in contemporary Britain, and relies mainly upon official statistics. It is important to point out that while official statistics are a valuable source of evidence about employment patterns, they also have some quite serious deficiencies, especially where women's employment is concerned. The following are some of the problems with them:

1 Statistics are collected as an administrative measure, as part of the government's work in planning. They reflect a masculine conception of employment which government departments use, and which is prevalent in commonsense conceptions of employment (the view, for example, that

'to be employed' means to be engaged in full-time, full-year-round employment outside the home). They also help to perpetuate this conception of employment.

2 Particular forms of work are systematically unrecorded, under-represented or distorted in the statistics. These are forms of work which do not conform to this masculine conception of employment (e.g. homework, casual, seasonal and irregular work and part-time work – all forms of work which are normally undertaken by women, and to some extent children). These forms of work are underrepresented for three reasons: (a) because the form of work falls outside the net of statistics altogether (e.g. homework); (b) because the categories used reflect divisions between particular kinds of men's work and recognition of men's skills; (c) because people often do not declare work which is unacceptable, or illegal, or both.

3 Those kinds of work in which women are particularly disadvantaged – because the work is poorly paid, is carried out in inadequate working conditions and falls outside the scope of protective legislation and the sex equality legislation – are also the kinds of work which are under-represented in official statistics. There is thus a parallel between the practical problems which many women face in employment and the problems which students encounter in studying women's work.

4 Unemployment statistics underestimate women's unemployment because they only count those who are registered as unemployed. Married women, in particular, are less likely than men to register as unemployed because fewer women are eligible for unemployment benefit. Furthermore, in periods of high unemployment women may be discouraged from seeking work and may not consider themselves to be unemployed in the same sense that male breadwinners do. They therefore do not show up in the statistics as being unemployed (see Allin and Hunt, (1982) for further discussion of this).

Which women do paid work?

Women's participation in the labour force has changed a good deal historically. In the pre-industrial economy, in which the household was the basic unit of production, women, men and children were all involved in production – working the land, spinning and weaving cloth, and making food and clothing. And in the early phases of industrialization many women continued to work – in agriculture, in the home, and in manufacturing workshops, factories and mills. However, the proportion of married women working declined in the course of the nineteenth century. The 1851 Census recorded 25 per cent of married women with an 'extraneous occupation' whereas, by the turn of the century, only about 10 per cent of married women were in paid employment. This was the result of several factors, among them: the removal of some kinds of work from the home; the exclusion of women from certain trades; the growth of new areas of industrial work (e.g. railways, steel production), which became defined as 'men's work'; and the prevalence of the Victorian ideology, which decreed that a woman's place was in the home.

Just under 10 per cent of married women were in the labour force in 1911. The proportion of married women entering the labour force increased dramatically in both World Wars because women worked in occupations that men had previously worked in while men went to fight. A great deal of propaganda was produced in both World Wars to encourage married women to enter the paid workforce. Between the two World Wars the proportion of married women in the labour force declined to around its pre-war level, as women were ousted from the jobs they had done during the war when peacetime conditions were restored.

After a brief drop at the end of the Second World War as women were once again forced out of some wartime occupations, (for instance, work in the munitions and engineering industries), the proportion of married women in the labour force has risen steadily since the war. Table 1 shows the proportion of married women of all ages in the labour force since 1911. Whereas in 1911 the proportion of married women in the workforce was just under 10 per cent, by 1980 the figure had risen to 52 per cent, although it has fallen off slightly since.

Table 1 Economic activity* rate of married women of all ages. Great Britain 1911 to 1982/% (Source: *EOC Sixth Annual Report*, 1981, p.62. *General Household Survey* 1982, Table 6.1)

1911	1921	1931	1951	1961	1971	1977	1980	1982
9.6	8.7	10.0	21.7	29.7	42.3	50.4	52	50

*People are classified as 'economically active' or in the labour force if they are either in employment or seeking a job. People waiting to take up a job or those who would be seeking work but for temporary sickness or injury are included among the economically active. The economic activity rate of women refers to the proportion of women who are in employment or recorded as seeking a job. The economic activity rate of married women refers to the proportion of married women who are in employment or seeking a job.

Today a majority of women are in paid employment, and they work for most of their working lives. 60 per cent of the women interviewed for a recent large-scale survey conducted by the Department of Employment, *the Women and Employment Survey*, were employed (34 per cent of them full-time and 26 per cent part-time), 5 per cent of the rest were unemployed and 5 per cent were students. Those of the women interviewed who had been born since 1941 had spent, on average, around 60 per cent of their lives working. When they were asked what were their main reasons for working were, 69 per cent of the working women interviewed mentioned a financial reason as primary, and non-married women with children were most likely to say that they worked for basic essentials (Martin and Roberts, 1984). Other studies suggest that this is particularly true of black women (Carby 1982, Parmar 1982). Many women interviewed for the *Women and Employment Survey* said they worked because they enjoyed it, or because they enjoyed the company of other people, but these tended to be of less over-riding importance than financial reasons. When

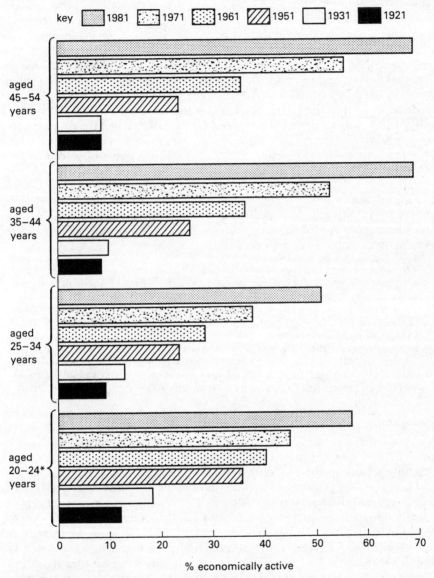

key ☐1981 ☐1971 ☐1961 ☐1951 ☐1931 ■1921

aged 45–54 years

aged 35–44 years

aged 25–34 years

aged 20–24* years

% economically active

* 1931: 21–24 age range
* 1981: 18–24 age range

Table 2 Economic activity rates for married females, by age, 1921–81. (Source: Department of Employment; *Manpower Paper No. 9*, 1974, p.7, General Household Survey 1982, Table 6.1)

asked what they valued most about their jobs most women (91 per cent) rated work they liked doing as most important. Full-time workers rated 'a good rate of pay' and a 'secure job' as equally important to work they liked doing, whereas part-time workers saw convenient hours of work as being equally important to having work they liked doing (Martin and Roberts, 1984).

Women's participation in the labour market varies markedly by age. Table 2 breaks down married women's employment by age over time. It shows that in 1961 a new pattern of married women's employment began to emerge. Whereas in the previous years the proportion of married women in the labour force declined steadily after the 20–24 age group, in 1961 the proportion of married women in the labour force began to increase again in the 35–44 age group. This pattern occurred again in 1971 and 1981, when the proportion of women over 35 years of age in the labour force exceeded the proportion of younger women. In 1981 almost 70 per cent of this age group were in paid employment.

In a paper called *Occupational Segregation*, published by the Department of Employment, Catherine Hakim (1979) has examined the aggregate changes in women's employment over their working lives. In the following passage she summarizes her observations about the changing pattern of women's employment in the twentieth century:

> The labour force participation of men has always been high and remained steady at around 96 per cent of the age group until 1951, with a slight drop in recent years due to the increasing number of full-time students aged 15–24 years. The work rates for women were also fairly stable until around 1931; around the time of the Second World War they began to rise to their current level of 55 per cent of the age group. This represents a proportional increase in economic activity rates of 45 per cent over the century. The greatest change is in the work rates of married women. In 1901 only one ever-married women in ten was economically active, by 1971 one in two was active in the labour force. This represents a proportional increase in labour force participation of almost 400 per cent for wives. (p.4)

She calls this new pattern of women's employment a 'two-phase' working life. It is two-phase because there are high rates of participation for women in the labour force when they first leave school or college, the rate of participation then declines, but it begins to increase again after 35 years of age, reaching a peak in the 45+ age group.

There is strong evidence to suggest that women's employment is affected by their responsibility for young children. The presence of children affects the likelihood that a woman will work outside the home, whether or not she works part-time, and the type of work she is able to undertake. Mothers are far less likely to work than women without children, whether they are married or are single parents. The Women and Employment Survey found that 93 per cent of childless women were economically active, compared with 31 per cent of women whose children were under five.

Both the number of children for whom a woman is responsible and their ages affect her participation in paid work. But overall it is the age of the youngest child, and particularly the presence of a child under five, that is the main determinant of whether or not women work outside the home and whether or not they work full-time. It is in fact very rare for mothers with pre-school children to work full-time: only 7 per cent of mothers with pre-school children interviewed in the Women and Employment Survey worked full-time. Married women with dependent children are far more likely to work part-time, although there are ethnic differences in this, with far higher proportions of white women working part-time.

A major shift which has occurred in post-war Britain is that marriage is no longer the critical determinant of women's participation in the labour market. Whereas in the immediate post-war years women were most likely to stop working when they got married, they are now likely to stop working for a time when they have children. The Women and Employment Survey suggests that while the two-phase pattern is still the dominant one, women are increasingly returning to work sooner after childbearing, sometimes between births. Gradually, in countries like Britain, women's working lives are looking more like men's. A major difference, however, is that large numbers of women work part-time. The numbers of part-time jobs have increased substantially since 1951, and part-time jobs have been the only significant area of employment growth in recent years. Over 1 million part-time jobs were created in the 1970s alone.

There are considerable differences in the levels of economic activity of women of different ethnic origins. The overall economic activity rate of West Indian women is much higher than that of white women, but Table 3 shows that this can partly be attributed to differences in the ages at which women from different ethnic origins take up employment.

The activity rate of West Indian women aged 16–19 is lower than that of white women, and it is only slightly higher among the 20-24 age group. A far higher proportion of West Indian women over 25 years of age, however, is economically active. Whereas white women's participation in the labour market dips substantially in the 25-34 age group, that of West Indian women

Table 3 Economic activity by age and ethnic group (Source: Brown (1984), Table 81, p.187)

Per cent of age group in labour market

Women aged:	Whites	West Indians	Asians	
			Muslims	Other Asians
16–19	(71)	59	(42)	(36)
20–24	74	78	20	65
25–34	54	75	17	60
35–44	70	88	14	64
45–54	65	83	(11)	58
55–64	34	40	(1)	(21)

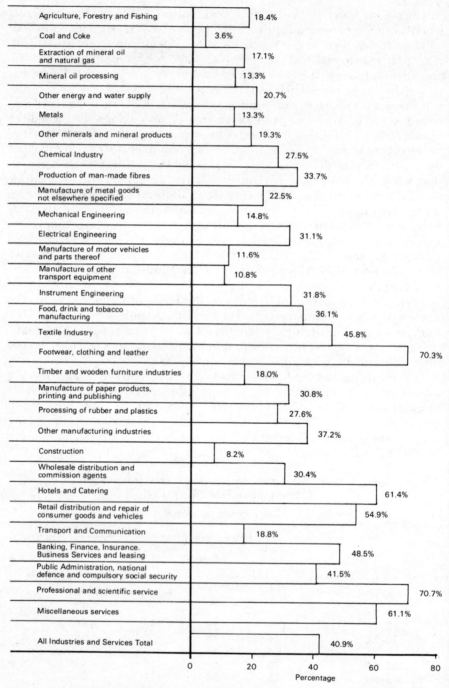

Table 4 Women as a percentage of industrial labour force, Great Britain 1983. (Source: *EOC Eighth Annual Report 1983,* Figure 3.5, p.81)

remains roughly constant. Official statistics show that Asian women, in contrast, are less likely to be in the labour market than white women, and that a big difference exists between Muslim and non-Muslim women. In the critical 25-34 age group the proportion of non-Muslim Asian women in the labour market is higher than the proportion of white women. It is likely that official statistics and surveys under-represent the extent of employment among Muslim Asian women in particular since there are strong religious and cultural prohibitions on them working outside the home. Black women are far less likely to work part-time than white women. A recent study by the Policy Studies Institute, *Black and White in Britain*, (Brown, 1984), found that 44 per cent of white women employees worked part-time, compared with 29 per cent of West Indian women and 16 per cent of Asian women.

Women's participation in the labour market also varies from region to region. Some areas, like the West Midlands, have traditionally had high levels of women's employment, while others (e.g. Wales) have been low. That, however, can change historically as employment opportunities are re-structured, and it has recently been predicted that women's employment in Wales is likely to exceed men's in the near future as a result of the move by new micro-electronics industries to sites of 'green labour'. (Williams, 1981). A study by the Runnymede Trust, based on 1971 census data, showed that the employment rates of black mothers whose children were under five varied markedly from area to area; 85 per cent worked in Leicester, 71 per cent in Manchester, 44 per cent in Bradford, and only 41 per cent in Wolverhampton (Lomas, 1973). This underlines the extent to which women's employment opportunities are affected by local labour market conditions.

What kinds of paid work do women do?

Women are concentrated in industries that are very largely female and black women, in particular, are concentrated in the lowest-level jobs. Table 4 shows the percentage of the labour force that is female in different industries.

Statistics on the industrial concentration of women and men are useful because they give a good idea of which industries rely heavily upon female labour. Thus, when you hear on the news or read in the newspaper about the plight of particular industries–for instance, about the intense competition that the textiles industry is subject to because of increased competition from Southern Europe and Third World countries; or about the impact of cutbacks in public expenditure on employment levels in the education system–if you know the extent to which the industry relies upon female labour, you can get some idea of how far women are likely to be affected by cutbacks in the labour force. However, many people studying women's employment have suggested that statistics such as these, which are concerned with the distribution of women and men between industries, have limited usefulness for analysing women's employment, and have suggested that occupational statistics are in fact more useful. In manufacturing industries women are employed not only in manufacturing occupations, but also in technical ones, in secretarial and clerical occupations, in cleaning and clerical jobs, etc. And in service industries, especially State services like the health service, women work in a wide variety of occupations; a few women work as doctors but most women work as nurses, in various paramedical occupations (e.g. physiotherapists, radiologists, occupational therapists), as secretarial and clerical workers, and in cleaning and catering. Thus, statistics like those in Table 4, which show the distribution of women and men within particular industries, tend to obscure the extent to which women are employed in particular occupations across *all* industries.

The government also collects statistics on the distribution of women among occupations. These have the advantage of showing the extent to which women's work is heavily concentrated in quite a small number of occupations in which mainly women are employed. Table 5 shows the distribution of women and men between occupations.

It is clear from this that there are some occupations in which women are heavily concentrated and others in which men are heavily concentrated. The term *occupational segregation* is used to refer to the division of the labour market into predominantly female and predominantly male occupations. If complete segregation existed, women and men would never work in the same occupations. Catherine Hakim (1979) points out in her paper on *Occupational Segregation* that in Britain today 'Complete occupational segregation on the basis of sex . . . (is) rare, as it requires that formal and direct mechanisms are at work to ensure that all entrants to given occupations are of one sex only'(p.19).

Historically the exclusion of women from particular occupations by formal and direct mechanisms has not been uncommon. Women were not permitted to enter into the professions of medicine or the law, for instance, until these were opened up to women as a result of feminist agitation in the nineteenth century. Likewise, many women were precluded from entering into craft occupations because the rules of the guilds would not permit women members, and membership of a guild was required in order to enter an apprenticeship. For a variety of reasons women are still prevented from entering some occupations, including the clergy of some churches, working underground in the mines, on North Sea oil rigs, in lighthouses, and in certain areas of the prison services (e.g. in security units) and the police force.

The reasons why women are not employed in certain occupations vary. In some instances (e.g. underground work in the mines) they are excluded because of protective legislation; in others, because the Sex Discrimination Act allows employers to discriminate in selection if sex is a 'genuine occupational qualification' for the job.

A close look at the statistics reveals that, despite the fact that women are not formally precluded from entry into many occupations in contemporary Britain, there is still a prenounced form of division of the labour market. That is, there is a pronounced form of occupation segregation, defined as *the division of the labour market into predominantly female and predominantly male occupations.*

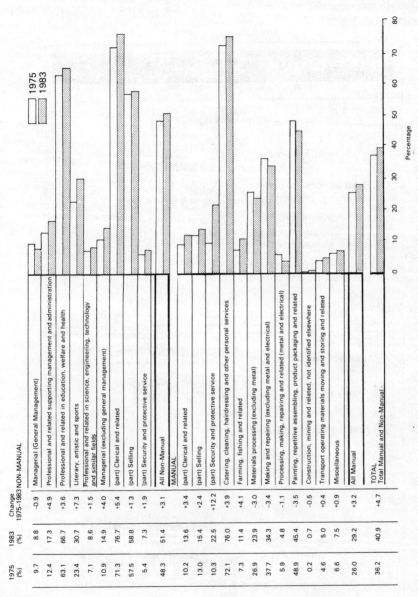

1975 (%)	1983 (%)	Change 1975–1983	
			NON-MANUAL
9.7	8.8	-0.9	Managerial (General Management)
12.4	17.3	+4.9	Professional and related supporting management and administration
63.1	66.7	+3.6	Professional and related in education, welfare and health
23.4	30.7	+7.3	Literary, artistic and sports
7.1	8.6	+1.5	Professional and related in science, engineering, technology and similar fields
10.9	14.9	+4.0	Managerial (excluding general management)
71.3	76.7	+5.4	(part) Clerical and related
57.5	58.8	+1.3	(part) Selling
5.4	7.3	+1.9	(part) Security and protective service
48.3	51.4	+3.1	All Non-Manual
			MANUAL
10.2	13.6	+3.4	(part) Clerical and related
13.0	15.4	+2.4	(part) Selling
10.3	22.5	+12.2	(part) Security and protective service
72.1	76.0	+3.9	Catering, cleaning, hairdressing and other personal services
7.3	11.4	+4.1	Farming, fishing and related
26.9	23.9	-3.0	Materials processing (excluding metal)
37.7	34.3	-3.4	Making and repairing (excluding metal and electrical)
5.9	4.8	-1.1	Processing, making, repairing and related (metal and electrical)
48.9	45.4	-3.5	Painting, repetitive assembling, product packaging and related
0.2	0.7	-0.5	Construction, mining and related, not identified elsewhere
4.6	5.0	+0.4	Transport operating materials moving and storing and related
6.6	7.5	+0.9	Miscellaneous
26.0	29.2	+3.2	All Manual
36.2	40.9	+4.7	TOTAL Total Manual and Non-Manual

Table 5 Women as a percentage of occupational labour force. Great Britain 1975 and 1983. (Source: *EOC Eighth Annual Report 1983*, Figure 3.4, p.80)

Occupational segregation in West Yorkshire

It can be helpful in thinking about occupational segregation to consider what this is like in one specific region. Table 6 is a diagrammatic representation of the female population of West Yorkshire, and it shows quite clearly the concentration of women in a limited number of occupations. Of the 32 out of

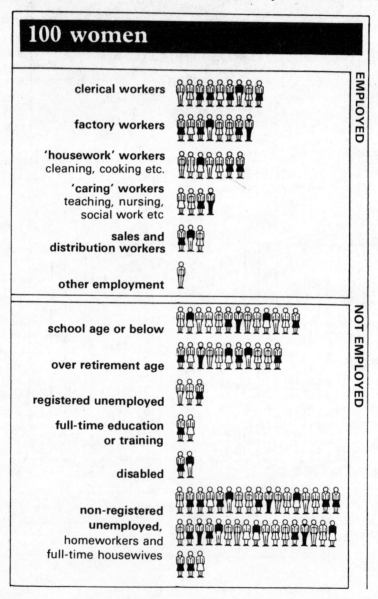

Table 6 Women's employment in West Yorkshire *(Source: Huws, 1982, p. 15)*

every 100 women who are in the labour market in West Yorkshire, by far the
largest group–nearly one-third–are clerical workers. The second largest–
accounting for eight out of 32, or a quarter of all working women–are factory
workers. The factory workers are assemblers, packers, workers in textile trade
jobs (such as winders, reelers, spinners, twisters, and weavers, sewing
machinists, electrical and electronic assemblers, and food processing workers;
the rest do other unskilled or semiskilled factory work. The third
category–covering seven out of the 32 working women– is a category which
Ursula Huws (who devised the table) calls 'other people's housework'. It
includes cleaners, canteen assistants, counter-hands, cooks, kitchen hands,
general servants, waitresses and launderers. The fourth category covers the
professional 'caring' jobs, and comprises nurses, teachers, social workers,
nursery nurses and a few other professional jobs, such as physiotherapy. This
accounts for four out of the 32 working women. The other type of work with a
significant number of women is sales and distribution. This includes some
packers and labellers, storekeepers, warehouse assistants and some proprietors
and managers as well as cashiers and sales assistants. These account for three
out of 32 or roughly a tenth of working women. There are a large number of
other occupations in which women can be found, but the numbers are fairly
low. Taken all together, they account for only one per cent of all women, less
than one in 32 of the working women. The picture in West Yorkshire is very
similar to that of the country as a whole. The only major difference is that
slightly more women work in factories, and slightly fewer in offices, than in
the rest of Britain.

Black women's jobs
It is hard to find systematic evidence about black women's employment. This
is because many official statistics (e.g. the Census) do not classify the
population according to race or ethnic origin. However, Political and
Economic Planning (now called the Policy Studies Institute) conducted a
number of studies which compared the situation of blacks and whites in the
labour market in the 1970s, and the most recent of these, *Black and White
Britain* (Brown, 1984) contains an analysis of black and white women's jobs.
As might be expected, there is a much lower proportion of women than men in
professional and managerial and skilled manual jobs, although the contrast
between black and white women is less marked than the very marked contrast
between black and white men. There are, however, very few West Indian
women employed in professional and managerial jobs (2 per cent compared
with 17 per cent of white women and 20 per cent of Asian women). Asian
women are far more likely to be employed in manufacturing industries that
white and West Indian women, and this reflects their concentration in the
textile and clothing industries, especially in areas like Yorkshire and the East
Midlands.
 The PSI Study found that the job levels of Asian women in the services sector
were overall higher than white women but that West Indian women had lower
job levels. However, more detailed occupational statistics show that Asian
women with non-manual jobs are disproportionately concentrated in the

distributive trades and in 'other services', a category which includes unskilled cleaning and catering work, which is often badly paid.

As Pratibha Parmar has pointed out, 'within . . . (the) concentration (of women into an occupationally segregated labour market) there are regional and racial variations whereby Asian women are confined to even more specific sectors . . . They are over-represented in the lower paid unskilled and semi-skilled sectors, where most Asian women are to be found working as machinists in the clothing industry, in laundries, light engineering factories, the hosiery industry, in canteens, as cleaners, and as home workers' (Parmar, 1982, p.247).

Table 7 Female employees: job levels by industry by ethic group (Source: Brown, 1984, Table 103, p.208)

Column percentages

	All manufacturing and mining	Professional and scientific services	Other services
White women			
Professional/employer/manager	6	1	10
Other non-manual	35	68	57
Manual Supervisors	2	–	1
Skilled Manual	17	1	*
Semi-skilled/unskilled manual	38	28	31
Base: (weighted)	217	263	474
West Indian women			
Professional/employer/manager	–	1	1
Other non-manual	19	67	48
Manual Supervisors	4	–	–
Skilled manual	14	2	1
Semi-skilled/unskilled manual	66	31	49
Base: (weighted)	200	417	316
Asian women			
Professional/employer/manager	1	12	7
Other non-manual	6	71	69
Manual supervisors	2	–	–
Skilled manual	9	–	2
Semi-skilled/unskilled manual	82	15	23
Base: (weighted)	341	122	186

Many West Indian women work in the National Health Service which actively recruited them in the post-war years. However, they are mostly employed to do domestic work (e.g. cleaning and catering) and nursing. A recent study found that overseas nurses (who come from Ireland, from New Commonwealth countries like Malaysia, the West Indies and Mauritius, and from non-Commonwealth countries like the Philippines) accounted for 17 per cent of all student nurses, but for only 4 per cent of those in London postgraduate teaching hospitals, they were disproportionately concentrated in psychiatric and geriatric institutions, and trainee nurses from overseas were frequently found on courses leading to a State Enrolled Nurse certificate (a qualification which is inferior to the State Registered Nurse, and earns no automatic international recognition) (Doyal, Hunt and Mellor, 1981, p.58). Overall, black women are employed in more highly segregated occupations than white women and many of them work in the least desirable jobs.

Horizontal and vertical occupational segregation
In analysing women's employment, it can be useful to distinguish between two kinds of occupational segregation: horizontal segregation and vertical segregation. Catherine Hakim (1979) defines these in the following terms:

> *Horizontal occupational segregation* exists when men and women are most commonly working in different types of occupation. *Vertical occupational segregation* exists when men are working most commonly in higher grade occupations and women are most commonly working in lower grade occupations, or vice versa. (My emphases, p.19).

There are various complicated means of measuring the extent of horizontal occupational segregation. For the purposes of the present discussion, however, let us assume that horizontal occupational segregation exists where women or men make up more than 70 per cent of the labour force in a given occupation. In 1981 this applied to women in clerical and related occupations, and in catering, cleaning, hairdressing and other personal services. Hakim suggests that the number of occupations in which women comprise over 70 per cent of the labour force actually increased slightly between 1901 and 1971. She also argues that the proportion of men working in all-male occupations declined slowly between 1901 and 1971, but that in 1971 over half of all men were still in occupations where they outnumbered women by at least nine to one, and over two-thirds of men worked in occupations where they outnumbered women by at least four to one. This means that men's work, too, is highly segregated in particular occupations. Hakim concludes, then, that the pattern of horizontal occupational segregation remains strong, despite the decline in direct and formal mechanisms for excluding women from specific occupations.

Hakim suggests also that the pattern of horizontal occupational segregation has been slightly different for women and men in the twentieth century, as the following extracts from her paper make clear:

> . . . over the seventy-year period occupational segregation declined but is still

largely preserved. The disappearance of occupations exclusive to one sex is counteracted by the fact that the likelihood of working in an occupation where one's own sex predominated . . . became proportionately greater for men. (p.23)

Male inroads into women's preserves have not been counterbalanced by women's entry into typically male spheres of work . . .
By 1971 the majority of men were still working in occupations where women would infrequently be encountered, whereas the majority of women were in occupations where male employees were not uncommon. (p.25)

The second kind of occupational segregation is *vertical occupational segregation*. Hakim has calculated the extent of this, using slightly different occupational groups from those in Table 5. The results of this calculation are summarized in Table 8.

There was, however, some shift in the patterns of vertical occupational segregation in the 1970s. Hakim suggests women made substantial gains in the higher grade white-collar work. In management-related professions, the proportion of women increased from 14 to 21 per cent between 1973 and 1979, and in science-related professions it increased from five per cent to nine per cent. In other occupations, however, there was no significant change in the pattern of vertical occupational segregation in the 1970s.

Hakim suggests that the overall trend through the twentieth century has been towards greater vertical segregation, that is, towards a proportionately greater concentration of men in higher grade occupations and of women in lower grade ones. In the following passage Hakim underlines some of the changes which she thinks have been most significant:

Table 8 Women workers in major occupational groups, 1911–1971
Female workers as a percentage of all workers in each of the major occupational groups (Source: Hakim, 1979, p.28).

Occupational groups	1911	1921	1931	1951	1961	1971
Employers and proprietors	18.8	20.5	19.8	20.0	20.4	24.9
White-collar workers	29.8	37.6	35.8	42.3	44.5	47.9
(a) managers and administrators	19.8	17.0	13.0	15.2	15.5	21.6
(b) higher professionals	6.0	5.1	7.5	8.3	9.7	9.9
(c) lower professionals and technicians	62.9	59.4	58.8	53.5	50.8	52.1
(d) foremen and inspectors	4.2	6.5	8.7	13.4	10.3	13.1
(e) clerks	21.4	44.6	46.0	60.2	65.2	73.2
(f) salesmen and shop assistants	35.2	43.6	37.2	51.6	54.9	59.8
All manual workers	30.5	27.9	28.8	26.1	26.0	29.4
(a) skilled	24.0	21.0	21.3	15.7	13.8	13.5
(b) semiskilled	40.4	40.3	42.9	38.1	39.3	46.5
(c) unskilled	15.5	16.8	15.0	20.3	22.4	37.2
Total occupied population	29.6	29.5	29.8	30.8	32.4	36.5

Changes have often been in the direction of greater segregation rath[e] integration of the sexes in the work sphere. In 1911 the proportion of wo[m] clerical occupations, shop-assistant and sales work was broadly compar[ed] their contribution to the labour force as a whole; by 1971 these occupati[ons] become typically feminine. About three-quarters of all clerical workers were women in 1971 compared to only 21 per cent in 1911. The proportion of women in managerial and administrative positions or in lower professional and technical occupations actually declined between 1911 and 1961, although figures for 1971 suggest women are now regaining some of the ground lost. In manual work, the trend is towards greater segregation, with men increasingly over-represented in skilled work and women contributing an increasing share of unskilled and semi-skilled workers. These changes outweigh the gradual, but small, improvements in women's share of higher professional occupations and among employers and proprietors. (p.27)

In a later article, Hakim (1981) looks at the extent to which the patterns of occupational segregation changed in the 1970s. The broad sex structure of occupations remained constant over this period (despite the fact that the Equal Pay and Sex Discrimination Act came into force then). One quarter of all jobs were typically female and three-quarters were typically male:

By the end of 1970s, just over a quarter (27 per cent) of all women were working in occupations where they outnumbered men by nine to one, while over half (58 per cent) of men were in occupations where they outnumbered women to the same extent – a picture that hardly differs at all from that in 1971. (p.523)

Looking at women's employment in terms of the concept of occupational segregation can be extremely useful because it pinpoints the extent to which women and men are employed in different kinds of jobs; and the concept of vertical occupational segregation highlights the extent to which women's jobs are graded lower than men's, and therefore the extent of inequalities between women and men within the labour market.

Part-time work
Part-time work is performed overwhelmingly by women. The 1984 Labour Force Survey showed that 88 per cent of all part-time employees are women. Part-time work is an important form of work for women – far more than it is for men. Nearly 45 per cent of women working (and 55 per cent of married women) work part-time, compared with above 4 per cent of working men. It is women returning to work who comprise the majority of part-time workers. Most part-timers are married, and mothers in particular tend to work part-time.

The Women and Employment Survey found that 68 per cent of women working who had children under the age of 16 worked part-time. All but 7 per cent of the part-time workers analysed in a study of the National Training Survey (Elias and Main, 1982) had at least one break in their working lives before their current part-time job. The extent to which it is white married women who work part-time is seldom recognized. Black women are much more likely to work full-time. So, too, are single mothers who are in paid employment.

Part-time work is heavily concentrated in the service sectors of the economy – in distribution; insurance, banking, finance and business services; professional and scientific services; miscellaneous services and in public administration. Over 80 per cent of all women part-time employees work in these sectors. Many jobs in these sectors have been constructed as women's part-time jobs. Part-time work in the manufacturing industries is not insignificant (.e.g in textiles and clothing), but it is declining rapidly in the manufacturing sector, whereas in the service sectors part-time work is growing.

Much part-time work is in small firms employing fewer than 25 people. This is because so many part-time jobs are concentrated in catering, cleaning, sales work, etc. However, significant numbers of part-timers are employed by the health service, and in education and the social services.

It is extremely difficult to obtain reliable evidence on the pay of part-time workers. But, from the available evidence it is clear that part-time workers tend to be concentrated in low-status, low-paying jobs. They also tend to be underrepresented in trade unions. Only about one in five part-time women workers belongs to a trade union, whereas twice as many full-time women workers are union members.

There is a growing body of evidence that indicates the extent of downward occupational mobility among women who are currently working part time. The analysis of work history information from the National Training Survey indicated that in the three low-status occupation groups which contain a high proportion of women in part-time jobs – 'other sales' occupations, 'other operatives' and 'other personal service' occupations – a relatively high proportion of the women were in higher status full-time occupations ten years earlier. One out of five of all women in the low-skilled catering and cleaning occupations had a full-time job in some other occupational group ten years earlier. One in twenty-five of part-timers who hold teaching qualifications was working in low-skilled catering and cleaning occupations in 1975. One in twelve of part-timers with nursing qualifications was also in this occupational group, as was one in six of part-timers with clerical and commercial qualifications.

Whether a women works full-time or part-time depends to a considerable extent upon whether or not she has responsibility for dependent children and crucially upon the age of her youngest child. A major reason why women with dependent children work part time is to give them the flexibility to combine paid work with domestic commitments. The following extracts are taken from three interviews with home helps in Belfast. They make very clear the extent to which the women tried to organize their paid work around their responsibilities for the children.

> Well, you have to manage so you do, I have a wee boy, one of three, but he'll be booking into a nursery shortly, so when he's in the nursery like, that will be my three settled . . . but then you must be home in time to collect them, you know, so that'll be a quarter to two, two o'clock and three o'clock, so you can't work full-time, like you must only work part-time hours, but it suits me to work those hours, you know . . .

Well I have two children also, my eldest girl's twelve, the youngest daughter is five, well when I'm working I have to be home by 12 o'clock to collect the younger one from school, get his lunch, take him back to school, go out and do my work, come back again for a quarter past two to collect them out of school and take them around to my mother and go out and do another house after that and then come back at tea time and do my, yu know, my household chores. I just have to try and fit it in the best I can.

Your family life has to come first, your family must always come first but I mean you've got to fit in a bit of social life and that as well, you know what I mean? If you have the time like, I like to go to me union meetings and what have you, and I think everybody else here is the same like, we've all made good friends through going to the union courses and different things like, we're all different religions but that doesn't matter.

Homework

Like part-time work, homework (i.e. paid work carried out in the home) is done almost exclusively by women. A study of homeworkers in four English cities carried out by Cragg and Dawson (1981) for the Department of Employment between 1979 and 1980 came across only one male homeworker.

The TUC estimates that there are at least 250 000 home-workers engaged in manufacturing or service trades and at least another 130 000 working as registered or unregistered childminders. Asian women often do home-work because many Muslim families think it unacceptable for women to go out to work. Cragg and Dawson suggest that the number of people working at home appears to be increasing partly as a result of the new computer technology and partly due to the increase in telephone ownership and the expansion of boutiques and craftshops. Between 1921 and 1971 the number of people who reported themselves as working at home increased. Cragg and Dawson put the figures somewhat higher than the TUC, and estimate that about 1.5 million people worked at home in 1971, that is, about 6 per cent of the labour force. The numbers of homeworkers engaged in blue-collar work (manufacturing work) and in white-collar work are now roughly equal. Cragg and Dawson include childminding and office work within the category of white-collar work.

Homeworkers have often been singled out as one of *the* most exploited groups of workers, working for extremely low rates of pay and long hours. Cragg and Dawson suggest that the employment situation of homeworkers is slightly more variable than this – more like the situation of women workers within the labour market in general – but the study did come across some appallingly low rates of pay among homeworkers. All but one of the homeworkers inteviewed in this study had at least one child under the age of 16 at home. The reasons women gave for working at all were primarily financial (although some women mentioned the importance of fulfilment). Most of the people inteviewed had come to rely on their earnings from homework, and about a third of those interviewed, including all the single women, regarded their income from homework as essential. This is how some of the women in this group described why they did homework:

That's why I have to do this homework. I rely on it. I don't get regular maintenance from my (ex-) husband, so whatever job I'm given, I won't refuse, because I need the money . . . Perhaps when they're a bit older (now 5 and 8) I'll try to get a part-time job . . . He (employer) knows he's got a hold on me. He knows I need the money.

Money. I wouldn't touch it with a barge pole if we could manage . . . I'm so limited in what I could do. I'm not leaving my son . . . My husband works long and irregular hours, so I couldn't do an evening job. We just couldn't manage without it.

The extra money is essential. My husband's business is up and down, and the children need things.

The study found homeworkers doing five different kinds of work: manufacturing (soldering plugs), needlework (e.g. machining, sewing and knitting), office and clerical work, childminding, and semiprofessional work (e.g. editing, sales promotion). As is clear from Table 9, the largest concentrations of homeworkers in the sample taken were found in manufacturing, office and clerical work, and needlework.

Table 9   Distribution of homeworkers between types of occupation (Source: Based on Cragg and Dawson, 1981)

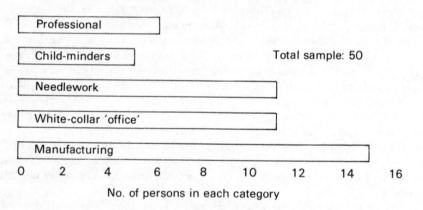

If money and, to a lesser degree, fulfilment determine whether or not women do paid work, it is having dependent children that is crucial in affecting whether women work in the home or outside it. Many mothers gave as their reasons for doing homework the flexibility which enables them to work when it is convenient to them and thus to accommodate their paid work to their domestic lives. This involves a whole array of working arrangements, as is evident from the following examples:

I do it at night when my husband is on nights, or during the day when he is on days. I can fit it in wherever I like. In the warmer days I have it set up permanently in the little box room, I just go up and do a bit whenever I want to.

My children come first. Absolutely . . . Normally I sit down and knit from 8 o'clock until I go to bed. But I don't slog at it – I take my time. Not unless it's required urgently.

I aim to finish my housework about 10.30 am. I usually type until about 2.30 pm, then have half an hour for coffee, and go and collect the little fella at 3.00, and that is my typing for the day.

I have to do it to pay the bills . . . My husband (crane driver) gives me 30 a week for all the bills, everything . . . I don't know how much he earns but it's good money . . . . He just says it's my responsibility, so I've got to do it. He won't give me any more . . . I'd sooner go out to work, but I'm not going to leave my children.

Part-time work and homework are distinctive forms of work which are done almost exclusively by women. The largest concentration of part-time workers and home-workers exist in occupations that are themselves predominantly female. This suggests that the construction of certain occupations – women's jobs – on a part-time basis or a homeworking basis is an important aspect of occupational segregation and that an adequate analysis of occupational segregation needs to take this into account.

Pay
Women's hourly earnings in 1983 were on average 74.2 per cent of those for men. Between 1970 and 1977 women's hourly earnings increased, as a proportion of men's hourly earnings, from 63.1 per cent in 1971 to 75.5 per cent in 1977 (see Table 10). Since 1977 this improvement has come to an end, and women's hourly earnings have remained on average around three-quarters of men's hourly earnings.

Table 10 Average gross hourly earnings excluding effects of overtime of full-time employees aged 18 and over, 1970–1983/pence per hour.
(Source: *EOC Eighth Annual Report,* 1983, p.89).

	1970	1974	1975	1976	1977	1978	1979	1980	1981	1982	1983
Men	67.4	104.8	136.3	162.9	177.4	200.3	226.9	280.7	322.5	354.8	387.6
Women	42.5	70.6	98.3	122.4	133.9	148.0	165.7	206.4	241.2	262.1	287.5
Differential	24.9	34.2	38.0	39.5	43.5	52.3	61.2	74.3	81.3	92.7	100.1
Women's earnings as a % of men's	63.1	67.4	72.1	75.1	75.5	73.9	73.0	73.5	74.8	73.9	74.2

Expressed as a proportion of men's full-time average weekly earnings, however, women's full-time weekly earnings are substantially lower, averaging only 66.6 per cent in 1983. One reason for this is that men tend to work longer basic hours than women, even when the women are engaged in full-time work. A second reason lies in the effects of overtime. If overtime is taken into account, the gap between women's and men's weekly earnings is wider, since men work substantially more overtime than women. Taking the effects of overtime into account, manual women's earnings were 62.6 per cent of men's earnings in 1983, and non-manual women's earnings were 59.5 per cent of men's.

A third reason why women's weekly earnings are on average lower than men's is that women tend to be concentrated in low-paying industries and in sexually segregated occupations. Table 11 lists the low-paying industries, and shows the extent to which women's work is concentrated within them. However, it is not only the concentration of women within the low-paying industries that accounts for women's low pay. As we have already seen, women mainly work in sexually segregated occupations and their pay in consistently lower than men's pay.

Table 11   Manual employees in low-paid industries, 1975 and 1981. (Source *EOC Sixth Annual Report,* 1981, p.75)

Low Paid Industries (i.e. Industries where the average full-time male earnings are less than 95% of the average for all industries and services)	% of all female manual employees		women as a % of all manual employees in each industry	
	1975	*1981*	*1975*	*1981*
Agriculture (77.4)	0.8	1.0	10.7	14.5
Textiles (88.1)	6.6	4.2	44.0	45.1
Clothing and Footwear (84.2)	8.4	6.2	78.3	76.6
Timber, furniture (90.0)	0.8	0.7	13.3	12.5
Distributive trades (87.2)	4.4	5.5	24.4	24.8
Professional, scientific (86.7)	20.5	26.1	71.9	75.5
Miscellaneous services (84.1)	15.2	20.2	51.0	53.1
Public administration (90.1)	4.3	5.2	27.8	36.5

Note: Figures in brackets are the percentage of average male earnings for all industries and services paid in each listed industry in 1981.

Comparison of black and white women's earnings is complicated by the different age structures of the two groups. Overall, black women's earnings are slightly higher than white women's at each job level, but when only the 25–54 year old groups of women are compared, white women's earnings are overall higher (Brown, 1984). Perhaps more significant than the differences in earnings between black and white women, however, is the large differential between men's and women's earnings.

There are, of course, a whole array of other material benefits that accrue from doing paid work other than basic earnings. One important benefit is membership of an occupational pension scheme. It is estimated that in 1983, 58 per cent of all women in full-time employment and 11 per cent of those in part-time employment, were members of occupational pensions schemes. Part-time workers fare particularly badly on a whole array of benefits–not only pensions but also sick pay, and paid holidays.

Some effects of occupational segregation

Occupational segregation has a number of consequences for women's experience of paid work. It means that hierarchical relations between women and men which exist throughout society and especially in the family are reproduced within the workforce. Thus, where men and women work alongside each other, it is almost invariably in jobs which give men more power and authority over women. For example, men generally work as doctors and women as nurses; men are managers and women are secretaries; men are foremen or supervisors and women are operatives. Black women, who historically have worked as servants for white men and women, often find themselves working in manual service jobs.

Second, the prevalence of occupational segregation has severe consequences for young women entering the labour market and for women wishing to re-enter the labour market, because it circumscribes the kinds of jobs which women can get into. It can be relatively easy to get into traditionally female occupations as the extracts from interviews with Karen and Adija show:

Karen
I got a Saturday job at British Home Stores. I just went into the shop and asked if they needed anyone. I worked from 8.30–6.30. You got 1 hour for lunch and a quarter of an hour break in the morning and afternoon. I got paid £7.20. I worked there for 6 months, while I was at college, doing a 2 year hairdressing course. Most of the other girls on my course had to do evening work or Saturday jobs, because none of us got grants. That meant that I only had Sunday free.

Adija
I work in a shoe shop on Saturdays. My sister's friend used to work there, and when she left she asked me if I wanted the job. I took it because I get bored at home; most of my friends had Saturday jobs, and I couldn't afford to go out much, as my family didn't have any extra money to give me. To work at the shop I'm supposed to be 15 but really I'm 14. I just had to lie, but I don't think they cared as they never checked up. The hours are 9–6 with one hour for lunch and two quarter hour breaks. I get paid £6.65 a day, which is about 84p an hour. (from *Spare Rib*, 116, March 1982)

Work in these 'women's jobs' is frequently part time and low paying, and women may be constrained to take part-time jobs because of the lack of full-time opportunities even if they would prefer to work full time. It is extremely difficult for women to get into nontraditional occupations, however, bcause the prevalence of occupational segregation means that certain jobs are defined as 'men-only' jobs.

The example of Dianne, typical of many cases, shows how a young woman's desires can be thwarted when she expresses interest in nontraditional occupations like engineering, or shows that she has ambitions. It also shows how careers officers and others who advise and influence girls can perpetuate a situation in which women seldom break into men's jobs because the advisers accept the existing structures of occuaptional segregation.

Dianne: Six O-levels, including maths, physics and chemistry; three CSEs
   Originally Dianne wanted to be a radiographer or laboratory assistant, but while looking through the "sits. vac." column of her local paper, she came

across advertisements for jobs in engineering, which strongly appealed to her . . .

But when Dianne mentioned her interest in engineering to teachers at her school: "The teachers just laughed at me."

On her own initiative, Dianne, who had never been shown by her school where to look for information on occupations, wrote to various engineering firms asking about apprenticeships. But many firms did not bother to reply, and of those that did the majority ignored her request for information about engineering apprenticeships and sent her instead details and application forms for clerical employment . . .

One firm invited her to take a selection test, which she passed. But the interview which followed this was something of a disappointment to Dianne:

"(The personnel officer) asked how I would cope if I rose to the top of the firm or if I would be satisfied with a lower job . . . he made it clear that he didn't think I would get the job and that he didn't want me to get it. He said 'We have never had a girl here yet.' The atmosphere was very tense. He asked how I would feel working with men – he went on a lot about this . . . he kept plugging leadership potential."

Dianne's interview lasted about 20 minutes. The previous applicant had been a boy from her school, who was given 45 minutes. Although he had a lower educational standard, the boy was offered an apprenticeship. She was not.

Dianne is now a clerk in an accountancy firm. (Bennett and Carter, *Employment Gazette*, April 1982, p.167)

Recently some education authorities, prompted by intiatives taken in WISE

Table 12 Employees in employment, Great Britain 1971–1983 (*Source: EOC Eighth Annual Report, 1983, Table 3.3, p.77*)

Millions

| | *June* | | | | | | | |
	1971	*1972*	*1973*	*1974*	*1975*	*1976*	*1977*	*1978*
All male	13.4	13.3	13.5	13.4	13.2	13.1	13.1	13.1
All female	8.2	8.3	8.7	8.9	9.0	9.0	9.1	9.2
Full-time	5.5	5.5	5.5	5.5	5.4	5.4	5.4	5.5
Part-time	2.8	2.9	3.2	3.4	3.6	3.6	3.6	3.7
All persons	21.6	21.6	22.2	22.3	22.2	22.0	22.1	22.3

| | *September* | | | | |
	1979	*1980*	*1981*	*1982*	*1983*
	13.1	12.7	12.1	11.8	11.5
	9.3	9.0	9.0	8.9	8.8
	5.6	5.4	5.2	5.1	5.0
	3.7	3.7	3.8	3.8	3.8
	22.4	21.7	21.2	20.7	20.4

(Women in Science and Engineering) Year, and by teachers, parents and students concerned about the lack of opportunities and/or encouragement for girls to study maths, science and technical subjects, have begun to examine the biasses (overt and hidden) in school curricula and to encourage girls to study and train in non-traditional subjects. (See Chapter 3 for further discussion of this.)

Women's Employment in the recession
It has often been suggested (especially by feminists) that women would be the hardest hit by the recession and would be the first to be made redundant. Statistical evidence suggests, however, that while this may have been true for particular industries, it is overall men who have lost their jobs to a greater extent than women. As Table 12 shows, there were 13 million men in employment in 1971, but only 11.5 million in 1983. This decline is a consequence not only of high levels of unemployment but also results from various measures designed to try and ameliorate youth unemployment – for example, early retirement and Youth Training Schemes.

The numbers of women who were employed, in contrast, increased over the same period from 8.2 million in 1971 to 8.8 million in 1983. A closer look at the statistics suggests, however, that marked differences in employment patterns have occurred between full-time and part-time women workers. The number of full-time women employees has, like the number of men, decreased, although proportionately slightly less, as Table 13 shows. On the other hand, the number of part-time women employed has increased dramatically both

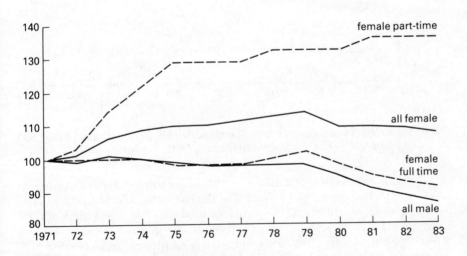

Table 13 Employees in employment, Great Britain 1971–1983 (1971=100)
(*Source: EOC Eighth Annual Report, 1983, Figure 3.2, p.77*)

absolutely and relatively. Indeed, part-time jobs for women have been the only significant area of employment growth in the past 15 years.

The question of how women are being affected by the recession is, however, quite complicated.

The registered unemployment figures show that in absolute terms more men than women have lost their jobs in the recession, but that women's registered unemployment has increased at a faster rate than men's. Between 1976 and 1983 women's registered unemployment increased four-fold, while men's slightly more than doubled. The rise in women's employment and their rising unemployment should both be seen as expressions of the same tendency for women to increasingly participate in the labour market over a longer period of their working lives.

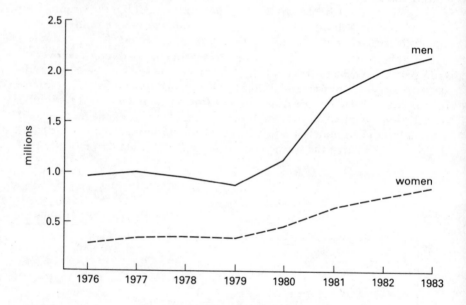

Table 14 Numbers registered unemployment, by sex, Great Britain 1476–1983. *(Source: EOC Eighth Annual Report, 1983, Figure 3.3, p.78)*

It is important to point out that straightforward job loss is by no means the only way in which women are affected by the recession. The hours of work of part-time workers are often cut or reorganized in such a way they are less convenient for women. Furthermore, jobs are being restructured with lower levels of pay and worse terms and conditions of employment. This seems to be happening on quite a large scale as jobs in the public sector are being privatised and will undoubtedly increase if wages councils are abolished. It is part-time women's jobs, in particular, which have been in the front line as privatisation has been put into practice.

Explaining Women's Employment

Commonsense and structural explanations
Any explanation of women's employment must address the kinds of questions which have been discussed in this chapter so far: why women have different patterns of participation in the labour market than men, why women in general and black women in particular are concentrated in particular industries and occupations, why part-time work and home-work are distinctively feminine forms of work in our society, and why women's earnings are systematically lower than men's. A variety of explanations of these phenomena exist in commonsense discourse, in statements like the following, for instance:

(a) women are better than men at doing boring repetitive work;
(b) men have an aptitude for mechanical skills;
(c) women are not interested in career or promotion prospects;
(d) women cannot lift heavy weights;
(e) women are not capable of taking responsibility at work.

'One of the characteristics of these commonsense explanations is that they explain women's and men's positions within the labour force in terms of characteristics of women and men themselves. For example, the claim that women are not interested in career or promotion prospects assumes that the underrepresentation of women among professionals and managers results from women's lack of interest. And the claim that women cannot lift heavy weights explains women's absence from certain jobs in terms of physiological characteristics'. In explaining the characteristic features of women's position in the labour force in terms of characteristics of women themselves, the commonsense explanations are all individualistic forms of explanation. They involve 'blaming the victim'. They explain the position of women in the occupational structure in terms of assertions about women's nature, or capabilities or temperament rather than social structures. Individualistic explanations very often implicitly or explicitly involve biologically determinist claims, that is, claims that women's capabilities are determined by their biological attributes.

It is worth looking in a bit more detail at one statement which generally involves biologically determinist claims in order to get some idea of how the argument is constructed. This is the statement that 'men have an aptitude for mechanical skills'. This involves two assumptions; first, that men are good at mechanical skills, and second (implicitly), that this is due to their biological or psychological aptitudes. There are two main problems with this. The problem with the first assertion is that it implies that all men have superior mechanical aptitudes, and thus fails to recognize that the distribution of aptitudes within the population does not mirror the distribution of the population by sex, and that there is considerable overlap between the attributes of men and women. Thus, even if it is true that some men have better mechanical skills than some women, it does not follow that one can generalize about the attributes of all men as opposed to all women in this way. The second problem arises from the assertion that these differences can be explained in terms of biological differences between the sexes. It is highly unlikely that even if most men do have more highly developed aptitudes for mechanical skills these result from biological factors. They are much more likely to result from childhood socialisation and from the different opporunities offered to girls and boys in the education system and to young men and women in training schemes. The explanations of women's employment to be considered in the rest of this chapter differ from these commonsense explanations in that they explain the characteristics of women's employment in structural terms, by reference to how society is organized.

The conventional sociological approach: women's two roles

The first framework for analyzing women's employment considered is exemplified in a study by Alva Myrdal and Viola Klein called *Women's Two Roles*. This is typical of what might be called the conventional sociological approach to women's employment. Myrdal and Kein wrote *Women's Two Roles* in 1956, but it has been reprinted many times since then. Rereading it today is a rather strange experience because the economic and political climate of 1956 was so different from the climate now. Nevertheless, the general approach which the authors adopt has continued to be influential. It has influenced a whole number of studies of women's employment which were conducted by the Department of Employment and by international agencies like the ILO and OECD (although its influence on government and international thinking has undoubtedly declined as the recession has affected the ways in which people have thought about employment). It has also influenced much more recent sociological studies, for instance, Young and Wilmott's study, *The Symmetrical Family*, which received a great deal of publicity when it was first published in 1973.

The influence of this approach is also evident in popular and journalistic accounts. The opening passage of *Women's Two Roles* is reproduced below:

> During the present century the social position of women has undergone a series of profound changes, in which we can distinguish two main phases. The first is characterized by the admission of women to an increasing variety of hitherto 'masculine' jobs, provided, on the whole, that the women were unencumbered by family ties. The outstanding feature of the second phase is the endeavour of a growing number of women to combine family and employment. Altogether, this social change amounts to a gradual recapture of positions which were lost when women were squeezed out of the economic process by the Industrial Revolution.
>
> Before that revolution women had at all times played a very active part in the economic life of society, as they do in agricultural communities to this day. Their two roles, raising a family and doing economically productive work, were fused into one way of life, work at home. When industrialization forced these to be separated, it was at first thought that women could carry on only one, namely, the family function. They had, therefore, first to assert their right to work

alongside men; and now they have to prove that they can carry on both functions
in one and the same lifetime, which is so much longer now than it was.

The process of eliminating women from economicaly active positions of
course affected different social groups in different ways, as does the
complementary process of bringing them back into paid jobs. In both urban and
rural proletariat the latter was an immediate effect of industrialization, and the
exploitation of women and children in its early phases was one of the blackest
spots in the social history of the nineteenth century. Later, as wages rose, many
working-class women left the labour market, since it was felt to be an important
element in a higher standard of living that wives and mothers should be able to
stay at home, like the women in more privileged social groups.

It eventually fell to the women in the urban middle class to symbolize the more
systematic return to economic productivity, by entering paid employment.

The recovering of women's lost territory is a long and uneven process, as yet
incomplete. The most painful part of the readjustment is caused by the fact that
habits of thought that belong to past phases of these complex developments, and
frequently to particular social groups, become established as absolute in
situations where they no longer apply. (Myrdal and Kein, 2nd edn, 1968, pp. 1
and 2)

Myrdal and Kein's central concern was with the changing pattern of
women's participation in the labour market. This they suggested was due to a
number of factors, the most important of which were connected to the family.

The factors which Myrdal and Klein strongly emphasized in their book
were: demographic factors, in particular the greatly increased average
expectation of life that has taken place in the twentieth century; the change in
the size and structure of the family and consequent reduction in the period in
which a women's life is entirely devoted to maternal duties; and the factors of
uncertainty relating to the later years of married life – uncertainty stemming
from the likelihood for women of widowhood and the increasing incidence of
marital breakdown and divorce.

They also discussed wider social and economic changes that have affected
the family – the fact thay many educational and other 'social welfare'
functions have been increasingly undertaken by the welfare state, and the fact
that the family has lost some of its economic functions as more commodites
have been produced outside the home. They suggested that, although women
were not taking less time on housework, it was in principle possible for
housework to take up much less of women's lives because of the invention of
labour-saving household conveniences and gadgets. Finally, Myrdal and
Klein pointed to the changing employment opportunities for women,
especially in the expanding service sector of the economy. They gave
considerably less weight, however, to the changes in the organization of work
which have led to an increased demand for female labour than to changes in
the structure of the family which have made possible an increase in the supply
of female labour.

The 1950s, in which Myrdal and Klein wrote *Women's Two Roles*, was a
period of economic expansion. In this period, the welfare state was developing
rapidly, and there were enormous increases in consumption.

The prevailing ideology in this period decreed that this was an era of new-
found affluence and equality. Myrdal and Klein argued that the changes that

were taking place in society would make possible women's equality with men. They asserted that women have a responsibility to enter into the world of paid work and, in passages like the following they chastized those women who chose not to go out to work:

> . . . Our modern economy cannot afford, nor can our democratic ideology tolerate, the existence of a large section of the population living by the efforts of others. Whether we like it or not, the leisured class has passed into history, together with the coach-and-four, the home-brewed ale, and other symbols of the 'good old times' (p.26).

Myrdal and Klein were particularly keen that women re-enter the labour market after their children are grown up. They did not challenge the prevailing view that a woman's primary duty was that of wife and mother, but rather argued that, in periods of the life cycle when a woman does not have to care for young children, she should enter the world of work. They pinpointed some of the barriers to women's re-entry into the labour force, and have suggested that there exist residual 'habits of thought which impede women's full participation in the labour market – an argument which you might recognize as being similar to the view put forward in the Government's White Paper on *Sex Equality* that 'tradition' has played a large part in perpetuating inequalities between the sexes. Myrdal and Klein suggested that inegalitarian 'habits of thought' pervade all sectors of society. Employers are often prejudiced against women. Many women too have ambivalent feelings about work – caught between a career and a family, they have a 'feminine dilemma' and do not feel fully at home in either world.

Myrdal and Klein claimed that social policies and changes in employers' practices could do a good deal to facilitate the fuller participation of women in the labour market. They argued for a 'constructive approach to the problem of women in employment', which considers questions like the following: 'What are the working conditions most conducive to maximum efficiency, considering the fact that workers have home responsibilities as well as jobs and that married women, in particular, often have arduous as well as important responsibilities at home?' (p.94).

They proposed an array of specific measures that could facilitate women's fuller participation in the labour market, for instance, part-time work, childcare facilities, home helps, the rationalization of housework, and the introduction of public services to decrease the domestic workload. They also placed great emphasis on the importance of changing some aspects of the dominant ideology so that it would be acceptable for married women, and especially married women who do not have responsibilities for dependent children, to have a job. They did not question the prevailing assumption that a woman's primary role is that of housewife and mother. Rather they proposed changes in social policy that would make it easier for women to combine their housewife and mother roles with paid work.

Myrdal and Klein's recommendations about social policy were extremely progressive for the period in which they wrote, since this was a period in which femininity and domesticity were strongly emphasized. There are, however, a number of problems with the framework of analysis which they developed.

Myrdal and Klein had an extemely optimistic view of the possibilities of 'progress'. They assumed that society was moving forward in an inexorable march away from 'tradition'. Although the march forward may need a little help-for instance, from the government, or from employers-they saw no structural impediments to progress in general, or to women's equality with men in particular. This optimistic belief was underpinned by the view that technology, both at home and in the workplace, has great liberatory potential. This criticism can be put in more theoretical terms. Myrdal and Klein seem to have taken at face value many of the prevailing ideological assumptions, and they gave insufficient weight to the ways in which the social structure and the organization of the economy give rise to a sexual division of labour, to occupational segregation and to inequalities in earnings between women and men.

My other criticisms are linked to this general point. One important feature of Myrdal and Klein's analysis is that they emphasized that if women did work they did this in addition to their domestic responsibilities. However, they did not question the assumption that a women's primary role is that of housewife and mother, not did they question the sexual division of labour within the family. Also Myrdal and Klein paid very little attention to the ways in which work was organized. They assumed that the 'lost terrain' of women's employment had been conquered by middle-class women, and that working-class women were following in the footsteps of their middle-class sisters. They also assumed that women were 'naturally' suited to certain kinds of jobs, especially caring and service jobs, which were rapidly expanding during this period. Myrdal and Klein did not recognize that in the 1950s, as today, women worked in an extremely narrow spectrum of jobs, which were occupationally segregated from men's jobs, and that women's share of top jobs had scarcely improved since 1911.

In part, Myrdal and Klein's blindness to the realities of women's position within the occupational hierarchy stemmed from the fact that they were principally concerned with a different question-with women's changing participation rate-and that a major aim of their book was to pursuade employers, the government and women themselves that women were capable of combining two roles. Nevertheless, their lack of concern for the realities of women's situation once they entered the labour market must be considered a shortcoming of their book.

The theories discussed in the following sections have analyzed women's employment from rather a different perspective because they have concentrated upon women's situation *within* the labour force. They have, therefore, shifted the focus of attention away from an exclusive emphasis upon the family and the conditions of female labour supply.

Dual labour market theory

Dual labour market theory grew out of studies of local labour markets in the
USA and originally emerged in the 1960s from attempts to understand the
problems of poverty and underemployment. It was used mainly to analyse the
position of blacks within the American occupational structure. It has more
recently been used to analyse the position of women within the occupational
structure, both in the USA and in the UK. One of the earliest attempts to use
the theory to understand the position of women in the labour market in
Britain can be found in a paper by R.D. Barron and G.M. Norris (1976) called
'Sexual divisions and the dual labour market'. The approach has become
quite popular among researchers into women's employment. It underlies
Catherine Hakim's paper on *Occupational Segregation*, for instance,
discussed above.

The central focus of dual labour market theory is on the structure of the
labour market. Barron and Norris do not disregard the impact of the family on
the structure of the labour market, but they argue that the sexual division of
labour within the family is of less importance in explaining sexual divisions
within the labour market than are employers' strategies within the labour
market:

> The emphasis in this paper is on the structure of the labour market, and the
> question of men and women's place in the family-the household sexual
> division of labour-is relegated to the status of an explanatory factor which
> contributes to, but does not of itself determine, the differentiation between the
> sexes in their work roles. (p.47)

Dual labour market theory shares with other economic theories this
emphasis upon the labour market. However, it analyses the labour market in a
distinctive way. Whereas economists conventionally think of the labour
market as an unitary phenomenon, dual labour market theory emphasizes
segmentation within the labour market. Barron and Norris outline their
perspective on the labour market in the following extract:

> There are . . . many ways of characterizing a labour market . . . All of these models
> have some explanatory value, but this paper concentrates upon one type of
> segmental model; the 'dual' labour market. A dual labour market is one in
> which:
>   1. There is a more or less pronounced division into higher paying and lower
>   paying sectors;
>   2. Mobility across the boundary of these sectors is restricted;
>   3. Higher paying jobs are tied into promotional or career ladders, while lower
>   paid jobs offer few opportunities for vertical movement;
>   4. Higher paying jobs are relatively stable, while lower paid jobs are unstable.
>   (pp. 48 and 49)

They argue that the labour market is divided into primary and secondary
sectors. This results from the strategies which employers use to tie skilled and
technical workers into the firm. Employers offer workers in the primary
labour market higher earnings and better career prospects to persuade them to

stay in the firm. Barron and Norris suggest a variety of reasons why employers privilege primary sector workers in this way. Among the most important are: the need to have a stable workforce in jobs that require extensive training and investment by the firm; a desire to weaken the unity of the working class, thereby reducing the potential for conflict in the workplace; and a desire to 'buy off' the most militant and well-organized sectors of the working class.

Dual labour market theory argues that employers do not privilege secondary sector workers in this way. These tend to work in unskilled and service jobs which have low skill requirements and require little training. Whereas primary sector workers are tied into the firm's career structure, secondary sector workers tend to move between industries and occupations, between one unskilled or semiskilled low-paying job and another. Barron and Norris outline the different strategies used by employers in the following terms:

> . . . If it is in the interest of the employers to maintain and expand the primary sector, it may also be in their interest to ensure that instability and low earnings are retained in the secondary sector. Of course, the strategy is necessarily related to the availability of a supply of workers willing to accept the poor pay, insecurity, low status and poor working conditions of secondary jobs. (p.52)

I have so far only discussed the distinction between primary and secondary sector workers. You may be wondering how women fit into this picture. Barron and Norris suggest that in Britain women comprise the major secondary sector workforce. They argue that employers often use ascriptive criteria in selecting workers – that is, they select workers on the basis of characteristics like age, sex or skin colour, which the individual acquired at birth, rather than on the basis of achievement criteria like educational qualifications. To quote from 'Sexual divisions and the dual labour market' again:

> Given the limited information about potential job applicants normally available to recruiters, it may often be difficult for an employer to obtain direct evidence about the likely reliability and stability of a potential employee. Therefore use is frequently made of relatively visible individual characterstics which are thought to correlate highly with these qualities. For purely operational reasons employers rely upon formal educational and training qualifications and other easily identifiable, personal criteria, such as sex, age, colour and possibly certified disability. The use of these broad categories as a basis for job allocation has two important consequences. When ascriptive characteristics, like sex, are used as selection criteria, it has the effect of confining the groups so delineated to the secondary sector over the whole of their working lives. The second is that the actual confinement of particular groups to the secondary sector will result in their having higher rates of labour turnover and job mobility. Thus a 'vicious circle' is created which reinforces the discrimination power of the trait which was made the basis of the selection criterion, and the labelling process becomes self-fulfilling. (p.53)

Barron and Norris argue that there are five main attributes that make a particular social group or category a likely source of secondary workers:

1   Dispensability - the ease with which an employee can be removed from a redundant job.
2   Clearly visible social difference - preferably one which emphasizes the relative inferiority of the secondary group
3   Little interest in acquiring training and experience
4   Low economism, i.e. little concern for monetary rewards
5   Lack of solidarism - for instance, relatively low level of trade union or collective strength

Women, they argue, are likely to score high on each of these criteria, and are therefore commonly used as secondary sector workers. Members of minority ethnic groups, too, often score high on these criteria, and may also be used as secondary sector workers.

You can get some idea of how dual labour market theory might work in practice by considering the UK car industry. It is invariably white male workers who work in the toolroom and in other skilled jobs in the car industry, and managements have consistently offered incentives like high wage rates to keep these workers within the firm. If black men are employed, it tends to be in semiskilled or unskilled jobs, and in heavy dirty occupations like foundry and paintshop work, which white male workers are reluctant to do. The car industry does not employ many women in manufacturing occupations, but they are sometimes employed in the trim shop and on other bits of semiskilled assembly work; and, of course, women are employed to do cleaning and catering work and in secretarial and clerical jobs. Dual labour market theory would argue that managements privilege their white male skilled workers (primary sector workers) to try to stop them from moving to other firms by paying them higher wages while having little regard for whether their women workers leave or move on. Women can always be replaced by other women since they do not have skills which are difficult to replace.

There are a number of important differences between dual labour market theory and the sociological approach discussed above. Dual labour market theory is far less optimistic than *Women's two roles*. This is hardly surprising, of course, since Barron and Norris were writing about somen's employment twenty years after Myrdal and Klein. As already suggested, however, Myrdal and Klein were far more optimistic about the possibilities for women's 'progress' than was warranted by an analysis of the statistical evidence which would have been available to them then. Second, Myrdal and Klein place more emphasis upon middle-class women's employment - on the importance of women's work in the professions - whereas Barron and Norris deal almost exclusively with working-class women's work - in semiskilled and unskilled jobs in the manufacturing and service sectors. Third, Barron and Norris concentrate primarily upon how employers organize their work-forces, and upon what economists call the demand for labour. This contrasts sharply with Myrdal and Klein's almost exclusive emphasis upon the family and demographic changes, upon what economists call the supply of labour. It is, in part, this difference in emphasis which leads to dual labour market theory's greater pessimism. The rest of this Section will raise some questions about the adequacy of dual labour market theory's analysis of the demand for female labour, and in particular consider how far it can account for occupational segregation, and the related problems of inequalities in earnings between women and men, and low pay.

Dual labour market theory has little to say about horizontal occupational segregation - that is, about the segregation of women into jobs like clerical work and selling, and men into jobs like security and protective services. It does, however, throw some light on the process of vertical occupational segregation, since it is centrally concerned with the question of hierarchy and privilege within the workforce and with the strategies used by employers to privilege certain groups of workers in order to keep them within the firm. It also throws some light on the question of unequal earnings and low pay, since it asserts that employers pay more to primary sector workers in order to keep them within the firm. Those are the main advantages of this approach. .

Dual labour market theory is, however, limited in the extent to which it can explain occupational segregation, because its analysis is derived from an account of employers' strategies in particular kinds of manufacturing industry. The theory is most satisfactory when it deals with industries like the car industry, in which men are employed in skilled and technical jobs. In such industries, it may well make sense to characterize women's work as secondary sector work. However, many kinds of women's jobs do not fit easily into the category of secondary sector work. Some women's work in manufacturing industries is skilled work that is integral to the production process, for example, work in the textiles industry. Although this may be low paid in comparison with men's work, it is not marginal or insecure as secondary sector work is. Much secretarial work throughout all sectors of the economy requires considerable training, and secretarial workers are in integral part of the workforce. Although secretarial work may not be well paid in comparison with some men's jobs, and although it may not actually be defined as skilled, it is not marginal and insecure. Finally, a goood number of women are employed in professional and technical jobs, especially in the public sector. The most obvious examples of these are nursing, teaching and social work - all important 'woman's professions'. Women are also employed to some extent in some management jobs, especially in these sectors. These require training, they are highly skilled, and are central to the activities of the health, education and social services sectors. Dual labour market theory's conception of women being a secondary sector workforce cannot adequately account for these kinds of women's work. A major problem with dual labour market theory is that it derives its whole conceptual edifice from an account of manufacturing occupations within manufacturing industry, and it generally assumes that women do semiskilled or unskilled work. If one looks at women's work across the occupational structure, a rather different picture emerges. Large numbers of women work as white-collar workers, for instance, and in certain professional occupations. Although it is true that women tend to be employed on the lowest rungs of the ladder in professional, white-collar and manual occupations and some people have tried to adapt the framework to analyse these other kinds of work, my own view is that it is oversimplifying to explain the concentration of women in the lowest grades of every occupation in terms of the concept of a secondary sector workforce.

A related point is that dual labour market theory does not provide sufficient *positive arguments* as to why employers employ women in particular occupations and industries. The main positive argument advanced is the 'divide and rule' argument, but this does not explain why so many occupations have been constituted as 'women's work'-why, for instance, secretarial work is done almost exclusively by women, and why women predominate in sales work, domestic work, teaching and nursing. Employers undoubtedly prefer to employ women in these occupations (except perhaps at the upper echelons of nursing management and schoolteaching), and this use of women as a preferred labour force within specific occupations needs to be explained.

The final point to make about dual labour market theory for the moment is that it is limited in its capacity to explain occupational segregation because it is classifactory and ahistorical. It provides a snapshot view of the economy at a given point in time, but it does not consider *why* particular occupations came to be defined as women's work and as men's work, and is thereby unable to analyse the process by which the sexual division of labour within the labour force changes historically.

Marxist approaches

A Marxist approach, like dual labour market theory, focusses primarily upon the demand for labour. Marxists have developed a number of theories about the ways in which women workers are employed in advanced capitalist societies, and in this section I shall discuss the argument put forward by Harry Braverman (1974) in his book called *Labour and Monopoly Capital*, which has become a classical study of waged work in capitalist societies. Braverman's book is principally about the organization of work in the USA. Nevertheless, the framework of analysis he uses is broadly applicable to the UK, as both countries have developed in rather similar ways after industrialization.

The point of departure of a Marxist approach is a consideration of the labour process. Braverman outlines his general approach to the labour process in the following extract:

> ...The subject of our discussion is not labor 'in general', but labor in the forms it takes under capital relations of production.
>
> Capitalist production requires exchange relations, commodities, and money, but its *differentia specifica* is the purchase and sale of labor power. For this purpose, three basic conditions become generalized throughout society. First, workers, are separated from the means with which production is carried on, and can gain access to them only by selling their labor power to others. Second, workers are freed of legal constraints, such as serfdom or slavery, that prevent them from disposing of their own labour power. Third, the purpose of the employment of the worker becomes the expansion of a unit of capital belonging to the employer, who is thus functioning as a capitalist. The labor process therefore begins with a contract or agreement govering the conditions of

the sale of labor power by the worker and its purchase by the employer.*

It is important to take note of the historical character of this phenomenon. While the purchase and sale of labor power has existed from antiquity, a substantial class of wage-workers did not begin to form in Europe until the fourteenth century, and did not become numerically significant until the rise of industrial capitalism... in the eighteenth century. It has been the numerically dominant form for little more than a century, and this in only a few countries. In the United States, perhaps four-fifths of the population was self-employed in the early part of the nineteenth century. By 1870 this had declined to about one-third and by 1940 to no more than one-fifth; by 1970 only about one-tenth of the population was self-employed. We are thus dealing with a social relation of extremely recent date. The rapidity with which it has won supremacy in a number of countries emphasizes the extraorindary power of the tendency of capitalist economies to convert all other forms of labour into hired labor.

The worker enters into the employment agreement because social conditions leave him or her no other way to gain a livelihood. The employer, on the other hand, is the possessor of a unit of capital which he is endeavouring to enlarge, and in order to do so he converts part of it into wages. Thus is set in motion the labor process, which, while it is in general a process for creating useful values, has now also become specifically a process for the expansion of capital, the creation of a profit. From this point on, it becomes foolhardy to view the labor process purely from a technical standpoint, as a mere mode of labor. It has become in addition a process of accumulation of capital. And, moreover, it is the latter aspect which dominates in the mind and activities of the capitalist, into whose hands the control over the labor process has passed. (pp. 51 and 53)

*Note that Braverman uses the terms 'worker' and 'working class' to refer to everyone who has to work for a living – professionals and 'middle-class' people as well as those in the white-collar and manual strata.

It is important to understand what is meant by taking the labour process as one's point of departure. At one level, the labour process refers to the way in which work is organized: to what kind of technology is used; what kind of division of labour is employed; how work is supervised and controlled; and what system of payment is used. According to this definition any process by which what Braverman called 'useful values' are produced involves a labour process – labour processes exist in factories and offices, but also in sweatshops and in the family. However, Braverman also refers to another level of analysis. He talks about the capitalist form of labour process (that is, the dominant form of labour process within industrial capitalist societies) in which production is carried out with the aim of creating a profit. He argues that it is this criterion of profitability which is crucial to the ways in which the labour process in capitalist societies is organized. It is this which determines how employers and managers actually organize work.

Braverman argues elsewhere in *Labor and monopoly capital* that in the form of society which he calls monopoly capitalist – that is, the form of capitalism which exists in twentieth-century Britain and the USA – the economy is more and more dominated by large corporations, and work has become increasingly subdivided so that unskilled labour has been substituted for complex skilled labour. This is because it is cheaper to pay unskilled workers than skilled craftsmen. Braverman's arguments about the subdivision and fragmentation of labour under monopoly capitalism have been labelled by others 'de-skilling', although Braverman does not use the term himself.

Braverman's argument that married women have been drawn into the labour force in periods of labour shortage is clearly incontrovertible. Married women, in particular, have been employed extensively in both World Wars in Britain, and have increasingly been employed in the post-war period. Indeed, they have continued to be employed in large numbers throughout the recession, when there has no longer been a labour shortage. The reasons for this are quite difficult to unravel, and different writers emphasize different factors. Myrdal and Klein assert that the increase in married women's employment primarily results from demographic changes and changes in the family, whereas Braverman asserts that the increased labour supply emerged in response to the changing demand for labour. For him the labour process has a primary role in explanation and the family is a dependent variable. Braverman is not, however, able to provide a satisfactory explanation of *why* women constitute a distinctive kind of labour force (particularly suited to unskilled work) in terms of his analysis of the labour process. His analysis tends, therefore, to rely upon naturalistic assumptions.

Braverman also asserts that workers have less control over the production process than they used to have, and everybody suffers from alienation at work These changes in the organization of the labour process all derive from employers' quest for profits. Braverman suggests that all kinds of occupation at every level of the occupational hierarchy have undergone this process of subdivision and fragmentation. As mass assembly methods of production have been introduced, skilled jobs in manufacturing industry have been more and more decomposed into semiskilled and unskilled jobs. So have traditional occupations like engineering, middle-class occupations like technical and scientific work, lower-ranking supervisory and management occupations, and professional occupations. Furthermore, he argues, 'new working-class' occupations like clerical work, service work, and retailing have also been increasingly subdivided. Work in these occupations has become increasingly routinized, repetitive and boring.

Braverman locates his analysis of women's employment within this general analysis of the subdivision of labour, and he argues that there has been a long-term shift in the structure of the working class as a result of this process. Women have been drawn into paid employment mainly in service occupations, which have been expanding under monopoly capitalism, whereas men have been employed in declining manufacturing occupations. There has thus developed a new form of sexual division of labour within the working class, in which women and men are employed in fairly equal proportions, with women being employed in the expanding service occupations like clerical work and retail sales work, and men employed in manufacturing occupations. Braverman thus suggests that a new form of sexual division of labour has developed under monopoly capitalism, and that in the typical working-class family the man is employed as an operative and the woman as a clerical or service worker.

Why, according to Braverman, have women been drawn into work in these service occupations? He points to a number of factors which he thinks have been important in drawing women into paid employment. First, he suggests that, as the capitalist mode of production developed, domestic production within the family was broken down. Women found that they could buy goods and services that they had previously produced within the domestic economy (e.g. cloth, food, clothing) and they thus began to purchase them rather than make them themselves. Second, women were drawn into paid employment to produce the same kinds of goods and services as they had previously produced within the domestic economy. Braverman suggests that women were able to move fairly automatically from working within the domestic economy to working in production outside the home. Third, women have been drawn into paid employment as traditional sources of labour (people migrating from countryside to towns, ex-slaves moving to work in the Northern States, and migrants from Southern and Eastern Europe) have dried up, particularly in the period of expansion since the Second World War. Women have thus become part of the industrial reserve army of labour; this is a reserve of labour which can be drawn on by employers when there is a shortage of labour. Finally, and most importantly, Braverman argues, women are a source of cheap and unskilled labour. This is the major reason why employers hire them.

Braverman's argument that women have been employed so extensively because they are a cheap and unskilled labour force has some truth to it, but it is oversimplifying. Clearly some women do routinized unskilled work in factories, as the following accounts of work in West German factories testify.

'In the grinding shop I worked at three machines simultaneously. I was rushing all the time to get through the piece-number. The whole time I was standing with one foot on the pedal. We always had our hands in petroleum jelly to prevent scratches when the diamond passed through. The steam made your hair greasy. I was so afraid of not keeping up that I produced more than was necessary, 1,500 to 1,800 pieces a day. I didn't write down the excess pieces in case they made us do even more.'

Frau Heinrich's work goes in short cycles. You can tell that by the boxes stacked up in front of her which make up her day's task. She almost disappears behind them. Her work-cycle lasts for nine seconds. She takes a base, picks up a support with a pair of tweezers and welds the support to the base. She does the same with the second support and puts the finished base n the box. To be able to go on with this Frau Heinrich has extended her movements over the years, within the limits of piecework. She has invented a few additional movements, but still manages to get through the required amount of work. She doesn't simply pick up the materials and weld them together beneath the electrode. If you watch her you see that she spreads out her arms as if she were flying, draws them together and picks up the materials with both hands as if she had come upon them by pure chance. As she does this she rocks backwards and forwards, treads on the foot pedal three or four times, and only then welds the first part. Then out go the arms again. Frau Heinrich uses all this to help her get through piecework, otherwise it would be superfluous movement and she couldn't afford it. She does exactly the same thing with her feet. She has to weld two spots on every unit, while the other women have to do from ten to twelve. But here again Frau Henrich adds a few movements. While she picks up the pieces and before she puts them under the electrode she rocks up and down three or four times on the foot pedal, and only then does the real welding.

Frau Heinrich has devloped these movements in resistance to the inhuman piecework. A unit is processed every nine seconds. Frau Heinrich welds 3,140 tube bases a day. (Herzog, 1980, pp. 147 and 148)

Furthermore, women have in certain cases been drawn into paid employment in order to deskill the workforce and undermine the position of skilled male workers. This happened particularly in the munitions factories and the engineering industry in the First World War in Britain. It is these kinds of processes which Braverman's analysis particularly identifies. Braverman's deskilling argument also enables him to link together different forms of work that are generally considered in isolation from each other, for example, professional and technical jobs, white-collar jobs, manual jobs in the service sectors and manual work in manufacturing industry. He thus counters the prevailing view that middle class and white collar jobs are necessarily qualitatively different from more traditional manual working-class occupations, and shows how these can change in similar ways as capitalism develops and more and more areas of work are subjected to its particular form of market rationality.

His analysis cannot, however, be used to analyse all forms of women's employment in capitalist societies. It cannot explain women's employment in professional occupations like nursing, teaching and social work (although his de-skilling arguments do shed some light on the increasing use of women as unqualified nurses, social workers and teaching assistants to do work which was previously done by qualified professionals). Nor can it easily explain women's employment in jobs which have never been defined as skilled, like much women's work in the service sectors of the economy, nor why many women's jobs are not classified as skilled work when they involve complex competencies. Finally, it cannot explain the reskilling which has occurred in certain kinds of work. Braverman's exclusive emphasis on deskilling ignores, for instance, the fact that the introduction of new technology into the secretarial and clerical fields has created some new skills as well as destroying old ones, as has the use of computerized technology in the health service and in some sectors of manufacturing industry (e.g. telecommunications).

In the following sections I shall discuss a number of important theoretical questions which arise from Braverman's analysis and from dual labour market analysis which are central to the analysis of women's employment. These concern the role of trade unions and of men in creating and maintaining divisions within the workforce, the concept of skill, the role of the family in explaining why women enter the labour force on different – and disadvantageous – terms from men, and the role of the ideology. I shall also discuss the relationships between gender, class and 'race'.

Understanding divisions within the workforce

Both dual labour market theory and Marxist theory pay relatively little attention to divisions and conflicts between men and women within the workforce. In this and the following section I shall briefly look at two perspectives which are explicitly concerned with analysing the contradictory interests between women and men within the workforce. Each involves a critical appraisal of dual labour market and Marxist perspectives.

The role of trade unions
In a paper called 'Structured labour markets, worker organization and low pay' Jill Rubery (1980) criticizes both dual labour market theory and other radical theories (as she calls them) for failing to include an analysis of the role of trade unions within their conceptual frameworks. She suggests that dual labour market theory and other radical analyses (including Braverman's) have viewed the development of the economic structure solely from one perspective – through the motivations and actions of individual capitalists – and they have thereby paid insufficient attention to the ways in which maintaining a divided workforce may be of interest to workers, and may be a product of struggle.

Rubery's own arguments follow the broad contours of *Labor and Monopoly Capital*. Like Braverman, she asserts that the development of monopoly capitalism involves the destruction of old skills – although unlike Braverman she emphasizes that this process also involves the creation of new ones. This process of recomposition of skills, she argues, has often provoked defensive attempts on the part of trade unions to maintain old skill divisions within the labour force, even when there is little or no real basis for maintaining these skill divisions. One of the examples of trade unions' successfully maintaining old definitions of skill, which Rubery cites, is the engineering industry in the First World War. Here skilled engineers sucessfully maintained craft demarcation until 1914, despite the fact that, as James Hinton has pointed out, 'a substantial proportion of the work performed by craftsmen, at the craft rate, required little of their skill' (Hinton,pp.61–2).

Women working in the engineering industry suffered from these attempts by the craft union to continue to get men's work defined as skilled. A more recent example, which Jill Rubery also discusses, is the printing industry, in which the craft printing unions have organized vigorously to prevent their skills being undermined by new technology.

Rubery argues that the *basis* of labour market segmentation lies in the fact that new supplies of wage labour have been introduced into the economy in different historical periods. Thus, in the UK, Commonwealth immigrants, blacks and married women have all entered the labour force more recently than men, and they have all been confined to the lowest strata of the labour market. They are often prepared to work at lower wage levels than white male workers, and this, she argues, leads to hostility of white male workers towards these groups. If employers try to substitute any of these groups of workers for white male workers, Rubery suggests, this may well lead to a decline in relative wages within a given occupation, and reduce employment opportunities for men. This, in turn, may lead trade unions to try and confine women to a particular sector of the labour force by using a variety of mechanisms, ranging from union organized apprenticeships schemes to promotion lines based upon strict seniority provisions. In this way, Rubery argues, 'Divisions by custom, rule and status are essential parts of any union's organizing strategy' (p.260).

Rubery's argument, then, is that trade unions have played a crucially important role in maintaining (though not in creating) labour market segmentation. In some cases this has involved attempting to restrict the access of women to skilled jobs. Rubery argues that the reasons for such restrictive practices (which effectively control the supply of female labour into occupations which have been hitherto defined as 'men's work') lie in trade unions' attempts to maintain some control over the labour process in the face of employers' moves to wrest control from skilled workers and to reorganize the labour process.

One problem with the way in which Jill Rubery discusses trade unions, however, is that she assumes that trade unions may engage in restrictive practices to protect encroachments on their position, but she does not explain *why* trade unions may decide to protect their members' positions by excluding women from skilled jobs, or by implementing grading schemes that maintain differentials between men and women workers, rather than in other ways. That is, she does not explain the basis of the sexism involved in many trade-union practices.

Michèle Barrett makes a similar point in her book, *Women's Oppression Today*. Discussing the question of skill, Michele Barrett suggests that the labour movement could in principle pursue two quite different strategies:

> ... The first would be to build upon the bargaining power of groups of workers whose skills and essential functions enable them to successfully raise wages and conditions of work, not only for themselves, but in such a way as to pull up the groups less powerful in these respects. This strategy depends upon differentials and exclusionary practices, but it is argued that in the long run it raises the standard of living of the working class as a whole. The second strategy is to attempt to establish a minimum wage for all workers, irrespective of skill and selectional bargaining power, and thereby reduce the likelihood of undercutting and substitution of cheaper labour. (p.170)

In fact, the labour movement in Britain has consistently pursued the former strategy. In doing so, Barrett argues, it has reproduced and reinforced the vulnerable position of women workers. Jill Rubery does not take into account the fact that there are different strategies available to trade unions. She also does not acknowledge that the fact that trade unions frequently pursue strategies that effectively disadvantage women needs to be explained.

And the role of men

Like Jill Rubery, Heidi Hartmann (1976) makes the picture of the organization of work within capitalist socieities more complicated than dual labour market theory and Marxist theory would suggest. She, too, emphasizes job segregation within the labour market. Her analysis is rather different from

Jill Rubery's, however, because she emphasizes the role of men in creating and reproducing job segregation.

Hartmann argues that the development of capitalism threatened men's power over women. It threatened to bring all women and children into the labour force, and hence to destroy the family and the basis of men's power over women (which lay in control over men's labour power within the family). Men, she argues, therefore developed strategies to maintain their power within the developing wage-labour system. One of these strategies was the development of techniques of hierarchical organization and control within the labour market. Hartmann identifies a number of factors that partly account for the existence of job segregation by sex, and for women's lower wages: the exclusionary powers of the male unions, the financial responsibility of men for their families, the willingness of women to work for less because of subsidies or a lower standard of living, and women's lack of training. Most important of all, however, she argues, is the ability of men to organize in trade unions, which has played such an important role in maintaining job segregation and differentials and excluding women. Like Rubery then, she emphasizes the role of trade unions. Unlike Rubery, however, she sees these as an expression of men's desire to control and dominate women.

Hartmann argues that job segregation creates a vicious circle for women from which they cannot escape. Their subordinate position in the labour market, and particularly their lower wages, keeps them dependent upon men. This dependence upon men within the family in turn reinforces women's subordination in the labour market, and so on:

> Job segregation . . . is the primary mechanism in capitalist society that maintains the superiority of men over women, because it enforces lower wages for women in the labor market. Low wages keep women dependent on men because they encourage women to marry. Married women must perform domestic chores for their husbands. Men benefit, then, from both higher wages and the domestic division of labor. This domestic division of labor, in turn, acts to weaken women's position in the labor market. Thus, the hierarchical domestic division of labour is perpetuated by the labor market, and vice versa. (p.139)

Hartmann introduces the concept of patriarchy into her analysis in order to explain this domination of women by men. Patriarchy refers to institutionalized power relationships by which men control women. Hartmann argues that there existed a set of patriarchal relationships before the development of capitalism. She asserts that:

> . . . before capitalism, a patriarchal system was established in which men controlled the labor of women and children in the family and . . . in so doing men learned the techniques of hierarchical organization and control. With the advent of the private-public separations such as those created by the emergence of state apparatus and economic systems based on wider exchange and large production units, the problem for men became one of maintaining their control over the labour power of women. (p.138)

As capitalism developed, and men's power within the old set of patriarchal relations began to be eroded, men developed a series of strategies to maintain the hierarchical relations in which they had power. Among these was job segregation by sex. According to Hartmann, the position of women within the labour force is the product not just of capitalist social relationships, as Marxist theory would argue, but of capitalist and patriarchal relationships, which mutually accommodate to each other. As Hartmann herself puts it:

> . . . This process is the present outcome of the continuing interaction of two interlocking systems, capitalism and patriarchy. Patriarchy, far from being vanquished by capitalism, is still very virile; it shapes the form modern capitalism takes, just as the development of capitalism has transformed patriarchal institutions. The resulting mutual accommodation between patriarchy and capitalism has created a vicious circle for women. (p.139)

Hartmann's analysis is important because it emphasizes that there are conflicting interests between women and men within the workforce. Her perspective, like Jill Rubery's, throws a critical light on dual labour market theory and Marxist theory because neither of these perspectives pays sufficient attention to gender divisions within the workforce, whether there are the result of trade-union practices or of men's endeavours to control women and to assert their power and authority over them.

There is, however, a major problem with Hartmann's conceptual framework. Hartmann analyses occupational segregation as a result of 'two interlocking systems, capitalism and patriarchy'. She then suggests that it is the 'resulting mutual accommodation between patriarchy and capitalism (which) has created a vicious circle for women'. The problem is that Hartmann identifies patriarchy and capitalism as two independent structures each with its own system of social relationships, the first being a system of relationships between capitalists and workers, and the second a system of relationships between men and women. One of the difficulties with this formulation is that it ignores the fact that capitalist social relationships are themselves patriarchal in form.

Gender and skill

One of the important issues which has been touched on several times in the preceeding sections is the question of gender and skill, and a major criticism which feminists, in particular, have made against Braverman's analysis is that he treats skills positivistically, failing to appreciate the extent to which social definitions and ideological constructions enter into the definitions of certain kinds of work as skilled. The concept of skill embodies a variety of different meanings. Skills can be defined as complex competencies – as capacities which some people have (like mending machines, or performing surgical operations) and which other people do not have. This definition of skill assumes that the complex competencies which people use at work are, in fact, accurately labelled as skilled. Another way of looking at the concept of skill is to say that only some of the compentencies used at work are defined as skilled and that women's competencies in particular (e.g. typing, preparing and serving food, mending clothes), are often not defined as skilled and that ideological constructions frequently enter into the definition of skilled jobs. In an article on sex and skill Ann Phillips and Barbara Taylor suggest that the designation of some kinds of work as skilled is not only ideological but also sexist. It is applied to certain kinds of work because it is men who perform it:

> . . . the classification of women's jobs as unskilled and men's jobs as skilled or semi-skilled frequently bears little relation to the actual amount of training or ability required for them. Skill definitions are saturated with sexual bias. The work of women is often deemed inferior simply because it is women who do it. Women workers carry into the workplace their status as subordinate individuals, and this status comes to define the value of the work they do. Far from being an objective economic fact, skill is often an ideological category imposed on certain types of work by virtue of the sex and power of the workers who perform it. (Phillips and Taylor 1980, p.79)

This raises the question of why certain jobs get defined as skilled, and suggests the need to investigate what the mechanisms are by which so much women's work escapes the classification 'skilled'.

The first reason why women's jobs are often not classified as skilled is because they generally involve quite short periods of formal training. Training through apprenticeships has always been the route by which people enter into craft jobs, and these apprenticeships can be very long. In her article on 'The state and training programmes for women', Ann Wickham cites the following data on young women's entry into apprenticeships:

> Women were doing badly in many areas of training. In 1970 only 110 females were apprenticed to the skilled craft occupations compared to 112,000 males and less than one fifth of those on day-release courses were female. Where girls were in apprenticeships the majority of these were in hairdressing. This situation is clearly related to the kinds of attitudes displayed by the unions and the Department of Employment. (Wickham, 1982, p.152)

Relatively few young women enter into formal apprenticeships. There are also now many forms of training other than apprenticeships, and these have proliferated recently under the auspices of the Manpower Services Commission, which was established in 1973. Despite a few positive action programmes, for example, those run by the Engineering Industries Training Board and by some local authorities, however, there is little evidence that young women have gained significantly from the expansion of training, and especially from the Manpower Services Commission's recent Youth Training Scheme. A further important point is that many women's jobs use skills which women learn informally within the home (e.g. sewing and cooking). This informal training, however, never counts as training in the more formal sense of the word, and is not generally considered a significant variable in the determination of women's pay.

A second reason why most women's jobs are not defined as skilled is that women have frequently been unable to get their jobs defined as skilled through trade unions. Trade unions have fought to get jobs defined as skilled or to maintain their definition as skilled in the face of employers' endeavours to define jobs as unskilled or semiskilled, and they have often tried to impose restrictions on entry into apprenticeships so that the number of skilled workers can be restricted.

Chris Aldred has a succinct summary of some of the ways in which trade unions have operated to restrict skilled status in the following passage:

> Trade unions have, from the early days, recognized the greater bargaining power of the skilled worker as opposed to the unskilled worker, who can be much more easily replaced, except at times when labour is very scarce. Of course, skilled workers lose this advantage if the particular skill is held by many people, all competing for the new jobs which use that skill. So the early craft unions-unions of skilled workers-saw how important it was that they had control over the number of people learning a skill, and fought hard to influence the number of apprentices trained and the standard of training approved. (Aldred, 1981, pp.32 and 33)

The case of the First World War shows quite clearly that the issue of what constituted skilled status was a major issue of controversy between employers, unions and the State. Women were largely excluded from skilled status – and, indeed, from the negotiations in which new definitions of skill were reached. Chris Aldred's comment that 'The label that eventually gets stuck on a job can be as much a reflection of the balance of power between union and employers as it is of the length of time taken to learn the job', would seem to be particularly true of women's work in the First World War. The history of women's employment suggests that this is by no means an isolated example, and that trade unions have often failed to get the jobs of their women members classified as skilled.

In an exercise Chris Aldred points out that a good case can be made for considering the work of a home help as skilled, on the grounds that she, like many men's jobs which are classified as skilled (joiners or engineers, for example) has to be able to make safe and efficient use of hand and power-tools, to use chemicals carefully, and to be able to identify and carry out necessary operations given general instructions.

This exercise well illustrates the main point I want to emphasize: that the concept of skill is socially constructed, and that an adequate analysis of the exclusion of women from skilled jobs has to take account of this. In part, women are excluded from skilled jobs because they have not managed to enter into formal apprenticeships or other appropriate training schemes. In part, however, women do work which may involve complex competencies (like typing, cooking) but which is not designated as skilled. In his analysis of de-skilling Braverman (like most industrial sociologists and industrial relations experts) does not appreciate this second kind of exclusion of women from skilled jobs. The European Community's equal pay legislation which argues that equal pay should be given for work of equal value, unlike the old U.K. legislation, allows for women to compare themselves with a hypothetical male and to argue that they should receive the same wages as him, and this makes it more possible for women to argue that their skills have been unrecognized relative to those of men. In an early case to be taken to the European court a cook working at Cammell Laird shipyard compared herself to a skilled man, and her employers were forced to give her a big pay rise. The question of skill is therefore, not just an academic question of definiition, but has real consequences for women's lives.

The family and women's employment

Both the family and familial ideology have an important role in determining women's position in the labour market, something which the women's two roles theorists recognized but which generally goes unnoticed in theoretical perspectives which focus on the labour market and the labour process. At the most concrete level, women's participation in the labour force is affected by whether or not they have children, and is most crucially affected by the age of the youngest child. This determines whether or not a woman does paid work, whether she works full-time or part-time (especially if she is white) and the kinds of jobs she does. Furthermore, caring for elderly and handicapped relatives is also becoming increasingly important in preventing some women from doing paid work, especially in mid-life. It is estimated that in London there are more women caring for elderly and handicapped relatives than for children under 16. In the absence of adequate facilities for caring for children, and for elderly and handicapped people in the community, and as back-up facilities like home helps and meals-on-wheels are being cut by many local authorities, it becomes increasingly difficult for women who have responsibilities for caring for others to work full-time.

In addition to determining both the likelihood and the hours of work, home responsibilities influence the type of work undertaken. A study of female factory workers noted that 'employment has to be fitted in with their household duties and childcare arrangements, which they and their families regard as unquestionably their responsibility. Factory work is often seen as the only job possible in the circumstances and entered into more from necessity than from choice...' (Shimmin, McNally and Liff, 1981). Similarly, a study of homeworkers concluded that 'many mothers gave as their reason...the flexibility it gave them to work when it was convenient to them' (Cragg and Dawson, 1981).

Whereas a considerable amount is now known about the ways in which *women's* employment histories are affected by their familial responsibilities, far less has been written about the situation of fathers and about the extent to which their domestic responsibilities affect their employment histories. Just as the question of why they *don't* work is seldom asked of women, so the question of why they *do* work is almost never asked of men. Lesley Rimmer and Jennie Popay from the Study Commission on the Family summarize what is known about fathers' employment in the following extract:

> Whereas the impact of children on their mothers' employment has been subjected to much scrutiny, far less has been written about the situation of fathers. Today married men with dependent children count for 43 per cent of the male labour force, and on this basis there are some 6.8 million fathers working or seeking work. What influence do family responsibilities have on their employment experience? Activity rates among married men tend to be higher

than among non-married men, and also to be higher among married men with dependent children than among those without. However, the proportion of fathers in work does not seem to vary with the age of their youngest child, nor with the number of dependent children in the family. In addition whereas women with children tend to work fewer hours than those without, the majority of fathers work full-time and fathers of large families, who tend to have lower hourly earnings, work longer hours on average than fathers in small families. Equally a number of studies suggest that paid overtime is most common among younger married men especially those with dependent children whose financial commitments are often high: one study showed that married men under 30 with children worked four times as much paid overtime as similarly aged childless husbands. And men with children are similarly more likely to work shifts. (*Employment Gazette*, June 1982, p.256)

Single fathers are far more likely to work than lone mothers, and single fathers' working hours tend to be similar to those of fathers in two-parent families. However, one study of motherless families suggested that fathers who had direct responsibility for caring for young children worked less overtime, were less able to work at weekends, and could not undertake jobs that involved travel from home.

Another way in which the sexual division of labour within the family affects women's employment is in the kind of jobs that women do. Many women do jobs that replicate their domestic responsibilities. This has been true historically, and is still true today, and is especially true of black women's jobs. In Table 6 representing women's paid work in West Yorkshire, Ursula Huws used the categories of 'housework' workers and 'caring' workers to describe some women's jobs. Eleven of thirty-two women in the paid labour force in West Yorkshire were engaged in these kinds of work, which in many important respects are based upon women's familial role, and which often presuppose skills that women learn informally within the family, that are not formally recognized, and for which they are not renumerated.

Much women's work, particularly in the Welfare State, involves skills that women learn, at least in part, in the family (e.g. caring, cleaning, preparing and cooking food)–although in non-manual and professional jobs, in particular, these skills are greatly supplemented by formal training programmes. Feminists have also pointed out that women's work often involves other skills and attitudes which are typically 'feminine', particularly in non-manual jobs. These are jobs in which glamour and sexuality are often an integral part of the job (.e.g air hostess, model, and some top-level secretarial jobs). What these share in common with the more domestic and caring jobs first discussed is the incorporation, within the definition of the jobs, of important aspects of women's more general social role.

The role of ideology

Women's position in the labour market is affected, in a number of important ways, by ideology, especiallly the ideology of femininity. Black women's situation is also affected by racism. As Lucy Bland et al have pointed out, the ideology of femininity is contradictorily constructed for women: 'while we are mothers who serve our husbands and children we are also the desirable 'sexual' objects for men' (Bland et al., 1978, p.65). Women are constructed within the ideology of femininity in relation to men throughout their lives, but the specific constructions change over the lifecycle. They also vary according to class and race. Some white feminists have emphasized the importance of notions of glamour and sexuality in the construction of young women's jobs, especially jobs like secretarial work, telephone/receptionist work, hairdressing, and flight attendant which represent women as being visibly attractive to men. Others have emphasized the servicing aspects of much women's work which frequently underlie these glamorous representations. Black femininists have recently pointed out, however, that ideas about femininity are also racially specific. Black women are frequently excluded from more glamorous jobs, it is suggested, precisely because it is white femininity which is required to be visible. The dominant representations which exist for black women are those of nurses, cooks, domestics and machinists, and their servicing role is often invisible 'belowstairs'.

Studies of women's paid work have generally emphasized the role of familial or domestic ideology, rather than the ideology of femininity in structuring women's paid employment. Whereas family households take different forms, varying historically and across different social classes and ethnic groups, familial ideology is universalistic. It asserts that the nuclear form of family and sexual division of labour within it is universal, reflecting biological differences between the sexes. Familial ideology asserts that men are primarily breadwinners and women are their dependants. It proclaims that a woman's primary role is that of housewife and mother. Familial ideology has in fact changed historically in Britain. In the nineteenth century it was thought to be unacceptable for married women to engage in paid employment outside the home at all, and single women's employment was only grudgingly accepted. Philanthropists and policy-makers expressed deep concern about the effects of married women working on family life:

> What was most forcibly articulated in bourgeois philanthropy was the degeneration of the family caused by the conditions in which mothers undertook wage labour, the way in which working wives neglected the home and so drove their husbands to the alehouse, the moral impropriety of men and women and young people all working together in the same place, the moral danger of the influx of independent single girls to the factory towns. (Barrett and McIntosh, 1980, p.74)

Today women's paid work is becoming more recognized and acceptable. Nevertheless, it is still assumed that a woman's work outside the home should not interfere with her domestic responsibilities in caring for her husband and particularly in caring for her children and other dependent relatives. Women's paid work must fit in with her domestic role and she must be a good wife and mother.

Despite the fact that fewer and fewer families correspond to the nuclear model with male breadwinner, non-working wife and dependent children, familial ideology remains pervasive. It is a crucial element of the dominant ideology. It plays an important role in structuring women's participation in the labour market and in restricting opportunities for paid work. It affects her participation in the labour market, deeming it unacceptable for her to work when she should be caring for others. It enters into the construction of certain jobs as 'women's jobs' and other jobs as 'men's jobs' with women's jobs frequently involving caring for and servicing others. It is used to depict women who work full-time (black women in particular) as 'bad mothers'. And finally, it is embedded in the concept of the family wage – the notion that a man's major responsibility is as family breadwinner and that he should provide for a dependent wife and children – which is still prevalent within employers' and trade unions' ways of thinking about wages. When ideologies make differentiations among people on the basis of ascriptive characteristics like age, sex, or race they tend to be particularly pervasive because they represent social relations as though they were natural. Familial ideology, which assumes that women are primarily wives and others, plays an important role in the organization of paid employment, while simultaneously portraying the sexual division of labour and women's position in the labour market in quasi-naturalistic terms.

Gender, race and class

Recent feminist analyses of women's employment have begun to redefine the theoretical analysis of work in several important respects suggested by the discussion in previous sections. They have argued that women's employment cannot be understood solely in terms of an analysis of production, or the labour process, but have instead suggested that the sexual division of labour within the family plays an important role in determining the conditions in which women enter the labour market. They have suggested that economic explanations of women's employment (which assert, for instance, that women are employed because they are secondary sector workers or cheap labourers) are oversimplifying. They have asserted that ideology, especially the ideology of femininity and familial ideology, play an important role in determining both women's entry into the labour market and the kinds of jobs they do. And they have suggested that state family policies, which generally embody the familial assumptions that a married woman is dependent upon a man and that the mothers of young children should not be in paid employment affect the patterns of women's employment. There is little agreement about the direction of determination between these different variables – about whether the family, or the labour process, or state policy, or ideology, is determinant – and different people working in this area emphasize different factors. It is however, clear that they are interdependent.

A further issue of concern to feminists is the role of gender in the organization of production. For some feminists have argued that one of the problems with classical analyses of the labour market and labour process like dual labour market theory and Marxist theory is that they are sex-blind, and they have, therefore, failed to recognize the ways in which gender relations enter into the organization of labour markets and into production itself. Thus, it has been suggested, women's unequal and inferior position within paid employment and their lower pay has little to do with economic factors (for instance, that they are cheap labour), but is a consequence of gender relations and gendered assumptions which affect employers' hiring strategies, trade union practices etc. and which relegate women to a subordinate position. A corollary of introducing gender into the analysis of paid employment is that women are not treated as some kind of marginal labour force, subject to discrimination, but are seen as structuraly subordinate. A further corollary is that men, too, are regarded as gendered subjects.

Black feminists have recently begun to point out the extent to which the theories which have been developed in recent years take the experience of white women as their instance of 'typical' women workers, and have therefore failed to appreciate the extent to which black women's experiences may be different because they have developed from rather different historical conditions–generally those of imperialism and colonialism–and because they are subject to racism in British society. (See Carby, 1982, Parmar, 1982, and *Feminist Review No.17* for discussion of this.) I have tried at certain points in this chapter to indicate some of the ways in which black women's experiences may be different from white women's. It seems likely, however, that a systematic inclusion of race and ethnicity into the analysis of paid employment would suggest new questions and lead to changed analytic frameworks. The criticisms which have been levelled by black feminists underline an important question of how far women share a common experience of paid employment. A great deal of work has been done identifying the differences between women's and men's experience of paid employment. However, we know far too little about the differences between women of different classes, races and ethnic groups, and have not yet developed a theoretical framework, which can adequately account for these differences.

Equality at work

Inequalities between women and men in the labour market have proved particularly difficult to change. More and more women are in paid employment and they work for most of their lives, but their position has scarcely improved this century. Furthermore, the increase in women's part-time employment means that many women, while perhaps having a flexibility in their hours of work, are employed in jobs which are defined as unskilled and are often insecure and badly paid. Feminists have adopted a variety of different strategies to try and improve women's position in the labour market. They have used the law, they have organized women in trade unions, and more recently they have pressed for positive action policies to be implemented in workplaces.

The law has proved to be extremely limited in its effectiveness in dealing with women's situation in the labour force. The Equal Pay Act has been largely ineffective in tackling occupational segregation and low pay, and the British Government has recently been obliged by the European Community to broaden the scope of its legislation to comply with Community law, which states that women should receive equal pay for work of equal value. In 1983 only 26 applications to industrial tribunals were made under the Equal Pay Act, and only six of these were upheld. Whereas under the old Equal Pay Act a woman could only bring a case if there was a man with whom she could compare herself (a fairly rare occurrence given the extent of occupational segregation), under the revised law a woman is allowed to compare herself with what a hypothetical man would be paid, were he to be employed in the same job. In principle this would allow for the upgrading of many women's jobs, although the British legislation (unlike the USA) only allows for individual solutions.

The issues of recruitment policies, promotion, training etc., are covered by the Sex Discrimination Act, which allows cases to be brought for both direct and indirect discrimination. The indirect discrimination clauses of the Act which allow women to argue that the requirements of a particular job (an age bar, for instance) are discriminatory are among the broader provisions of the Act, but these are still not widely tested, and few cases of discrimination have been upheld. In 1983 256 people made applications to industrial tribunals under the Sex Discrimination Act, but only 61 of these were successful. A major problem with the Act is that with the exception of its provisions for special training schemes for women the Sex Discrimination Act is mainly negative in its effects. At best it can be used to enable women to counteract individual acts of discrimination, but it can do very little positively to break down occupational segregation and the concentration of women in low-paying jobs. (cf. Robarts, 1981).

Historically, trade unions are the agencies through which workers have pressed claims against employers on a collective basis, but these too have proved inadequate in dealing with the problems on their women members. Women comprised 31 per cent of trade union members in 1981, compared with 25 per cent in 1971, but they are still very badly represented at all levels of officialdom, as Table 15 shows.

Historically, too, trade unions have been founded on the very structures of occupational segregation that lie at the root of many of the problems faced by women in the labour market, the structures and culture of many trade unions are inhospitable to their women members, and their continuing adherence to concepts like the family wage and their desire to maintain differentials means that trade union commitments made to equal pay are often superficial. All too frequently a real commitment to equal pay would upset the structures of collective bargaining, and in the 1970s unions in many workplaces actually went along with management attempts to evade the requirements of the Equal Pay Act by regrading or redefining jobs (cf. Snell *al.*, 1981). It took 300 women sewing machinists at Fords seventeen years to win a campaign for parity with the majority of semi-skilled production workers – this campaign was eventually successful because the women were backed by their union, the TGWU, but they had a long hard fight to get their union to support them.

Table 15 Representation of women in trade unions
(*Source:* EOC Eighth Annual Report, 1983)

Union	Membership			Executive members			Full-time officials			TUC delegates		
	Total	Women	% Women	Total	Women[6]		Total	Women[6]		Total	Women[6]	
APEX[2]	100,968	53,668	53.2	15	4	(8)	50	2	(26)	12	5	(6)
ASTMS[2]	410,000	92,250	22.5	22	2	(5)	97	7	(22)	31	6	(7)
BIFU[5]	141,042	69,112	49.0	31	3	(15)	54	6	(26)	20	5	(10)
CPSA[1]	182,282	132,553	72.7	29	12	(21)	37	8	(27)	15	7	(11)
GMBATU[2]	880,449	253,686	28.8	31	1	(9)	290	16	(84)	86	3	(25)
NALGO[1]	780,037	405,619	52.0	71	18	(37)	181	16	(94)	72	18	(37)
NUPE[1]	688,101	458,733	66.7	26	10	(17)	161	10	(107)	31	10	(21)
NUT[3]	260,281	187,860	72.2	47	6	(34)	27	2	(19)	27	3	(19)
NUTGW[4]	76,130	70,776	92.7	14	7	(13)	38	3	(35)	12	4	(11)
TGWU[1]	1,547,443	226,765	14.7	39	1	(6)	502	10	(74)	83	3	(12)
USDAW[1]	403,446	224,171	55.6	17	1	(9)	125	8	(69)	36	6	(20)

Sources and notes:
[1] Figures have been supplied by the individual trade union and are as at December 1983.
[2] Figures have been supplied by the individual trade union and are as at September 1983.
[3] Membership figures are as at December 1982; TUC delegates are for the 1983 conference; Executive members and full-time officials are as at February 1984.
[4] Membership figures are as at December 1983; TUC delegates are for the 1983 conference; Executive members and full-time officials are as at April 1984.
[5] Up to date figures are unavailable at the time of going to press. Membership figures are for the year ending. December 1980. Figures for Executive members and full-time officials were supplied by BIFU. TUC delegate figures are derived from the *TUC Annual Report 1981*.
[6] Figures in brackets show how many women there would be if they were represented according to their share of the membership.

Furthermore, with a few exceptions, trade unions have not been eager to take up the issues which particularly affect their women members, issues like maternity leave, flexible hours of work, and the rights of part-time workers.

Because it has proved so difficult to use the law and trade unions to fight for women's equality in the workforce, some feminists have argued that more positive measures are needed to improve the situation of women at work, and, in particular, to try and break down occupational segregation with all the attendant problems this has for women (unequal earnings and low pay, concentration in unskilled jobs, lack of opportunities for moving into work that had traditionally been defined as men's work.) Positive action is essentially a strategy designed to remove the effects of past discrimination, and can involve re-evaluating and upgrading women's work or introducing positive measures to desegregate men's and women's work. Positive action programmes have been introduced in a number of companies (e.g. Thames Television and Sainsbury's) and also some local authorities (particularly the GLC and a number of 'left' local authorities). In Britain positive action schemes are entirely voluntary, and they are unlikely to be successful unless negotiated and agreed between management and unions. They are also unlikely to be able to tackle successfully inequalities between women and men in the labour force unless they deal with the problems experienced by part-time workers.

The problem with all strategies for dealing with inequalities between women and men in the labour force – the law, trade unions and positive action programmes – is that they necessarily focus upon workplace issues, and are thus restricted to the 'public' sphere and associated with the organization of work. Many of the problems experienced by women in the labour market are a product of the sexual division of labour within the family, however. A strategy that is adequate to deal with the problems faced by women in the work of paid work has to recognize this, and to devise ways of breaking the vicious circle in which the sexual division of labour in the family and employers' and trade union strategies in the labour market continually reinforce each other.

Acknowledgement

In preparing this chapter I have received a great deal of detailed help from Jackie West of the University of Bristol and Ceredwin Roberts of the Department of Employment.

References and further reading

ALDRED, C. (1981) *Women at Work*, Pan.

ALLIN, P. and HUNT, A. (1982) 'Women in official statistics', *The Changing Experience of Women*, Martin Robertson.

BARRETT, M. (1980) *Women's Oppression Today*, Verso.

BARRETT, M. and McINTOSH, M. (1980) 'The "family wage" ', *The Changing Experience of Women*, Martin Robertson.

BARRON, R.D., and NORRIS, G.M. (1976) 'Sexual divisions and the dual labour market' in BARKER, D.L. and ALLEN, S. (eds) *Dependence and Exploitation in Work and Marriage*, Longman.

BLAND, C., BRUNSDEN, C., HOBSON, D., WINSHIP, J. (1978) 'Women inside and outside the relations of production', Women's Studies Group, CCCS, *Women Take issue*, Hutchinson.

BRAVERMAN, H.V. (1974) *Labor and Monopoly Capital*, Monthly Review Press.

BROWN, C. (1984), *Black and White Britain*, The Third PSI Study, Gower Publishing Company.

CARBY, H.V. (1982) 'White woman listen: Black feminism and the boundaries of sisterhood', in CCCS, *The Empire Strikes Back*, Hutchinson.

CRAGG, A. and DAWSON, T. (1981) *Qualitative Research among Homeworkers, Research Paper No. 21*, Department of Employment, May 1981.

DOYAL, L., HUNT, G. and MELLOR, J. (1981). 'Your life in their hands: Immigrant workers in the National Health Service', *Critical Social Policy*, Vol. 1, No. 2, Autumn, 1981.

ELIAS, P. and MAIN, B. (1982) 'Six facts about part-time work', University of Warwick, Institute of Employment Research.

Feminist Review (1984) *Many Voices One Chant: Black Feminist Perspectives'*. Special issue of *Feminist Review*, No. 17, Autumn 1984.

HAKIM, C. (1979) *Occupational Segregation: A Comparative Study of the Degree and Pattern of the Differentiation between Men and Women's Work in Britain, the*

United States, and Other Countries. Research Paper No. 9, Department of Employment, November, 1979.

HAKIM. C. (1981) 'Job Segregation: trends in the 1970s, *Employment Gazette*, December, 1981.

HARTMANN. H. (1976) 'Capitalism, patriarchy and job segregation by sex' in BLAXALL. M. and REAGAN. B., (eds) *Women and the Workplace*, University of Chicago Press.

HERZOG. M. (1980) *From Hand to Mouth*, Penguin.

LOMAS. G. (1973) *The Coloured Population of Great Britain*, Runnymede Trust.

MARX. K. (1976) *Capital*, Vol. 1, Penguin.

MARTIN. J. and ROBERTS. C. (1984) *Women and Employment: A Lifetime Perspective*, HMSO.

MYRDAL. A. and KLEIN. V. (1968) *Women's Two Roles: Home and Work*, Routledge & Kegan Paul.

PARMAR. P. (1982), 'Gender, race and class', 'Asian women in resistance', in CCCS, *The Empire Strikes Back*, Hutchinson.

PHILLIPS, A. and TAYLOR. B. (1980) 'Sex and Skill: Notes towards a feminist economics', *Feminist Review*, No. 6.

RIMMER. L. and POPAY. J. (1982) 'The family at work', *Employment Gazette*, June 1982.

ROBARTS. S. *et al.* (1981) *Positive action for women: The next step in education, training and employment*, NCCL.

ROYAL COMMISSION ON THE DISTRIBUTION OF INCOME AND WEALTH (1974) Report No. 6, *Lower Incomes*, London, HMSO, Cmnd 7175.

RUBERY. J. (1980) 'Structured labour markets, worker organization and low pay', in AMSDEN. A.H. (ed.) *The Economics of Women and Work*, Penguin.

SCOTT. J. and TILLY. L. (1975) 'Women's work and the family in nineteenth-century Europe, in *The Changing Experience of Women*, Martin Robertson.

SHIMMIN. S., MCNALLY. J. and LIFF. S. (1981) 'Pressures on women engaged in factory work', *Employment Gazette*, August 1981.

SNELL. M.W., ELUKLICH. P. and POVALL. M. (1981) *Equal Pay and Opportunities*, Department of Employment Rsearch Paper No. 20, April 1982.

TRADES UNION CONGRESS (1981), *Homeworking: a TUC Statement*, TUC.

WILLIAMS. G. (1981) 'Mother Wales, get off me back?' *Marxism Today*, December 1981.

WICKHAM. A. (1982) 'The state and training programmes for women', in *The Changing Experience of Women*, Martin Robertson.

YOUNG. M. and WILMOTT. P. (1973) *The Symmetrical Family*, Penguin.

3 State Education Policy and Girls' Educational Experiences

Madeleine Arnot

This chapter discusses the various ways in which the educational system has contributed to the lives of women in British society. It focuses on the pattern of female education and educational achievement and considers to what extent the intervention of the state into the educational arena has benefited the majority of girls.

The chapter also investigates the various factors which need to be taken into account in explaining the patterns of female education. It analyzes the structure of education and training provision for girls historically and the ideologies underlying that provision. Later the chapter discusses the variety of factors which can broadly be described as 'educational organization': factors such as early childhood experiences, school organization and classroom practice. Explaining how and why girls and women are educated as they are is not a simple task; it reveals the complexity of the educational system, the intricacies of its internal structures and processes and the importance of its relations with external structures such as those of the waged labour process and the family. The analysis also underlines the fact that we cannot talk about female education satisfactorily without some reference to other forms of social inequality in our society, particularly those of class and race.

I begin, therefore, by looking at the nature of girls' experiences in schools and by considering the impact of class, race and gender relations on their lives. The effect of different forms of social inequalities can also be seen in the outcomes of schooling – for instance in the patterns of educational achievement and the 'take up' of educational opportunities in higher education. In the second section these outcomes will be investigated before discussing the various social and educational explanations for such experiences and levels of educational achievement.

Girls' educational experiences

It is difficult to know where to begin providing an assessment of the impact of the educational system on the lives of women. Most accounts start with the statistics on educational achievement, identifying areas of female educational disadvantage and 'underachievement'. Yet is success or failure in obtaining educational certificates or in studying certain subjects the only effect of schooling, and are qualifications the only factor affecting female employment patterns and future life styles? A feminist account of education needs, in my view, to begin with the concept of gender and to develop an understanding of how definitions of gender, of masculinity and femininity, shape our lives. We need to investigate how specific concepts of masculinity and femininity are constructed and how they are adopted by individual girls and boys. Central to this analysis, I want to argue, are the ways in which girls make sense of the definitions of femininity presented to them, how they reconcile the messages of home and school, and the experiences within community and personal relations, and how they construct for themselves personal values and identities within the constraints of their class, racial and gendered positions.

In this chapter there is only the space to look at a few examples of the sort of research now beginning to be available on girls' lives in and outside school and girls' own views of the role school should play in shaping their futures. In such research we can see an attempt being made to relate macro-structures such as class and racial divisions to girls' definitions of themselves as women. Here we glimpse the diversity and contradictions within female gender roles, class- and 'race'-specific definitions of femininity, as well as common female experiences. In the relations between (a) schools and communities, between (b) family and school cultures, and (c) in the forms of gender conformity and resistance we find indications of the impact and meaning of schooling on girls.

Let us begin with the work of Katherine Clarricoates (1980) which suggests ways in which definitions of masculinity and femininity transmitted in different primary schools might be shaped by the occupational structure and class relations of each locality. The value of this research is that it moves away from a simple notion of gender entailing a dichotomy between the masculine and feminine which applies to all children irrespective of their social class origins. Clarricoates found, for example, that in the traditional working-class primary school, a 'rigid conformity' to the 'fixed' masculine qualities of strength, toughness, dominance and bravery was expected of men, whereas women were seen as submissive, weak and located within the home, even though there were a large number of women in paid employment. In contrast, in the middle-class community school, the ideology of the school was that of academic achievement, and boys were seen as the intellectual elite, having imagination, ability and creativity. Although there were less explicit gender differences in this school, girls were expected to concentrate more on being clean, well dressed and controlled in their language rather than becoming academically oriented. Thus, although in both schools femininity was considered different and inferior to masculinity, the boundaries and the nature of the division between boys and girls differed for the different social class clienteles.

Another facet of the interaction of class and gender is in the impact of schooling, which varies for boys and girls of the working class and the middle class, whether in rural, urban or suburban environments. From a considerable amount of sociological work, we know that the school culture and its organization is based on and gives legitimacy to a specifically middle-class

culture and language. Thus children from different social classes experience
the school in a variety of ways.

For those girls who enter fee-paying schools, the experience is likely to be
one of continuity of class culture, since the schools teach and encourage the
development of upper-middle-class notions of femininity. The conflict
between home and school may not be great, and therefore the impact of the
pattern of socialization offered by such schools may be very forceful.

In the nineteenth century, girls' public schools were set up, modelling
themselves upon the already existing and successful boys' public schools.
They developed prefect systems, houses, uniforms, and boarding education,
and attempted to gain all the accoutrements of the high social status already
held by boys' schools. What these girls' schools had in common with the boys'
schools was that pupils were excluded from any contact with the supposedly
polluting environment of other social classes, of members of the opposite sex,
of contact with the modern ideas of an urban and materialistic culture. Even
today, despite changes in these schools, attendance at a private girls' school
means developing a distinctive class consciousness and a recognition of the
boundaries of that social class. This *class socialization* involves learning the
specific concepts of femininity that complement its antithesis – the masculinity of upper-middle-class men. Such a masculinity is learnt in the team
games, the house spirit and the training in leadership offered by the boys'
public schools. In contrast to a boy's education – with its stress on visions of
political power, initiative, independence and leadership – what Judith Okely
(1978) experienced at a girls' private school was constant supervision,
centralized control and a training in obedience. Whereas in the boy's school
one might find vertical social groups with senior pupils having control over
juniors, in Okely's school less emphasis was placed on pupil hierarchy, and
more emphasis on following rules. Girls were encouraged to learn the
'language of the body' through the rules of posture and feminine physical
sports and games. She writes:

> The boys' and girls' educations are not symmetrical but they are ideologically
> interdependent. That considered female is partly defined by its opposite: that
> which is considered to be male. The characteristics of one institution are
> strengthened by their absence in the other. Qualities primarily reserved for one
> gender will have a different meaning in the institution for the opposing gender.
> The two educations are also linked in practice since, in adulthood, individuals
> from the separate institutions will be united in marriage, for the consolidation of
> their class. As members of the same social class the girls and boys may share
> similar educational experiences, but as members of different gender categories
> some of their education may differ. (p.110)

Through such similarities and differences in single-sex public schools, the
division of labour between men and women of the upper-middle classes can be
transmitted. Indeed, the introduction of girls into boys' private schools does
not seem to have affected this process since such schools still use very
traditional notions of masculinity and femininity.

In contrast the experience of a working-class girl who achieves entry into a
single-sex, state grammar school shows that the culture, the ethos and

demands of the school can conflict with a child's own background. The differences between the class culture of the school and her family are experienced by Irene Payne (1980) in terms of the different definitions of femininity expected of her. Thus, even though she came from a male-headed family and was educated in a 'patriarchal' educational system, her experience was not a consistent one of oppression and the continuous reinforcement of *one* definition of gender. The following extract shows how the school uniform symbolized the interconnectedness of the class and gender culture of the school:

The first clear set of values was characterized by the school uniform. The class roots of school uniform are fairly clear because their origins are in the public schools. Institutional colours, mottoes and crests were all part of the total image derived from the ruling class. The uniform represented a sobriety and discipline whose power extended beyond the school. I can remember that prefects had the responsibility of ensuring that girls wore their berets on the bus journeys on public transport to and from school. The power of the ideology showed itself in the fact that they meticulously performed their function and reported girls seen without their berets. The uniform was part of a process of destroying individual and class identity, in order that pupils would submit unquestioningly to school authority and what that represented. School control extended even to such hidden recesses as underwear and was enforced with a vengeance, by regular inspections. Punishable offences included wearing the wrong coloured or knickers or socks. These practices were part of the process of enforcing a particular set of bourgeois values, based on ideas of respectability, smartness and appearances.

However, I think there was a further dimension to this, in terms of gender. The uniform couldn't have been better designed to disguise any hints of adolescent sexuality. I suppose that shirt and tie, the 'sensible' shoes, thick socks and navy blue knickers were part of a more 'masculinised' image. It was as though femininity had to be symbolically sacrificed to the pursuit of knowledge. Modesty was implicit as there were regulations about the length of skirts and the covering of your arms. Jewellery, make-up and nylon stockings were taboo. Ideas about dress were based on notions of 'nice' girls and 'not so nice' girls, with both class and sexual connotations. We were, after all, to be turned into middle-class young ladies.

I wore the uniform without too much suffering at school but it was the greatest source of embarrassment to me beyond the school gates. I can remember being terrified that someone from my neighbourhood might see me wearing it. I was worried that I might be regarded as a 'college pud' or a snob by my peers. If they saw anyone in school uniform they would usually jeer and hurl abuse. But it had sexual as well as class connotations. As I got older, I was particularly concerned that potential boyfriends didn't see me in this 'unfeminine' garb. The first thing I always did when I got home from school was dash to my bedroom to change out of my uniform. However, my rebellion against school uniform was never very strong as I wanted to do well at school and wearing uniform was part of the process of earning approval.

It is interesting . . . that the rebellion against school uniform did take on a very 'feminine' form. Within the grammar school, there were groups of working-class girls as well as disaffected middle-class girls who were alienated from school and just wanted to leave as soon as possible. Their rebellion manifested itself in the usual things like smoking or being rude to teachers. However, it was also structured along 'feminine' lines, in opposition to the 'masculinity' of school rules about appearance. I can remember bouffant hairstyles, fish-net stockings, make-up and 'sticky out' underskirts being the hallmarks of rebellious girls. All of these stressed femininity and the girls involved were also noted for being 'experienced' with boys. The rebellion's ultimate culmination was in getting pregnant, which meant that a denial of sexual activity was no longer possible. Such matters were always carefully hushed up and the girl concerned quickly removed. (p.13–15).

This account suggests *first*, that gender definitions are not just class specific but can be a form of *social control*, particularly when they are imposed on children of another social class and, *second*, that there may be *discontinuities* between the definitions of femininity and masculinity learnt in the home and those learnt in schools. The pattern of gender socialization may, therefore, *not* be a smooth process but rather one in which contradictions emerge that have to be resolved by the boys and girls themselves. The family and the school do not, therefore, always work in concert in what is often described as a continuous process of socialization. Schools may be more 'progressive' or more 'conservative' than parental culture. Further, the disjuncture between working-class and middle-class culture experienced at school age may well account for the failure of working-class children – and in particular the failure of working-class girls – to seize all the educational opportunities offered to them.

For the working-class girl or boy especially, the experience is often one of being confronted with an alien culture which bears very little relation to her or his everyday life – the effect can be rejection of the school ethos and the ideology of academic achievement. Many of the struggles found within schools today can be understood, therefore, as a form of class struggle – a result of conflicting value systems and culture. However, it is rare that such conflict is seen as also being related to gender. The work of Paul Willis (1977) is interesting in this respect since he shows that working-class 'lads' who reject the school celebrate a particular notion of masculinity derived to a large extent from their fathers. This prepares them in many ways for their eventual fates as manual workers. Their version of masculinity differs from that offered by the school, in that the boys identify being male with leaving school as early as possible to earn a wage, with enjoying the physicality of sports, with choosing manual work and joking with the 'lads', rather than valuing academic success.

Such conflict between home and school takes another form when girls are involved, particularly since girls, whatever the class culture, are in a subordinate position. They can never achieve the 'superiority' that the 'lads' experience; but what they can do is find other ways of re-establishing a sense of their own worth and of their identity.

Angela McRobbie (1978a) has conducted research on a group of teenage girls who have, to all intents and purposes, rejected not just the school but also, significantly, its definitions of femininity as alien to their own way of life and their perception of their futures. Paradoxically, the centre of these working-class girls' resistance to school was their notion of femininity, derived from their family and 'worked-on' by the culture of their peer group:

. . . one way in which the girls combat the class-based and oppressive features of the school is to assert their 'femaleness', to introduce into the classroom their sexuality and their physical maturity in such a way as to force teachers to take notice. A class instinct then finds expression at the level of jettisonning the official ideology for girls in the school (neatness, diligence, appliance, femininity, passivity, etc.) and replacing it with a *more* feminine, even sexual one. Thus the girls took great pleasure in wearing make-up to school, spent vast amounts of time discussing boyfriends in loud voices in class and used these interests to disrupt the class. (p.104)

If the school, therefore, asserts the ideology of equality of opportunity and, to a certain extent, 'unsexes' children through its stress on the importance of academic success, then the danger is that it denies an important source of self-evaluation of working-class girls (and boys) through gender categories. It may be that the family culture and, in particular, its gender definitions become the major obstacles to educational achievement. The definitions of femininity which working-class girls construct for themselves can encapsulate the dreams as well as the reality of marriage, female sexuality, and romance.

It is a moot point whether this notion of femininity, which may lead girls to aspire to motherhood rather than to careers, is a result of a realistic appreciation of the limited work opportunities that face working-class girls on the labour market or is, in fact, a very unrealistic diverting of their aspirations through which they lose out within the competitive educational system. What is clear is that this notion of femininity is not constructed in a vacuum, but rather in the complex set of relations that exist between family, school, class culture and peer group. In this sense it would be hard to attribute 'blame' either to the school or to the working-class family culture. The particular version of schooling that working-class girls receive pushes them into a situation where they 'freely choose' their own subordination. As a result, they head for domesticity, towards low-skilled and low-paid employment and dependence eventually on the male wage. Thus the girls' own culture of 'femininity' and romance has the effect of strengthening gender stereotypes by exaggerating them.

This experience is, however, not shared by all girls in comprehensive schools. Lynn Davies (1978), for example, found a variety of girls' responses, some of which were similar to boys' in similar academic streams, e.g. in their attitudes to teachers, their anxieties over achievement, the 'boringness' of school assemblies, homework etc. Where girls' experiences differed from those of boys were in their attitudes to school uniforms and to the types of school subjects they were pushed towards (e.g. child care rather than metalwork). Meyenn (1980) found that school control over the accoutrements of femininity (such as make-up and jewellery) were critical determinants of girls' responses to schooling. He discovered that the girls most likely to be pro-school (i.e. academic achievers) had the same attitudes to school authority as girls who could be described as anti-school, since they both opposed the school's policy forbidding the wearing of make-up. The division, therefore, between 'conformists' and 'resisters' on the basis of academic work alone was not useful in describing different girls' responses to schooling.

Mary Fuller's (1980) research has shown, in the case of Afro-Caribbean schoolgirls, the subtleties of negotiation and resistance. Their anger and frustration at school led to their positive acceptance of being black and female. They rejected the double stereotypes of blackness and femininity, not turning against themselves or against whites or the opposite sex, but by exploiting the school. They aimed to achieve good educational qualifications, obtain decent jobs and move out of their subordinate position. The acquisition of good qualifications gave them a sense of their own worth and of control over their lives. They conformed, therefore, to the notion of a 'good pupil' only in so far as they worked conscientiously at schoolwork.

In the classroom they gave the appearance of inattention, boredom and indifference. Fuller, in her analysis of these girls also calls into question the equation between academic striving and success, on the one hand, and conformity, on the other. What her study reveals is that partial negotiation of stereotypes and a sense of 'going it alone' gave the girls a means of exploiting the school system without becoming subordinate.

Kathryn Riley (1982) in a more recent piece of research found very similar patterns of response to school by fifth and sixth form girls of Afro-Caribbean origins. These girls did not see themselves as peripheral to male black culture, nor as passive sexual objects. They intended to organize and control their lives, using the more positive aspects of school life for themselves to help them achieve more equal terms with men. Their sense of realism, however, also came out clearly when talking about race discrimination in the job market:

> *Christine:* It's mostly whites, whites do the jobs with the good qualifications... They just put up some barriers, or make some excuses.
> *Angela:* You can't get jobs. There should be jobs, but it depends on the employer as well. He might be one of those who doesn't like blacks. I mean, if a white person and a black person went to the same school and got the same degrees, the white person is more entitled to get it than the black. I mean, we're all classed as stupid. (p. 12)

Such experiences of black girls in schools cannot be treated as just another variant of white schoolgirls' experiences. The relations between class and gender are made more complicated by those of race in our society. To ignore the effect of racism is to render black girls' experiences invisible and to treat as insignificant the part played by white people in maintaining race inequality and oppression (see Brah and Minhas (1985), and Carby (1982)). Pratibha Parmar (1981) suggests that the experiences of Davinder, a sixth form student are not uncommon among Asian girls in schools today:

> When I was in my second year at school and you walked down the corridor and if there were gangs of white girls they could always pick on us and call us 'wogs' and 'Pakis' and everything like that. One day it happened to me, but I could speak up for myself, so it was quite good, you see. I was walking down with my friend and they started hitting us, they think you are entirely stupid, because you are Indian, and you won't stick up for yourself. They enjoy it if you don't say anything. I told my tutor about it, told her that they shouldn't be allowed to do things like that, should they, and she said, 'We will see what we can do about it.' But she didn't say or do anything. Some teachers' unwillingness to take any action in such situations is not the only way in which they expose their racism:

often they use their authority to abuse Black pupils by calling them 'uncivilized animals'.

(Parmar, 1981, pp. 26-27)

These authors suggest that in order to recognize fully the impact of racism in education on black girls' lives it is necessary to rethink existing feminist perspectives, and to ask new questions. We might ask, for example, whether class relations are as significant for black girls as they can be shown to be for white girls, or whether the experience of being black in a racially prejudiced society overrides all other experiences. What is evident is that we need more research on black girls' lives within the educational system in order to begin to answer these questions.

Social class, gender and race all affect girls experiences of school in complex ways. The reaction to a gender category can take the form of 'pro-school' conformity, or the appearance of such, or at the other extreme it can result in rejection of the school. The range of possible responses to school life is broad and is affected by a child's social origins. Although the research into girls' school culture is still at an early stage, it is nevertheless possible to see that the process of gender socialization is full of contradictions and the structures of sexism and racism impinge differently on different groups of girls. It is wrong to assume, therefore, that the school is totally successful in its preparation of girls into one definition of femininity or that it is systematically oppressive to all girls.

Female Educational Achievement

Such educational experiences have their effect not just on girls' self-perception and identity but on their pattern of educational achievement. If we look in particular at girls' access to higher education, we can identify the impact of both sex differences and social class inequalities in educational achievement. (Unfortunately there are no comparable figures for race.)

The Robbins Report, published in 1963 is perhaps the best place to begin since it is one of the most important statements of state educational policy since the Second World War. What the Report assessed was the impact of the 1944 Education Act, which set up free, secondary education for all. It discovered the continuing depth of social inequality in so far as educational achievement and the distribution of access to higher education across different social classes and different sexes were concerned. It found that:

> The proportion of young people who entered full-time higher education is 45 per cent for those whose fathers are in the 'higher professional' group, compared with only 4 per cent for those whose fathers are in skilled manual occupations. The underlying reasons for this are complex, but differences of income and the parents' educational level and attitudes are certainly among them. *The link is even more marked for girls than for boys.* (Robbins Report, p.51, vol. 1. Quoted in Silver, 1980, p.129; my emphasis.)

The class differences in educational attainment (defined by entry into higher education and, in particular, universities) were found to have changed very little since the 1920s, despite the provision of free secondary education for all, and even though the proportion within each social class attaining higher education had steadily increased since the beginning of the century. The Robbins Report reaffirmed that social inequality in British society had remained a major obstacle to educational equality of opportunity. It confirmed the judgement of R.H. Tawney who wrote in 1931: 'The hereditary curse upon English education is its organization upon lines of social class' (p.142).

In the postwar period, Tawney's anger at what he called the 'barbarity' of an educational system that imposed differences of educational opportunities among children according to the differences of wealth among the parents had been reformulated into a more positive concern to provide 'equality of opportunity' for children of equal ability, irrespective of their social origins. The new ideological motto was *meritocracy*. The goal was to create a new society in which people were allocated their various occupational positions on the basis of their intelligence, ability, and aspirations. The resulting 'meritocratic order' would, it was thought, achieve both the desired results of greater economic efficiency through the maximization of human resources, and greater social cohesion through the socialization of all children into the value of social mobility. The capital investment demanded by the expansion of educational provision would be repaid in the greater productivity and reduced social conflict that it would ensure.

The goal of equality of opportunity led to a reorganization of education, which initially meant the setting up of the 11-plus test to sift out the school population according to ability levels. By the 1960s, it meant the abolition of the 11-plus test and the reorganization of the secondary school system into comprehensive schools, where children of all abilities and all social classes would be taught under one roof. In primary schools, the ideals of equality of opportunity produced a new 'progressive' ideology, where teachers were encouraged to treat all children according to their individual levels of creativity and needs. There was also an expansion of higher education and the provision of student grants for further study.

Yet have these reforms actually made a difference to the pattern of class and gender inequality that Robbins discovered? For the answer we have to look at the available educational statistics on class and gender and, in particular, at the statistics on educational achievement.

Table 1 shows the educational qualifications of adult males and females aged 20–69 who were economically active and were not in full-time education in 1977–78. The distribution of women in the various social classes is very different from that of men. But how do their educational qualifications compare within each social class?

The statistics show that although women were less likely than men to have reached degree level and were more likely to have no educational qualifications at all, a slightly higher proportion of women whose fathers were in social class 1 obtained a degree than men. This shows that the newly created opportunities for higher education tended to be taken up by women in the professional middle classes. In 1972 Kelsall, Poole and Kuhn confirmed

Table 1 Highest educational qualifications by social class of males and females (Great Britain) (1977/1978) (Source: Based on Reid (1981) *Social Class Differences in Britain*, pp.207 and 208).

Qualification	Social class*/per cent													
	Non-manual occupations						manual occupations						ALL	
	1		2		3		4		5		6			
	m	f	m	f	m	f	m	f	m	f	m	f	m	f
Degree or equivalent	60	67	10	7	11	4	φ	φ	φ	φ	1	φ	8	3
Higher educational below degree	20	12	15	13	13	15	4	2	1	1	1	1	8	8
GCE A-level or equivalent	9	3	10	4	13	4	8	2	3	3	1	φ	8	3
GCE O-level or equivalent or CSE grade 1	4	6	18	15	20	19	12	9	7	7	4	3	13	13
CSE other grades/commercial/apprenticeship	1	2	10	11	7	16	20	8	9	7	5	5	13	12
Foreign and other	3	5	5	6	5	4	3	3	4	3	2	3	4	3
None	2	6	31	44	32	39	53	75	75	81	85	89	47	58
Total	7	1	16	5	18	50	41	8	15	27	4	10	100	100

*See Note for social class groups.
φ=less than 1 per cent.

that a greater proportion of female (67 per cent) than male (60 per cent) university graduates came from non-manual, middle-class occupations. In contrast only 14 per cent of female graduates had fathers in skilled work, and only 5 per cent had fathers in semiskilled and unskilled manual work, compared with 19 per cent and 7 per cent of male graduates respectively. The findings corroborated those of the Robbins Report which found that a higher percentage of women students (74 per cent) than male students (69 per cent) came from middle-class homes.

It is interesting to look briefly at another kind of educational development which might be expected to offer women and especially working class women, 'a second chance' to gain a higher education – the Open University. The Open University has since its foundation allowed many women to make up for their 'missed opportunities' and women students have responded by increasing their share of applications to join the university. In 1970 the proportion of applications from women was 30 per cent, by 1980 it had reached 45 per cent, with housewives accounting for about 40 per cent of all women applicants. By 1985, women represented 45 per cent of the university's undergraduate student population.

Most OU students work in higher-level white-collar occupations. Yet, by 1979, the proportion of the undergraduate population in lower-level white-collar occupations had risen from 14 per cent to 23 per cent, and that of manual workers from 5 per cent to 9 per cent. However, this increase in manual workers was almost entirely an increase in male students. Female manual workers are still badly represented. They account for around 2 per cent of the student intake, although around 23 per cent of the female workforce are in this group. In contrast, 61 per cent of the male working class represented by 13 per cent of the students. In terms of social class intake, therefore, the Open University has not made any real inroads into the problem of working-class women's low participation in higher education.

The reasons why some women do not take up the opportunities offered by the Open University are important since they indicate how women's role in society reinforces their disadvantaged educational position, which, in turn, reinforces their financial and social dependency on men. In 1977, for example, when applicants were asked why they had not taken up a place offered to them by the Open University, 62 per cent of women compared with 44 per cent of men gave 'non-work demands' as the reason for withdrawal from studying (e.g. social and domestic duties, care of children, moving home, new baby, death in the family, etc.). In contrast, the pressure of work, change of job, travel, etc. were reasons given by 43 per cent of the men but only 27 per cent of women. Personal and family commitments affected 30 per cent of all women and 50 per cent of all housewives. The lack of financial independence also affected 35 per cent of all women and 47 per cent of housewives, who could not afford even the relatively low cost of the Open University. Women's domestic and family commitments have, therefore, greatly affected their chances of taking up 'second chance' opportunities for higher education with the Open University (McIntosh, 1979).

Two further points should be made about the relationship between the pattern of female achievement and the pattern of female employment. First, it is significant that even if women do achieve the same educational qualifications as men, there is no guarantee that the outcome, in terms of occupational level reached, will be the same. As Wolpe (1978) argues:

> . . . even assuming that it were possible for women to replicate the training, in every way, that men received, it still would not follow that it would ensure them a place in the skilled world of work. Women would come into competition with men for the limited number of skilled jobs. Not only would the power of the male-dominated trade unions have to be reckoned with here but also the resistance of employers themselves, a resistance which is linked to structural elements. (Wolpe, 1978, p.161).

Secondly, there are major discrepancies in how men and women convert their education qualifications into income. Table 2 shows that, on average, women's earnings are 63 per cent of men's earnings and that the percentage decreases at the lower levels of educational qualification. Clearly not only is the pattern of female and male educational achievement different but so also is the value of educational qualifications for each sex.

Table 2   Median annual earnings in 1978 of women as a percentage of men's*. (Source: Reid, 1981, p.211, derived from General Household Survey 1978, 1980).

Degree or equivalent	76 per cent
Higher education below degree	75 per cent
GCE A-level or equivalent	65 per cent
GCE O-level or equivalent or CSE grade 1	61 per cent
CSE other grades/commercial/apprenticeship	65 per cent
None	61 per cent
All	63 per cent

*Aged 20–69, employed for 31 hours or more per week.

Ideological aspects of state education policy

The search for explanations of women's educational patterns has encouraged historians to trace the ideological assumptions underlying state educational provision. Sociologists, on the other hand, have focused on the shape of educational organization and classroom practices. Unfortunately the two analyses are rarely related together. In the next section I shall look at the processes within education which may have contributed to female patterns of achievement and female school cultures. But first I would like to consider the ways in which state education policy and its ideological assumptions have structured educational provision for girls and women and the assumptions made about girls' educational needs. It is state education policy that has, in my view, determined to a large extent the internal educational organisation and the attitudes of pupils and teachers to gender.

Understanding the nature and effect of state intervention and policy in any area is difficult to analyze at the best of times. This is especially the case since the state is not an autonomous institution – many of its policies are a result of particular historical struggles and reflect the compromises reached by competing interest groups in different areas. State education policy derives to a large extent from an uneasy combination of policy decisions: from a combination of economic and political pragmatism and concessions to those groups the government wants to win or maintain the support of. In this context it is difficult to separate out the ways in which state education policy perpetuates the continuing power of dominant social classes and the continuing domination of black people by white people and of women by men. Further, the ways in which state ideologies are manifested in curriculum, school organization, in various types of teaching styles and assessment procedures are often diverse and contradictory and, as a result, the outcomes of schooling are to a certain extent unpredictable and contradictory. Therefore, even when we have identified the rationale for certain state policies, we have not necessarily explained the shape and the nature of state schooling or, indeed, its impact.

All these qualifications, however, do not mean that we can overlook the patterns of social inequalities in the state education system. To a certain extent the 'official ideology' of state educational legislation and the resulting pattern of educational provision must be examined as both causes and a reflection of, women's economic dependence on men and the continuance of social class and racial inequalities in society.

Historically, the ideology of state educational policy has, to a great extent, assumed that the education of girls should differ from that of boys. The benefits would accrue not just to individual girls and boys, but also to society, since it was assumed and still is assumed that education was designed to prepare people for adult life. And as adult life is sex-segregated it seemed only natural to devise an educational system that catered for a sex-segregated world. Although at certain points in the twentieth century a class-segregated world was seen as unjust, it was only by the late 1970s that a sex-segregated world appeared to contravene any sense of fairness. This is perhaps because in no other area has the reference to the 'natural', 'God-given' world been so prevalent. Since boys and girls could be shown to be physiologically different, why should they not also be socially and psychologically different?

The debate that evolved around the nature of girls' education in the nineteenth century is a complex debate with a complex history – only the barest outlines are touched on here. From the work of feminist historians we know that the issue of whether parents should educate their daughters or not was contentious and produced diverse responses. By the nineteenth century, many middle-class parents were involved in pressing for the setting up of small private girls' schools (Pederson, 1979). Further, the demand for girls' public boarding schools resulted in the establishment by the end of the nineteenth century of schools designed along similar lines to the famous boys' public schools. Yet, despite the rapidly increasing number of girls' boarding and day schools in that century, there was also considerable controversy over the 'educability' of girls, their brain power and the possible detrimental effects of educating girls into an 'academic' curriculum.

It was generally assumed that boys and girls should receive different educations, and there was an assumption that women of different social classes were expected to need and receive different types of schooling. The ideal to be produced by schools in the nineteenth century was one which 'rested in the prototype of the frail, protected woman of the middle classes' (Burstyn, 1980). Thus the hard physical stamina women of the working classes needed to carry out their work in the home and in paid employment was conveniently ignored.

A further contradictory aspect in the battle over women's education in the nineteenth century can be found in the desire, on the one hand, to have intelligent mothers of sons and, on the other hand, the desire not to educate them up to the level of men. Burstyn (1980) argues that in the nineteenth century educational planners saw the concept of the 'nation's' need as more important than women's own needs.

> Intelligent women, unspoiled by education, produced eminent sons. The country would benefit far more from such men than from a similar number of sterile but educated women who might otherwise have produced them. 'Unsexed it might be wrong to call the educated woman, but she will be more or less sexless. And the human race will have lost those who should have been her sons. Bacon, for want of a mother, will not be born.'[1] Whereas education did not deprive men of their virility, and could prove useful in helping them to earn more money to support their families, it was likely to disable women reproductively. Intelligent, well-trained mothers were the ideal; how many eminent men had proclaimed their debt to their mothers. Moreover, educators claimed that the early years of childhood were more important than they had previously thought; the role of a mother in the education of her child was becoming more important than ever before. Spencer . . . claimed that parents' chief function with young children was to provide the conditions requisite for growth, and that this applied to the growth of children's minds as well as their bodies.[2] Intelligent mothers were needed to provide the kind of environment that would encourage mental development in their sons. An education that threatened to deplete the ranks of motherhood, and deny to it the most intelligent women, was as disastrous for the nation as for the women concerned. Every effort had to be made to get women to desist from their path of folly before it was too late. (p.95).

[1] Withers Moore (1886) in *The Lancet*, 2 p.315.
[2] H. Spencer (1860) *Education: Intellectual, Moral and Physical*, New York, p.108.

What is most striking in this quotation is the correlation between the 'nation's interest' and the needs of *male* children. By the late nineteenth century, references to the 'good of the nation', as far as women's child-rearing role was concerned, were to be heard more and more frequently. This was especially the case when it was discovered that men, called up to fight the Boer War, were physically unfit for conscription. Further, by the end of the nineteenth century, the infant mortality rate was still high and there was a low birthrate. There was an obsession, therefore, with the 'physical deterioration' of the population, which coincided with concern over the future of the Empire, 'national efficiency' and social standards of health, fitness, etc. Women were now being seen as a 'national asset', and their education was judged to be necessary for the future of the country.

The impetus to educate women was directed not towards their membership of the paid workforce – as contributors to industrial wealth – but rather as *mothers* (not just wives) of future workers, soldiers and citizens. Even on the issue of training domestic servants, state policy makers were apparently reluctant to organize girls' elementary education specially for this means of independent survival. This was despite considerable pressure by the middle classes for working-class girls to receive domestic training so that they might become servants, and despite the fact that, until well into the twentieth century, domestic service was the single largest category of female paid employment. In 1911, B. L. Hutchins estimated that 34.8 per cent of 14–18-year-old employed girls were in domestic service (including hotel service, laundry and washing service) (quoted in Dyhouse, 1981, p.82). For many it was the only means of economic survival without marriage. By the early twentieth century, the concern by the middle classes for the 'servant problem' was the result not just of the declining numbers of working-class girls available and interested in entering service (especially since there were new employment opportunities available to them during and after the First World War) but about the quality of the new recruits to domestic service.

The compromise rhetoric of state policy makers was to stress that the curricula of elementary schools should 'fit girls for life'. Needless to say this meant that, over the course of the nineteenth century, domestically oriented special school subjects were introduced into elementary schools. In 1862, for example, needlework was made compulsory for girls in such schools. It acquired more than any other domestic subject 'symbolic importance' since 'proficiency with a needle implied femininity, it implied thrift' (Dyhouse, 1981, p.89). It was a subject that was said to appeal 'directly to the natural instincts of girls'. By 1875, pressure from associations such as the National Association for the Promotion of Housewifery led to the provision of grants for scholars to study other domestically oriented subjects and the adoption of such subjects was rapid and extensive:

> The Code of 1878 made domestic economy a compulsory specific subject for girls. Between 1874 and 1882 the number of pupils studying domestic economy in the Board Schools rose from 844 to 59,812. Grants were first made available for teaching cookery in the Code of 1882, and for laundry work in 1890. In spite of various obstacles in the way of a speedy adoption of these subjects in some schools (the expense, for instance, of the necessary plant and equipment), the results of the grant being made available were quite impressive. According to a report on the progress of domestic economy teaching made to the Education Department in 1896, in 1882–3, 7,597 girls from a total of 457 schools had qualified for the cookery grant: by 1895–6 these numbers had risen to 134,930 and 2,729 respectively.[1] Between 1891–2 and 1895–6 the number of girls attending recognised classes in laundry work had similarly risen from 632 to 11,720: the number of schools offering these classes from 27 to 400 over the same period.[2] (Dyhouse, 1981, pp.89–90)

[1] Mrs Pillow 'Domestic Economy Teaching in England' (*Education Department Special Reports on Educational Subjects*), Vol. 1, HMSO, 1896–7, p.159.
[2] ibid., p.167.

Thus, within the national system of state elementary schools established by the 1870 Education Act, the ideology of women's domesticity focused the curriculum of girls' education around their domestic futures as wives and mothers. It was a *domestic educational ideology*. Thus elementary schools offered a means of combining within *one* system of state education, *two* different models of schooling – one for boys and one for girls. And it was not just in the subject choices that differentiation between the sexes occurred.

The differential rate of attendance of girls and boys, for example, is often forgotten in accounts of the rise of mass schooling. It was considered appropriate for girls to be involved in domestic labour in the home, looking after younger children and the sick, or doing domestic chores. The low level of girls' attendance at school affected their literacy rate, which in the nineteenth century was lower than that of boys. This fact may have accounted for their higher attendance in adult evening classes, where they were still in search of basic reading and writing skills.

Further, within the early state schools, there was a differential stress on appearance, with neatness and cleanliness being considered more important for girls than for boys. Discipline and order problems were more commonly associated with boys. This emphasis distinguished the future careers of girls as housewives and mothers, who would eventually need to maintain a clean and tidy home and family, from the careers of boys in the 'public sphere' as wage workers.

The development of girls' education during the course of the nineteenth century was framed, therefore, not just in terms of female 'service' and dependency on men but also in terms of a recognized need to maintain a sexual division of labour by reproducing male and female separate spheres. The divison between the public sphere of paid employment and the private sphere of family, through the work of the schools, was linked to the division of the sexes in such a way that the public sphere was seen as male and the private as female. Women, therefore, were not only defined as being 'home based' but were mainly prepared for the domestic sphere. The development of schooling was of key importance as one of the major agencies through which the division between public and private spheres was reinforced and associated with the men and women respectively.

Education for different social classes
At the same time as *gender differentiation* was an explicit ideology of early forms of state education, so too was *social class differentiation*. The establishment of state elementary schools in the 1870 Education Act ran in parallel to, and did not challenge the existence of, private schools, where sons of the upper-middle classes were educated (most middle-class girls were still educated in the home by governesses unless they were sent to small private girls' schools). The setting up of secondary education also reinforced the pattern of social class differentiation: there was an assumption that different schools and different types of education should be provided for different social classes.

The Schools Enquiry Commission, called the Taunton Commission (1864), was perhaps the most significant landmark in the development of girls' secondary education. What the commission recommended were specially designed schools for each social class based on their future occupational roles. They also recommended that 'since the picture brought before us of the state of middle-class girls' education is on the whole unfavourable', good well-regulated day schools should be set up for girls in the principal towns. The preference, unlike that for boys, was to keep girls as close to home and their mothers as possible.

This report established that occupational differentiation was to be the ideology for the structure of boys' secondary education, and that girls' education was to be placed *alongside* and not *in* that hierarchical structure. In this sense, the 'vocational' ideology of schooling in the case of girls was not linked to waged work but to a domestic vocation. The Report of the Schools Enquiry Commission led directly to the establishment of high schools for girls and, in particular, to the formation of the Girls Public Day School Trust, which still exists today. This Trust developed the work of the National Union for Improving the Education of Women of all Classes, set up in 1871, and was noticeable in its efforts to recruit students from as wide a social range as possible. The Trust schools were to promote the establishment of good cheap girls' day schools for all social classes above those attending the elementary schools. By 1903, thirty-four such schools were established around the country. Also the Endowed School Act in 1869 made available funds for the setting up of girls' grammar schools, reflecting the new realization that the education of girls was as much a matter of public concern at that of boys, and that public funds must be allocated to it. The effect, therefore, of the Taunton Commission and the Endowed Schools Act was to add on to the boys' school system a parallel system of girls' secondary education. Two separate educational lines were established, each concerned with the different roles of men and women in each social class.

The development of female education obviously had a different impact on middle-class and on working-class women. On the one hand, education and the increasing work opportunities it offered, gradually gave middle-class women far more freedom and rather more chances to break away from their family situation than it gave their working-class sisters. It allowed them access, eventually, in the early twentieth century to university education and to the newly deveoped professions (such as nursing and teaching). It allowed them a certain degree of financial freedom as single women. For some working-class women, access to education gave them a chance to aspire to nonmanual occupations such as clerical and office work, and to take up jobs where basic literacy was required. However, the development of state education was also experienced by working-class women as a form of *class control* of themselves and their families. Ironically, the increasingly domestic role of women in the nineteenth century gave middle-class women a certain social power, in the sense that they were permitted to expand their acitivtes outside the home and become 'missionaries' in their various efforts to educate the poor. As a result, the curricula offered to working-class girls in the charity schools and private foundations transmitted specifically middle-class versions of what women's place should be and the middle-class concept of family form.

State elementary schools and mother-care training schemes also adopted this notion of family life for educating working-class girls. According to Davin (1979) the explanations for the development of state schooling offered so far have neglected this aspect of class control. Thus, to the extent that they focused on political or economic explanations of state schooling, they have not explained why girls were educated at all:

> The *political* explanations . . . [offered for the rise of schooling refer to the need to combat] . . . the growing labour movement, in which women played no part at this time, and to the 1867 Franchise Act, which created a million or so new voters [who needed to be educated 'wisely], [yet] none of them [were]' women; while the *economic* context concerns the development of a new skilled and literate workforce (including a whole range of minor technicians significant in the expansion of empire and commerce as well as industry – telegraphists, sappers and signalmen as well as the more obvious draughtsmen, engineers and clerical workers) from which women (to begin with at least) were again absent. If such political and economic grounds had been the only reason for introducing general elementary education, one might well ask why girls were included at all. (p.89; my emphases and additions)

Davin argues that the educational requirements of maintaining women's place in the home was part of the perceived need of Victorian reformers to re-establish the family as a stablizing force in the context of a society undergoing rapid industrialization, urbanization, and increasing social unrest. The 'failure' of the working-class family, in particular, was considered to have contributed to the growth of working-class militancy, subversion and violence, or even social apathy. Schools were, therefore, designed in such a way as to inculcate the values of the social order. They were designed to 'civilize' the working classes and 'bring the structure and organization of working-class family life into line with middle-class values and canons of "respectability" (Dyhouse, 1981, p.79).

However, within the broad pattern of female domestic ideology, class-specific ideals of femininity were also taught. Although middle-class girls were educated to become the 'perfect wife and mother', the ideal which the middle class imposed on the working-class girls was that of the 'good woman'. The middle-class girl was to learn the new ideal of femininity – which combined the Christian virtues (such as self-denial, patience and silent suffering), ladylike behaviour (refusing any paid or manual employment) and a ladylike etiquette (dress, style and manners); the working-class girl was to learn in essence what it meant to be a good housekeeper, wife and mother by being trained in the *practical* skills of domesticity, with no pretensions of becoming a lady. She would acquire enough conscience and ability to safeguard the family against crime, disease, immorality, and other social problems to which, in the eyes of the middle classes, the working classes appeared to be so prone (see Purvis, 1981).

The development of state education as it unfolded – with its transmission of the values and standards of the middle classes – had different effects and meanings, therefore, for the families of the middle and working classes. Miriam David (1980) has outlined in detail the changing relations of the families of different social classes to the educational authorities and the central policy-making structure. She sums up the effects of the events of the nineteenth century:

> By 1900 the relationships between parents and children, and between parents and the state, over schooling were entirely changed from the beginning of the century. Parents were no longer solely responsible for their children. But different classes of parent had different responsibilities: working-class parents had to submit their children to education and, in return, were required to behave in particular ways towards them before, during and after schooling. In particular, rearing was becoming more professionalised, and mothers were having demands made upon them. Children were also shown their position and future place in the social order. Increasingly, developments were made in vocational education, to ensure children a more precisely delineated place in the social hierarchy. Upper- and upper-middle-class parents were not required to reach the same standards as working-class parents. Even at the end of the century the employment of servants and tutors to care for young boys and girls remained the norm. These parents were only expected to obtain the adequate upbringing of their children, especially their sons. (p.41)

Obviously the removal of children from the labour force and from the home during the day by the end of the nineteenth century had considerable effect on family relations and the household income. In many ways the development of schools represented a major incursion by the state into family life, and signified the 'taking' on by the state of the role of parents. The state acted, in so far as the education of children was concerned, in place of parents (i.e. in *loco parentis*), assuming the responsibility for the training, supervision and the instilling of discipline and order in the next generation and, as Davin (1979) argues, a new generation of parents:

> Education was to form a new generation of parents (and especially mothers) whose children would not be wild, but dependent and amenable, accepting not only the obvious disciplines of school and work but also the less visible constraints at the bottom of the heap. Education was to establish (or as they believed to re-establish) the family as a stabilizing force. (p.90)

The development of girls' education in the twentieth century reveals many of the same assumptions of class and gender differentiation that were prevalent in the nineteenth century. However, in the period after the First World War it had become less and less feasible to talk openly about providing different educations for different social classes. The new rhetoric stressed differences in individual ability, needs and interests, rather than different social class 'needs'. As a result, it became more difficult to recognize the principle of class differentiation at work in the structure of education. Far easier to see is the way in which the development of state secondary schooling incorporated an ideology of gender differentiation.

Even in the period immediately after the 1944 Education Act when secondary education for all was established and an ideology of equality of opportunity framed educational thinking and planning, girls' education was similar to that of previous decades. The importance of relating girls' schooling to their future role as mothers was emphasized and supported not just by educational policies but also by social policy. Nurseries set up during the war were shut down and women were encouraged to see their primary responsibilities as home makers, even if they had paid employment.

In the fifties and sixties, the concept of 'dual careers', of being 'equal but different' was promoted, particularly amongst the middle classes (see Birmingham Feminist History Group, 1979). The Crowther Report (1959) recognized that middle class girls would be interested in combining a career with motherhood but working-class girls were still to be educated largely for their domestic role, even if they were more likely to be found in employment in adult life.

Looking at three major education reports produced since the 1940s (the Norwood Report, 1943, the Crowther Report, 1959, and the Newsom Report, 1963), Wolpe (1976) shows that despite major economic changes and shifts in the position of women in society, all three had similar assumptions. First, boys and girls differed in their needs and interests, especially because of girls' future role as wives and mothers and boys' alleged interest in becoming wage earners. Second, each revealed an uncritical acceptance of the dominant cultural values of how the sexes should live together, and third, each took hardly any account of the concrete facts of female employment and women's economic position. By stressing female domesticity as women's primary functions, Wolpe suggests that each contributed in its own way 'to produce an adaptable, pliable and docile female labour source with only marginal skills'.

By the 1960s, secondary schooling was undergoing radical reform through the movement to set up comprehensives; yet even here it was not clear that girls would benefit from the new organization. Deem (1981) argues that the curriculum within these schools tended to mean providing shorthand, typing and child-care classes for working-class girls, and a different range of crafts for boys. Middle-class girls, on the other hand, could benefit from the opportunities offered by the new non-selective schools to take formal examinations and later go on to higher education.

By the end of the sixties however the contradictions and tensions of women's dual roles were beginning to be discussed more publicly. New demands were being made for women's rights to an equal education and equal treatment within schools. This movement was reflected in the passing of the Sex Discrimination Act in 1975 which made it unlawful to discriminate on grounds of sex in education, as well as in employment and training. Although not very effective as a means of reforming educational practice, the presence of such legislation and the promotional work of the EOC drew attention to issues such as the lack of scientific education for girls and the limited patterns of female subject choice, particulary in secondary schools. Feminist teachers also began to develop their own schemes to analyze existing curricular materials and teaching practice and what has been called the 'hidden curriculum' of schooling (i.e. the informal processes and procedures of educational institutions). And in some schools, projects were started to reform radically both pupils' and teachers' perceptions about sexual divisions and sexism and to change the level of girls' participation and their subject choices. By the end of the seventies concern about girls' education focussed on demands, not just for equal access to educational facilities, but for equal outcomes of schooling.

Gradually central government and some local authorities have started to investigate and make recommendations to improve girls' education. However, the emphasis has been limited on the whole to improving girls' education in scientific and technological subjects. Rather less attention has been paid to restructuring the relations between the sexes and explicitly tackling the problems of sexism. Social policy, meantime, continues to reinforce the family division of labour and to assume that it sould be women who are the main domestic workers and carers (see David, 1984).

Summing up the period 1940 to the 1980s Deem (1981) argues that most of the advances achieved by women, both inside and outside education, can be linked to periods of full employment and to the implementation of social democratic policies and ideology, and suggests that, in understanding how women have benefited or become disadvantaged by educational policies, we have to recognize that the 'treatment of women in education has been closely linked to other social policies and to prevalent ideologies about women's roles' (p.141). One cannot, therefore, separate out educational policies for women, from women's involvement in the paid labour force and their family responsibilities.

The state education system has played a major role in the 'reproduction' (in the sense of continual production and maintenance) of a society divided by class, race and gender. As a result there is a tension between the role of education as a means of female liberation and its role in the *imposition* of a middle-class, white male culture. It is inadequate, therefore, to see educational provision *either* as a form of social control *or* as a form of liberation. What makes an educational system so complex is that potentially it can fulfil both these functions at one and the same time, and in different ways for different classes, sexes and ethnic groups.

State training policy and women's work
The pattern of educational achievement has changed over time, and girls have improved their qualifications on leaving school, particularly in gaining 'O' levels and some 'A' levels. Table 3 shows that in the last ten years a higher proportion of girls have taken degree courses, although the proportion of boys on these courses is still higher than the percentage of girls. Both sexes have been affected by the cutting back of educational opportunities in the early 1980s. The reduction of female teacher training students is particularly noticeable in the last decade.

The types of further training that girls receive, needless to say, are different from those of boys. Whereas full-time and sandwich courses attract an equal percentage of boys and girls, far more male students than female students can be found on part-time day-release courses. Women tend to

Table 3   Destination of school leavers in England & Wales: by sex
(Source: *Social Trends,* 1984, Central Statistical Office.)

	BOYS				GIRLS			
	1970/71	1975/76	1980/81	1982/83	1970/71	1975/76	1980/81	1982/83
Pupils entering full-time further and higher education as a percentage of all school leavers – by type of course								
Degree	9.0	8.8	9.3	8.5	5.3	5.4	6.8	6.5
Teacher training	1.3	0.5	0.2	0.1	5.2	2.2	0.7	0.6
HND/HNC	0.7	0.4	0.5	} 0.6	0.3	0.3	0.3	} 0.3
OND/ONC	0.6	0.9	0.4		0.4	0.5	0.1	
GCE 'A' level	1.6	1.8	2.8	3.2	1.1	2.1	3.3	3.6
GCE 'O' level	1.7	1.5	1.7	1.6	1.1	1.5	2.2	2.0
Catering	} 4.7	0.5	0.6	0.7	} 10.8	1.0	1.7	1.8
Nursing		–	–	–		1.6	1.9	1.8
Secretarial		–	–	–		4.8	5.2	4.3
Other full-time		4.5	6.6	8.2		6.0	9.6	10.9
Total pupils entering full-time education (percentages)	19.5	18.9	22.2	23.0	24.1	25.4	32.0	31.8
Total school leavers seeking employment on leaving school (percentages)	80.5	81.1	77.8	77.0	75.9	74.6	68.0	68.2

predominate on other part-time day and evening courses. The Manpower Services Commission Training Services Division Report (1976) revealed that in 1974 only 10 per cent of girls compared with 40 per cent of boys under eighteen years old took day-release courses. This report also pointed out that women were less likely to receive in-service training and retraining later in their working life. For example, in clerical jobs, 40.5 per cent of women and 7 per cent of men were given no training.

Another aspect of differential training patterns of boys and girls can be found in their level of participation in different *types* of courses. The Equal Opportunities Commission (1978/9) reported that in 1975 only 8000 women were on further education courses in engineering and technology compared with 42500 men. Also, even though women constituted 35.4 per cent of undergraduate students on full-time university courses, they were unevenly distributed across the different subject specializations. In 1975, women made up 68.4 per cent of those studying education; 62.4 per cent of those taking language and literature, and area studies, and 52.2 per cent of students in Arts subjects (other than languages), compared with only 30 per cent of those studying science subjects and 4 per cent of engineering and technology students. Women are also underrepresented on professional and vocational courses such as medicine, dentistry and health, vetinary science, business studies, etc.

The impact of this pattern of training is obvious if one looks at where women are found in the paid employment. Not only are most women concentrated in stereotypical female jobs, but even when women have received an advanced training (for example at a university) they are still found clustered in a limited range of occupations. The majority of female graduates find their first employment in public service jobs, particularly in local government, health authorities, and education. Only 35 per cent of female graduates entered industry and commerce in 1975, compared with 62 per cent of male graduates. Why is this the case? Why do men and women have such different training patterns and eventual employment? Is it because the state has deliberately created this difference? Or is it because the state has neglected to help women break away from the discrimination and limitations of a sex-segregated labour market?

Ann Wickham (1985) argues that state training policies have changed over time and there were occasions when the problems of women's specific training needs were recognized. However, reports and recommendations were seldom acted upon. The intervention of the state in providing training for work and in particular for skilled work has been inadequate and prejudicial as far as women were concerned. As Phillips and Taylor (1980), put it 'skilled work has become almost by definition work that women do not do'. Wickham argues that it is only in recent times that the redefining of the concept of skill to include such notions as attitudes to work, social and communication skills has opened up possibilities for the entry of women into training courses and jobs in different work spheres. Training contributes to, but does not determine, women's place in the labour market. Yet even here state training policies have failed to challenge the notion that women's place is still primarily as wives and as dependants of men.

The opening up of training courses such as the Training Opportunities Programme (TOPS) by the Manpower Services Commission has led to an increase in women students. However, this again has not shifted them away from primarily female subjects: in 1980/81 women represented 97 per cent of students on shorthand and typing courses, 88 per cent on clerical courses, and 74 per cent on hairdressing and cleaning, whereas only 0.5 per cent were on construction and welding courses, and 1 per cent on metal making and engineering courses.

In 1983 the Youth Training Scheme (YTS) replaced the Youth Opportunities Programme (YOP) and constructed new divisions between employer-based courses (Mode A) and training workshops (Mode B). Girls represented some 44 per cent of Mode A schemes and 35 per cent of Mode B courses by the end of 1983. However, as Wickham (1985) has found 'all the signs suggest that exactly the same patterns (of sex stereotyping) are repeating themselves and exactly the same excuses made'. Careers' advisers, YTS managers and employers do not seem to be encouraging and helping girls to move into 'non-traditional' areas, even though the MSC at times publicly acknowledges the desirability of this goal. Interviews with a sample of young people on YTS schemes revealed the following distributions of girls and boys across the different occupational training families (OTFs):

Table 4 Percentage of girls and boys in occupational training families (OTFs) in the YTS (Published January 1985)
(Source: *The Class of '84*, The Fawcett Society and National Joint Committee of Working Women's Organizations 1985)

OTF	Male per cent	Female per cent
Admin/Clerical	7	35
Agriculture	6	2
Craft and Design	4	1
Maintenance	24	1
Technical/Scientific	2	1
Manufacturing	16	5
Processing	1	1
Food Preparation	4	5
Sales/Personal Service	8	29
Community/Health	1	8
Transport	2	0
More than 1 OTF	1	0
Unclassified	23	13

The recent verbal commitment to increasing women's opportunities through new training programmes has not therefore turned into a reality. Wickham argues that state policies have been concerned primarily with men and their needs. State training programmes have thus contributed to, rather than challlenged, the existing social divisions within the occupational structure.

Educational organisation and girls' achievement

In contrast with the analysis presented so far which identifies the origins of female educational disadvantages in the ideological assumptions of state education and training policy and provision, is the 'offical' view represented for example, by the Sex Discrimination Act 1975 and the Equal Opportunities Commission. Here there is a tendency to find the 'causes' of sex inequalities within the educational system itself, particularly the attitudes of those most involved in it - for example parents, pupils and teachers. For many educationalists, the problem of gender inequality is an *educational problem* for which an *educational solution* can be found. Sex discrimination is therefore defined as the problem of ignorance or 'conventional' attitudes which can be tackled through the prevention of unlawful behaviour and educational reform. From such a perspective the history of state provision and its ideological assumptions and structures appear to be largely an irrelevance.

The search for explanations of why some people hold biased or stereotypical attitudes has led to an interest in the processes of learning in the family and school system, and many of the suggested reforms have focussed on changes in these areas. The following sections will consider some of the factors which might be involved. I shall look in particular at four areas; (a) childhood experiences (b) school organization (c) mixed versus single sex schools and (d) classroom practice.

Childhood experiences

A variety of theories of gender development have been used to explain the ways in which children acquire their concepts of gender, gender identity and gender role. Psychoanalytic theory and cognitive development and social learning theories are the most important ones and have been much debated by psychologists. (For a good summary see Kessler and McKenna, 1982). It is not relevant here to go into the intricacies of this theoretical, and somewhat inconclusive, debate; instead I shall focus on the sociological research on patterns of gender socialization found in British society today. Such research has concentrated on the many cultural influences on the child, which may reinforce or contradict the messages received from its parents. These influences feed into the child's later school experiences.

Research such as Sara Delamont's (1980) shows the number of different ways children can be taught to recognize at a very early age a gender classification system and to use this classification system to label their environment accordingly. She points to the significance of boys' and girls' names, their clothes, the different colours used in the nursery, etc., all of which are cultural artifacts that discriminate between the sexes.

Glenys Lobban (1985), after looking at sex roles in the reading schemes used in infant and primary schools in 1974 and 1975 in Britain, summarized her research as follows:

> In our society more than half the population is female yet a child who took her view of reality from these schemes could be forgiven for concluding that females were in a distinct minority and that those females who do exist are intrinsically inferior to, and less worthy of mention than, males. (p.206)

In the reading schemes Lobban studied (the *Pirates* schemes and the *Language in Action* scheme), the overall ratio of male heroes to female heroines was five to one. Together, the two schemes showed 33 adult male occupations with only 8 female occupations (mum, granny, handywoman, princess, queen, witch, teacher and shop assistant). No children's reader showed the mother going out to paid employment. She concluded, therefore, that the world of work appeared to be even more male dominated than it really was, and this would only depress the aspirations of female children.

Similarly, in a survey of toy catalogues, Delamont (1980) found that the world of toys and games offered girls a far more restricted and domestic range of roles than boys. Girls were encouraged to be essentially passive, home-centred, nonscientific, nontechnical and 'good'. Whereas boys were offered the exciting roles of Robin Hood, a big-game hunter, spacemen, Dracula, cowboys and Indians, girls were limited to Miss World and being a ballerina. The variety offered to girls consisted of a range of domestic roles such as cleaning, cooking, sewing and shopping

Yet, surprisingly, despite such forms of cultural imposition of traditional images of a woman's role, little girls can and do succeed academically, particularly in the early years of childhood. In the home, where from early childhood the differences between boys and girls may be emphasized, little girls nevertheless can benefit from their sedentary and passive activities, close to their mothers. On average, they develop, unlike boys, an early proficiency at language and reading skills; they develop a verbal fluency that excels that of boys. In preschool years, girls also tend to score higher on general intelligence tests than boys and, up to the age of 12, girls are equal to boys in arithmetical computation. Paradoxically, the availability of models of femininity in the mother and female primary-school teacher, as well as what has been called the 'feminine atmosphere' of the home and early school life, may also encourage female academic success. The mother and the primary-school teacher may operate stereotypical sex distinctions, and thus praise girls for their greater tidiness, quietness and obedience. In this environment, a girl, by conforming to notions of femininity, may also be conforming to one notion of a 'good pupil' and vice versa. What she may lose, however, is a training that encourages originality and experimentation and physical rough and tumble. Boys, on the other hand, by resisting the teacher or their mother, learn a certain degree of assertiveness and initiative, which may benefit them in later school life.

As the child grows up, children's literature, television and other cultural influences, (such as those of its peer group,) reinforce the differences of concepts of masculinity and femininity. In particular, girls are presented with a definition of femininity that is closely connected with a subordinate position in a male-centred world. For example, in *Jackie*, the schoolgirl magazine, teenage female sexuality is constructed in such a way as to reinforce female subordination.

> Romance problems, fashion, beauty and pop mark out the limits of the girl's concern – other possibilities are ignored or dismissed.
> . . . The *Jackie* girl is alone in her quest for love; she refers back to her female peers for advice, comfort and reassurance *only* when she has problems in fulfilling this aim. Female solidarity, or more simply the idea of girls together – in *Jackie* terms – is an unambiguous sign of failure. To achieve self-respect, the girl has to escape the 'bitchy', 'catty' atmosphere of female company and find a boyfriend as fast as possible. But in doing this she has not only to be individualistic in outlook – she has to be prepared to fight ruthlessly – by plotting, intrigue and cunning, to 'trap her man'. Not surprisingly this independent-mindedness is short-lived. As soon as she finds a 'steady', she must renounce it altogether and capitulate to *his* demands, acknowledging his domination and resigning herself to her own subordination. (McRobbie, 1978b, p.50)

In discussing these various forms of cultural *imposition* of gender stereotypes, we must be careful not to forget the various responses of boys and girls to these stereotypes, and to the message of parents and peer-group cultures. We must be aware that girls can negotiate the dominant definitions of femininity at a very early age, not just in schools.

School organization

Secondary schooling and further education obviously play a vital role in shaping girls' image of themselves and their future. The qualifications that individual students receive in these institutions are critical to their eventual training and placement in the occupational hierarchy. Yet in Table 5 below we can see there are major differences between the subjects entered at GCE 'O' level by boys and girls. This pattern is reflected at CSE as well as 'A' level and higher education courses selected.

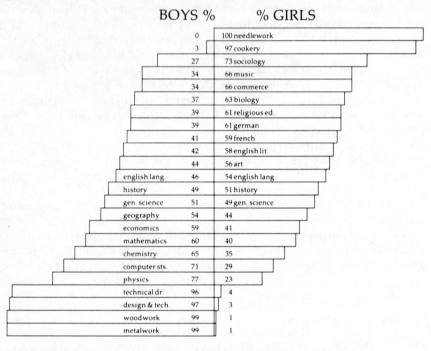

BOYS %		% GIRLS
	0	100 needlework
	3	97 cookery
	27	73 sociology
	34	66 music
	34	66 commerce
	37	63 biology
	39	61 religious ed.
	39	61 german
	41	59 french
	42	58 english lit.
	44	56 art
english lang.	46	54 english lang.
history	49	51 history
gen. science	51	49 gen. science
geography	54	44
economics	59	41
mathematics	60	40
chemistry	65	35
computer sts.	71	29
physics	77	23
technical dr.	96	4
design & tech.	97	3
woodwork	99	1
metalwork	99	1

Table 5 GCE 'O' level entries Summer 1980 *Source:* Harding, J (1982) 'C.D.T. what's missing?' *Studies in Design Education, Craft and Technology* Vol. 15, No. 1, winter. Department of Education, University of Keele, Staffordshire. ST5 5BG.

One of the most critical aspects of this pattern is the fact that girls do not generally study science or technological subjects, in further education, or at university. This avoidance or lack of interest in scientific subjects on the part of girls is an issue that has concerned the EOC and a range of government departments. In 1977, for example, the Manpower Services Commission argued that there was a need to teach 'mathematical, scientific and technical knowledge, enabling boys and girls to learn the essential skills needed in a fast-changing world of work' (quoted in Wolpe, 1978, p.150). Girls, it argued, should 'broaden and modernize their aspirations and . . . feel confident of success, in unfamiliar fields of science and technology'. In 1980, this concern for girls' involvement in science led the DES to produce a report specifically on

Girls and Science.

Explaining girls' failure to choose science is now an industry in itself, especially since 1984 was declared WISE (Women into Science and Engineering) year by the EOC. Alison Kelly (1981, 1982) has put forward a variety of different explanations for why girls don't do science – such as their lack of self confidence, the masculine image of science and the impersonal approach to science which do not relate easily to girls' previous experiences and interests. Such research, however, illustrates the more general problems which girls face, particularly within secondary schools. Broader political questions are now being asked as to whether there is in fact genuine 'equality of opportunity' for boys and girls to choose and take all school subjects so that any differences in their patterns of school-subject choice reflects genuine 'free choice' and genuine differences of boys' and girls' interests. The dominant ideology of state policy by the mid-twentieth century has been that boys and girls of any social class are indeed 'free' to choose; in the school they will be encouraged to follow their own independently made decisions as to the nature of their education, their interests and futures.

However, in order for this ideology of free choice to work, two conditions must be satisfied – all children must have *equal access* to all forms of curriculum subjects, and all school experiences and careers advice must be 'neutral'. If these two conditions can be achieved, the resulting pattern of educational choice can be described as reflecting student choice and the 'distribution of natural interests' without regard to social class or ethnic origins or gender.

In the 1960s, the programme for school reorganization in the form of comprehensive schools enshrined such an educational goal. The assumption was that these schools would reduce the impact of social inequalities on subject provision and choice by placing all children in the *same* schools. All children in these new schools would be offered the chance to take all subjects.

Yet, despite the principles and the ideals behind comprehensive schools, the reality was different, as Benn and Simon (1972) found when they investigated these schools. They discovered a number of factors that inhibited student choice *inside the school*; for example, the traditional pattern of gender differentiation (particularly in the area of curricula timetabling and provision) was being reproduced in the new comprehensive schools. Fifty per cent of all mixed schools admitted to limiting some subjects to boys only and 49 per cent limited some subjects to girls only (e.g. catering, nursing, pottery, hygiene, jewellery-making, domestic science and dancing). There were a dozen subjects not open to boys, and over a dozen not open to girls.

Such arbitrary subject provision inevitably had a considerable impact upon the patterns of educational qualifications received by boys and girls. Benn and Simon's conclusion from their research was that real freedom of subject choice for both sexes does not just happen – it must be 'actively organized'. However, the active organization of equality of school-subject provision is not an easy task, especially when schools have limited resources and only a certain number of places available to students to study specialist courses. Under pressure from the Sex Discrimination Act and the Manpower Services Commission's Technical and Vocational Educational Initiative (TVEI) schools are now being encouraged to find ways of challenging the traditional stereotyping of boys and girls and to offer them genuine access to the same curricula subjects. This, however, had led to various interpretations of the problem. For example, one can assume that genuine equality of opportunity is achieved when precisely equal numbers of boys and girls are found taking the same subject? Would a ratio of 6:4 be sufficient to represent equality? What does equality of provision and choice actually look like? If schools offered all students the chance to study the same subjects, but male and female pupils still chose stereotypical subjects, can the school be held responsible? A genuine 'free-for-all' in terms of subject choice does not necessarily lead to genuine equality since it is still likely – given traditional assumptions about men's and women's place in society – to lead to stereotypical choices: to some 'all-male' subjects, oversized groups, under-used facilities, etc., or to all students doing all craft subjects in rotation and the staff feeling that they never do their subject for long enough to get full benefit from it.

The Equal Opportunities Commission's initial view (although later retracted) was that the vast majority of cases of sex discrimination occur *by default* rather than by intent, especially since educators are often unaware of their own deeply held discriminatory attitudes. This view was also supported by the DES (1975) in *Curricular Differences for Boys and Girls*, which reported the findings of the HM Inspectorate, who investigated maintained primary, middle and secondary schools in England and Wales. They revealed the extent of gender differentiation practised in schools, which resulted from the assumption that boys and girls had different interests, abilities and futures. Children of different sexes were prepared for different roles in adult life and were encouraged to expect gender differentiation as normal. Teachers considered that such differentiation was not for academic reasons, but because it was 'normal practice, a part of a convenient long-standing organization. The most important effect of such 'normal' practices was found in the pattern of boys' and girls' curricula – the subjects they were offered, those they chose to study, and those taken by boys and by girls for examination.

However, the significant revelation of this report was that what appeared to be important in affecting the choice of school subjects was whether the school was mixed or single sex – it is to this which we shall now turn.

Mixed versus single sex schools

The looseness of the school reform programme during the 1960s and after, which aimed to set up comprehensive schools, meant that a range of possible school structures were permitted. In general though, the reforms meant the development of state coeducational schools, even though there was no real debate on the repercussions of mixed schools for pupils. It was assumed that coeducation was a 'good thing' – that by bringing both sexes into the same physical building, inequality of the sexes (comparable to the inequality of social classes) would be reduced. As a result, by 1975, some 87 per cent of comprehensive schools in the state sector in England and Wales were mixed and, in contrast, 74 per cent of grammar schools were single sex. The distribution of mixed-sex and single-sex schools differed in each local educational authority since some authorities decided to offer only co-educational schools, others chose mainly mixed-sex schools leaving a few single-sex schools, others offered mainly single-sex schools. In Scotland, secondary schools were virtually all mixed. By 1978 the majority of schools in the maintained sector in the United Kingdom were mixed; in contrast with this pattern, 1046 independent schools were single sex out of 2220 such schools.

The importance of the distribution of single-sex or mixed-sex schools was high-lighted by the DES (1975) in *Curricular Differences for Boys and Girls*. They discovered that secondary school curricular options were often either purposely or unintentionally segregated for boys and girls, which had the effect of clustering girls primarily in the art subjects and leaving boys in the majority in the hard sciences such as chemistry and physics, and that this pattern of subject provision was affected by the 'sex structure' of schools. Although girls were more likely to be offered a science subject in mixed-sex schools, they were less likely actually to choose and take that subject in such schools. Thus the DES discovered that the provision of school subjects at secondary level did not mean that the subject was chosen; what did affect choice was the absence or presence of the opposite sex. Table 6 below shows why they came to this conclusion.

The impact of single-sex schools was also felt at A-level, when the report argued that 'any correlation between the sex of the pupil and the popularity of a subject is markedly greater in mixed schools than in single-sex schools' (p.16). The tendency, therefore, of single-sex schools was to weaken the traditional patterns of subject choice, particularly in the case of girls taking science subjects. However, what the DES survey also discovered (which seems to have been neglected by most commentators) is that the provision made for craft and practical subjects – subjects thought more suitable for the less academically able – followed traditional patterns in almost all cases in single-sex schools, with more chance of 'progressive' practice in mixed schools. As Eileen Byrne has pointed out, single-sex education – because of its total lack of access of girls to handicrafts and boys to homecraft – has had important vocational effects. Domestic economy for girls has meant focusing on cookery or needlework, whereas for boys handicrafts has involved woodwork, metalwork and technical drawing. Yet, she argues, these two sets of craft studies are not equivalent, 'Cookery has very little educative transfer value and is mainly skills based with a low conceptual element. Except for the rare few who study catering it has little relevance to the world of work and is not properly *technical* education' (Commission of the European Communities, 1978, p.41). Also, needlework is taught to pupils so that they can do dressmaking and domestic sewing. In contrast, the courses that boys take give them at least some provisional technical education. Furthermore, technical craft courses reinforce spatial development and numerical concepts in boys.

Table 6 Options in the fourth and fifth forms: pupils being offered, choosing and taking particular subjects (corrected percentages for comparing segregated and mixed schools) (1975) (Source: Department of Education and Science (1975), p.13)

		Being offered		Choosing		Taking	
		per cent of totals of pupils		per cent of those to whom offered		per cent of totals of pupils	
		single-sex schools	mixed schools	single-sex schools	mixed schools	single-sex schools	mixed schools
Physics	boys	85	91	60	52	51	47
	girls	62	75	23	15	14	11
Chemistry	boys	81	79	36	35	29	28
	girls	75	78	27	22	20	17
Biology	boys	79	91	39	30	31	27
	girls	96	96	49	53	47	51
French	boys	75	87	37	28	28	24
	girls	92	90	49	43	45	39
German	boys	33	36	21	11	7	4
	girls	44	38	18	21	8	8
Geography	boys	91	61	55	54	50	33
	girls	72	61	53	46	38	28
History	boys	92	57	45	40	41	23
	girls	69	61	46	48	32	29
Art	boys	97	98	36	38	35	37
	girls	98	98	39	37	38	36
Music	boys	55	75	11	13	6	10
	girls	94	81	16	16	15	13

Yet it is precisely these skills that girls, given their early deprivation need to acquire in this respect.

Despite the evidence that girls and boys received less stereotyped 'academic' education in single-sex schools, the DES survey did not argue that boys and girls should be educated separately or together. The HM Inspectorate stated categorically that the 'findings would be misinterpreted if used to argue the case for either single-sex or mixed schools'; instead they advised a reconsideration of the curricula provision for 12–16-year-olds to ensure that 'the principal areas of the curriculum are open to all boys and girls in whatever kind of school they happen to be' (p.22).

The report's hesitancy to recommend single-sex schools may have been a result of the other findings of their report. Curricular provision and choice was determined to a considerable extent by the *type of secondary school*. In their appendices, the DES report showed that physics was offered to 90–100 per cent of grammar school girls (mixed and single sex) but only 37 per cent of mixed secondary modern and 11 per cent of single-sex secondary modern school girls. Whereas 33 per cent of girls in single-sex grammar schools and 29 per cent of mixed grammar schools actually took physics, a paltry 3 and 4 per cent of girls in mixed and single-sex secondary modern schools did. The type of secondary school attended was critical, therefore, to the pattern of subject provision and choice, especially in high status 'academic' school subjects.

Class differences in the types of pupil recruitment also make a difference. For example, single-sex schools were found by Douglas and Ross (1966) to be an advantage for middle-class boys, and for boys and girls of the manual working classes who attended grammar schools: they stayed on longer and got better O-level results. Middle-class girls, on the other hand, were at a considerable advantage in mixed grammar schools, perhaps because girls' single-sex grammar schools were underresourced and the curricular options were limited. In the secondary modern schools, the 'sex structure' of the school made little difference to middle-class boys and the working-class pupils; again middle-class girls did better in mixed schools. This study could not examine the effect of mixing in comprehensive schools.

More recent studies have managed to compare different types of schools, different levels of pupil ability and girls' experiences in mixed and single sex comprehensives, modern, technical and grammar schools. Steedman's (1983) and Bone's (1983) research, report that there seem to be no intrinsic advantages or disadvantages, in terms of academic performance, for girls in mixed or single sex schools. The type of school and the style of the school they found to be a more important feature of girls' experiences. Girls seemed more favourable to 'non-traditional' areas in single sex schools, although they were not necessarily encouraged by the schools to go ahead and challenge the feminine stereotype.

Support for coeducational schools was presented in the major study of single-sex and mixed schools – that of R.R. Dale (1969, 1971, 1974), published in three volumes. Dale stressed the *social* advantages of coeducation since, by mixing the sexes, schools could in his view more effectively reproduce what he called 'normal life', i.e. life in a two-gendered and heterosexual world in which men dominate and women learn to complement and subordinate themselves to men. In mixed schools, boys and girls could get to know each other; they were more likely to avoid the extremes of character defects such as the 'aggression' of boys and the 'cattiness' and 'bitchiness' of girls. In the happy family atmosphere of such schools, teachers would use less harsh discipline and less physical force.

Dale stressed the social advantages for boys of mixed schools and ignored the social disadvantages which girls face in such schools. Yet these disadvantages affect girls' low perception of themselves and their worth, in comparison with boys. And as Alison Kelly has argued, it is difficult to separate out the effects of lack of self-confidence with the lack of academic ambition. Mixed schools in many ways are boys' schools with girls in them and, as Jenny Shaw (1974, 1980) has argued, the deterioration of girls' academic performance and their limited horizons in the choice of school subject in mixed secondary schools are linked to a school climate in which most senior staff are male and where there is overall anxiety about appropriate gender behaviour. The use of gender in mixed schools to categorize pupils, to organize their daily activities, their examination results, their school dress or uniform, their play activities, etc., as well as separate staffrooms for male and female staff, all have the effect of reinforcing the differences rather than the similarities between the sexes.

In contrast, away from the pressures of male pupils, girls may get the impression that it is important whether they do well academically at school and that the 'male' world of science is potentially assailable. As a result of the research on mixed schools, single-sex schools are now seen as the way forward by some feminists. Such schools represent for them not merely a means of offering a wider curricular choice to girls but also a way in which girls may be taught how to challenge patriarchal relations in society. Single-sex schools in this context would have a new *subversive* potential. If one could set up a single-sex school with a predominantly female teaching staff, a female head, and all female pupils, the potential is there to encourage girls to 'resist oppression in wider society'. The 'positive' aspects of girls' schools encompass not merely the absence of boys, with their jokes, their ridicule of girls, their absorption of the teacher's energy and attention, their competitive spirit, their aggression and the imposition of their notions of femininity, but also the absence of male teachers, male control and responsibility for decision-making. (see Sarah, Scott and Spender, 1980).

The introduction of single-sex classes for girls within mixed schools in science and mathematics subjects however also makes sense. After all, if boys can get help on remedial reading classes, why cannot girls be helped to overcome their reluctance to study mathematics, and their lack of familiarity with technical subjects? Such remedial work really begs the question: can genuinely 'comprehensive' schools exist when there is still education inequality of the sexes within them? Should we still keep working at this ideal, or should we go back to single-sex schools? Perhaps we should rethink the notion of coeducation, which never really meant equal education for boys and for girls but only a range of common and different subject choices.

The correct strategy is very hard to assess, especially since most of the evidence is inadequate and is based on single-dimensional analyses. It is important to remember that the issue of coeducation involves the problem of selective and nonselective schools, of the private and public sector, of denominational schools and boarding schools; that the resources are unlikely to be available to bring all single-sex schools up to the level of coeducation facilities; and that since most of the single-sex schools are private schools or were grammar schools, single-sex education is closely tied to social class divisions in education.

Finally there is also a practical consideration to take into account. If girls are best educated in single-sex schools but boys are not, where will the girls be found to fill the mixed schools? What sort of education is best for boys in order for them to change their stereotypes of masculinity and femininity? So far, there has been very little discussion of this aspect of coeducation, although a few projects with boys have been started (see Arnot, 1984).

Classroom practice
Finally, let us look at the structure of classroom life. Here there are a variety of factors to consider – for example, does the sex of the teacher, the presence of boys, the teaching style, or the attitudes of teachers make a difference to girls?

Historically, the development of the state educational system (especially primary schools and girls' schools) has been based upon a supply of female teachers. Yet the development of mixed schools, particularly at secondary level, has limited the career prospects of female teachers. It is still unusual to find a female head teacher in a mixed school. This fact is important, not just for the women who are teachers struggling to get promotion within the school system, but also for the pupils. By witnessing the sexual division of labour within the teaching profession, especially in terms of the hierarchy of responsibilities and power, the child is likely to acquire a certain perception of the social order. Certainly, if there is one thing that is clear in the history of the educational system, it is that men have had control over the development, the shaping and the administration of education. Further, the sex of teachers is important, if one believes that learning comes through imitation. As Alison Kelly has argued, the lack of women science teachers may contribute to the attribution of masculinity to scientific studies and to girls' reluctance to study such subjects. It may be particularly significant therefore that in 1977 only one per cent of female secondary school teachers' main subject of highest qualification was in craft, design and technology, and only one per cent of male teachers had Home Economics as their subject of highest qualification (EOC, 1982).

Earlier research focussed on the attitudes of teachers and showed that both male and female teachers had similar expectations of gender differences and differentiated between male and female pupils in similar ways – a fact that is hardly surprising if one considers the similarity of teacher training courses and their lack of coverage of the issues of sex discrimination in schools. Both sets of teachers in primary schools appeared to have similar stereotypical attitudes to boys' and girls' futures after school. Glennys Lobban (1978) argues that the evidence in teachers in primary schools shows that:

> Teachers of both sexes thus appear to endorse sex-role stereotypes. They believe that extreme differences between males and females exist as early as age three. They also appear to believe that it is appropriate to behave differently to the sexes in accord with their 'natural' characteristics. They seem to interpret behaviour acording to stereotypes, they expect their female pupils to be passive, dependent, compliant and on the way to marriage as their only life-consuming career, while the males are expected to be active, independent, bright and challenging and destined for a 'real' career. (p.57).

However, Michelle Stanworth (1981) looked more closely at a group of teachers who taught 'A' level classes in a humanities department of a college of further education. The college was completely coeducational and appeared not to discriminate between pupils by sex in any formal way. Using a variety of research techniques, she found that male teachers were far more likely than female teachers to view the sexes as relatively discrete groups. Thus, they were more likely to compare a boy with other boys, rather than with girls in the same class. Male teachers were also much more likely to be attached to or concerned about boys than girls. The chance, for example, that a boy was the focus of the teacher's concern was twice that of a girl, if the teacher was a woman, but ten times more if the teacher were a man. Girls were twice as likely to be 'rejected' than boys of the same academic standing.

First impressions of girls entering the class were that they were exceptionally quiet; teachers also tended to learn boys' names more quickly. When the teachers were asked to speculate about what various pupils would be doing in two and five years time, boys were thought likely to have jobs of considerable responsibility and authority, e.g. civil service and management, and marriage and parenthood were only mentioned in one boy's case. The occupations girls were thought likely to enter were those of secretary, nurse and teacher which Stanworth found neither matched any individual girl's academic standing nor aspirations.

Both male and female teachers suggested, and took for granted, that girls would marry and become parents, whatever their educational abilities. Male teachers, in particular, had difficulty envisaging careers for girls. Such views obviously have repercussions as to how girls are treated in classrooms and in the perceived importance of 'A' levels in their future lives.

Equally important for girls is the ability of the teacher to maintain authority and control in the classroom with pupils of different sex. Again, there is very little research completed on this crucial area of school life, but what little there is suggests that female teachers may have far more trouble coping with male pupils, who are generally the most troublesome in the classroom. This may be because male pupils have learnt from a very young age that women are powerless and inferior and that they can exploit the classroom situation 'as boys'.

Valerie Walkerdine's (1981) research has shown that little boys can challenge the teacher's authority by using sexist language and behaviour. She recorded the following sequence in a nursery school. It starts when three-year-old Annie takes a piece of Lego to add to a construction she is building. Four-year-old Terry tries to take it from her to use himself, and she resists. He says:

Terry: You're a stupid cunt, Annie.

The teacher tells him to stop and Sean tries to mess-up another child's construction. The teacher tells him to stop. Then Sean says:

Sean: Get out of it Miss Baxter paxter.
Terry: Get out of it knickers Miss Baxter.
Sean: Get out of it Miss Baxter paxter.
Terry: Get out of it Miss Baxter the knickers paxter knickers, bum.
Sean: Knickers, shit, bum.
Miss B: Sean, that's enough, you're being silly.
Sean: Miss Baxter, knickers, show your knickers.
Terry: Miss Baxter, show your bum off.
(they giggle)

Miss B: I think you're being very silly.
  Terry: Shit Miss Baxter, shit Miss Baxter.
  Sean Miss Baxter, show your knickers your bum off.
  Sean: Take all your clothes off, your bra off.
  Terry: Yeah, and take your bum off, take your wee-wee off, take your clothes, your mouth off.
  Sean: Take your teeth out, take your head off, take your hair off, take your bum off. Miss Baxter the paxter knickers taxter.
Miss B: Sean, go and find something else to do please.

(Walkerdine, 1981, p.15)

Such manipulation of male-female relations by very young boys, Walkerdine argues, causes problems not just for the girls and female teachers involved, but also raises questions about the value of 'progressive' education for girls. The notion of childhood sexuality underlying this pedagogy has its roots in psychoanalysis which stresses that children's sexual natures should be 'released' rather than developed; 'expressed' rather than repressed. Any suppression of sexual feelings and their manifestation, particularly amongst boys, it is feared might lead to later aggression or deformity of personality. With progressive education, teaching therefore is designed on the principle of *non-intervention*.

The irony is that within the 'space' created by progressivism for children to define what they want and don't want to do, sexist practices and language learnt at home and in the community can be brought into the classroom and cannot be corrected or interfered with by the teacher (as shown by the teacher's response in the transcript above). Walkerdine therefore suggests that any desire to remove sexism in progressive schools will have to challenge the validity of such 'freedoms' for girls. The picture she presents of life within a nursery school however is not totally bleak since the girls fight back temporarily using traditional female roles of domesticity and mothering. However, it does raise critical questions about what teachers' practice should be.

In terms of classroom interaction, the research on primary education indicates that boys and girls receive different amounts and quality of attention from teachers. At one level, girls are taught to need teacher approval more than boys; yet girls adopt a definition of maturity that involves the early acceptance of quietness and obedience. Because of this, girls tend to receive more approval for gender conformity and interact less with their teachers, who concentrate on the more difficult boys in the classroom. Boys receive more prohibitory messages than girls – in other words they are punished more for failing to keep order and for misbehaviour – yet they also receive more than their share of all types of interaction with the teacher.

In Stanworth's study such research findings were borne out for A-level pupils. Although pupils criticized both male and female teachers for being insufficiently authoritarian, they saw male teachers as 'more effective disciplinarians'. Boys, in particular, saw male teachers as more successful and female teachers as less. Girls, in contrast, were more even-handed in their ranking. Girls felt that female teachers were easy to get on with, more fun, and more helpful; similarly boys preferred male teachers.

Given such attitudes amongst teachers and such classroom practices, how then did such pupils see the pattern of classroom interaction? In Stanworth's study, both male and female pupils perceived boys as receiving far more attention than girls from the teacher. Boys were more likely to get involved in classroom discussions, to comment, to demand help or attention and to be seen as 'model' pupils by the other pupils. Boys were also perceived as more likely to be asked questions, to be seen as highly conscientious by the teacher, to get on best with the teacher and receive more praise and more criticism. They were more likely to be the ones the teacher appeared to enjoy teaching. As Stanworth puts it, girls were placed on 'the margins of classroom life'.

The implications of such pupil perceptions, and the pattern of teachers' expectations and reinforcement of gender differences, are serious for girls as a group, specially if they legitimate as 'natural' the unequal relationships between pupils themselves. Increasingly research on the sexual relations within schools and between boys and girls points to the dominance of boys over girls and the 'laissez faire' attitude of schools to this domination. Research such as that by Sue Lees (1983) shows how the boys' language and in particular their naming of different types of girls 'slags' or 'drags' has the effect of categorizing girls by their sexual attractiveness and availability to males, rather than by their personalities or abilities. Girls themselves, in trying to negotiate the fine line between these insults, use and manipulate the distinctions, often at the expense of giving attention to themselves as people in their own right. The research by Mahony (1985) and Wood (1984) also points to the ways in which boys dominate the linguistic and physical space of the school and sexually harrass girls. They illustrate the ways in which masculinity is constructed through the devaluation and sexual denigration of girls and the imposition of their values upon the girls. Increasingly sexual harrassment in secondary schools is being taken up by feminist teachers as a matter of the deepest concern.

Stanworth's research shows how even at A-levels this devaluation of girls is still present. Boys downgrade the girls' ability and see them as a 'faceless bunch', when they are not chasing them for sexual favours. The overall impression she received was that 'classroom interaction . . . does not merely transmit beliefs about the superiority of one sex over the other, but actively serves to give such beliefs a concrete foundation in personal experience' (p.51). It is precisely the teachers' policy of 'non-intervention' in this process which, in her view, constitutes a 'significant political act'.

Conclusion

I have argued here that patterns of female education achievement need to be explained by a whole range of structures. I discussed the history of state policies for women's education and their underlying ideologies of gender differentiation and social class differentiation. I tried also to show that within educational institutions, gender differentiation is not just a matter of attitudes or of unintentional discrimination, but of what could be called 'institutional sexism' – i.e. hidden structures of sex inequality found in, for example, classroom interaction, in teachers' expectations and practice, and in the structured interaction between boys and girls in the classroom, corridor or playground. The ideological assumptions behind state policy are not separate influences but are built on and incorporated into educational practice, especially since such assumptions have had such a long and continuous history. We are not dealing here with just an educational problem for which an educational solution can be found. Educational policy and practice, cannot be divorced from the position of women in the economy – both as waged and domestic workers within patriarchal social relations.

If we ask whether state education policy has benefited women we have to seek the answer, not necessarily in the success of some women to reach university, or to gain more qualifications than they had previously, but in the general social location of women in the economy and the family. And here it is difficult to see substantial improvements in women's position over the course of the twentieth century. Further, even if women have achieved a higher level of education than previously, the experiences they face *inside* educational institutions still leaves room for concern. In many ways state education, whether intentionally or unintentionally, has discriminated against the majority of female pupils – for example by allowing the shift to coeducation without substantial assessment of its impact and the new problems it has engendered. Overall there appears to have been a lack of real concern over the future of girls and women in society, and the future role they could play within the changing labour force, yet what this analysis has shown is that in reality the intervention of the state into girls' education has not been 'neutral'. It has operated to maintain differences between the sexes and the sexual division of labour, both explicitly and implicitly. The extent to which the education system has succeeded in doing this is arguable – mediated as it is by the personal and collective struggles of women to 'break out' of the mould. Women have won some major victories – such as gaining access to secondary and higher education, and more recently to scientific education. However, what in the end constitutes a victory of women is a matter of some contention. Should women aspire to succeed within a male defined and structured educational system? Or should we challenge the principles according to which such a patriarchal system of education has developed?

Note

___Social class classification for Table 1 (Source: Based on Reid, 1981, p. 43–5)

Social Class	Occupations
1	*Professional workers*—self-employed normally requiring qualifications to degree standard.
2	*Employers and managers*—in central and local government, industry, commerce, large and small establishments and farmers (employers and managers) who won, rent or manage farms employing other than family workers.
3	*Intermediate non-manual workers*—employers engaged in clerical sales non-manual communications and security.
4	*Foremen and supervisors*—manual employees *Skilled manual workers Own account workers*—self-employed in trade, personal service or manual occupations, with no employees other than family workers. *Farmers*—who own or rent with only family workers.
5	*Personal service workers*—employees engaged in service occupations caring for food, drink, clothing and other needs. *Semi-skilled manual workers Agricultural workers*
6	*Unskilled manual workers*

References

ARNOT, M. (1984) How shall we educate our sons? in DEEM, R. (ed.) *Coeducation Reconsidered*, OUEE.

BENN, C. and SIMON, B. (1972) *Half Way There*, Harmondsworth, Penguin.

BIRMINGHAM FEMINIST HISTORY GROUP (1979) 'Feminisim as femininity in the nineteen fifties', *Feminist Review*, 3, pp. 148–164.

BONE, A. (1983) *Girls and Girls-Only Schools: A Review of the Evidence*, EOC Manchester.

BRAH, A. and MINHAS, (1985) 'Structural racism or cultural difference: Schooling for Asian girls', in WEINER, G. (ed.) *Just a Bunch of Girls*, OUEE.

BURSTYN, J.N. (1980) *Victorian Education and the Ideal of Womanhood*, Croom Helm.

CARBY, H. (1982) 'White women listen! Black feminism and the boundaries of sisterhood', *The Empire Strikes Back*, CCCS, Hutchinson.

CLARRICOATES, K. (1980) The Importance of being earnest . . . Emma, Tom, . . . Jane: The perception and categorization of gender conformity and gender deviation in primary schools' in DEEM, R. (ed.) *Schooling for Women's Work*, Routledge & Kegan Paul.

COMMISSION OF THE EUROPEAN COMMUNITIES (1978) *Equality of Education and Training for girls* (10–18 years) by BYRNE, E.M. Education Series, No. 9, Brussels.

CROWTHER REPORT (1959) *15-18*, (Central Advisory Council for Education), HMSO.

DALE, R.R. (1969) *Mixed or Single-Sex School?* (Vol. 1) (1971), *Mixed or Single-Sex School? Some Social Aspects* (Vol. 2) (1974), *Mixed or Single-Sex School? Attainment, Attitudes and Overview,* (Vol. 3), Routledge & Kegan Paul.

DAVID M.E. (1980) *The State, The Family and Education,* Routledge & Kegan Paul.

DAVID, M. (1984) 'Women, family and education', in ACKER, S. *et al.* (eds) *Women and Education,* Kogan Page.

DAVIES L. (1978) 'The view from the girls', *Educational Review,* 30, 2, p. 103-9.

DAVIN, A. (1979) 'Mind that you do as you are told': reading books for Board School Girls, 1870-1902, *Feminist Review,* 3 pp. 80-98.

DEEM. R. (1981) 'State policy and ideology in the education of women, 1944-1980', *British Journal of Sociology of Education,* Vol. 2, No. 2, pp. 131-44.

DELAMONT. S. (1980) *Sex Roles and the School,* Methuen.

DEPARTMENT OF EDUCATION AND SCIENCE (DES) (1975) *Curricular Differences for Boys and Girls,* Education Survey 21, HMSO.

DEPARTMENT OF EDUCATION AND SCIENCE (DES) (1977) *Education in Schools: A Consultative Document,* HMSO (CMND 6869) (Green Paper).

DEPARTMENT OF EDUCATION AND SCIENCE (DES) (1980) *Girls and Science,* HMI Series: Matters for Discussion 13, HMSO.

DOUGLAS. J.W.B. and ROSS, J.M. (1966) 'Single sex or co-ed? The academic consequences', *Where,* 25 (May) pp. 5-8.

DYHOUSE, C. (1981) *Girls Growing Up in Late Victorian and Edwardian England,* Routledge & Kegan Paul.

EQUAL OPPORTUNITIES COMMISSION (1978/79) *Research Bulletin,* Vol. 1, Winter.

EQUAL OPPORTUNITIES COMMISSION (1982) *Equal Opportunities in Home Economics,* Manchester.

FULLER. M. (1980) 'Black girls in a London comprehensive school', in DEEM, R. (ed.) (1980) *Schooling for Women's Work,* Routledge & Kegan Paul.

KELLY, A. (ed.) (1981) *The Missing Half,* Manchester University Press.

KELLY, A. (1982) 'Why girls don't do science', *New Scientist,* 20 May, pp. 497-500.

KELSALL, R., POOLE, A. and KUHN, A. (1972) *Graduates: the Sociology of an Elite,* .Methuen.

KESSLER, S.J. and MCKENNA, W. (1982) Developmental aspects of gender, in E.L. WHITELEGG *et al.* (eds) *The Changing Experience of Women,* Martin Robertson.

LEES, S. (1983) 'How boys slag off girls', *New Society,* 13 October, 1983.

LOBBAN, G.M. (1975) 'Sex-Roles in Reading Schemes', *Educational Review,* 27, (3), pp. 202-10.

LOBBAN, G.M., (1978) 'The influence of the school on sex-role stereotyping, in CHETWYND, J. and HARTNETT, O. (eds) *The Sex Role System,* London, Routledge & Kegan Paul.

MAHONEY, P. (1985) *Schools for the Boys. Co-education reassessed,* Hutchinson Explorations in feminism collective.

MANPOWER SERVICES COMMISSION, TRAINING SERVICES DIVISION (1976) *Training for Women,* MSC.

McINTOSH, N.E. (1979) 'Women in distance education: The Open University experience', *Educational Broadcasting International,* Dec. pp. 178-183.

McROBBIE, A. (1978a) 'Working class girls and the culture of femininity', in Women's Studies Group, Centre for Contemporary Cultural Studies, *Women Take Issue: Aspects of women's subordination,* Hutchinson Educational.

McCROBBIE, A. (1978b) *Jackie: An ideology of adolescent femininity,* CCCS Stencilled Occasional Paper, Women Series SP No. 53.

MEYENN, R.J. (1980) 'School girls' peer groups', in WOODS, P. (ed.) *Pupil Strategies,* Croom Helm.

MINISTRY OF EDUCATION (1963) *Higher Education*, Vol. 1, (Robbins Report).

NEWSOM REPORT (1963) *Half our Future* (Central Advisory Council for Education) HMSO.

NORWOOD REPORT (1943) *Report of the Committee of Secondary Schools Examination Council on Curriculum and Examinations in Secondary Schools*, Board of Education, HMSO.

OKELY, J. (1978) Privileged, schooled and finished: boarding education for girls in ARDENER, S. (ed.) *Defining Females*, Croom Helm.

PARMAR, P. (1981) 'Young Asian women: A critique of the pathological approach', *Multiracial Education*, 9, 3. pp. 19–29.

PAYNE, I. (1980) 'A working-class girl in a grammar school', in SPENDER, D. and SARAH, E. (eds) *Learning to Lose*, The Women's Press.

PEDERSEN, J.S. (1979) 'The reform of women's secondary and higher education: Institutional change and social values in mid and late Victorian England', *History of Education Quarterly*, 19, pp. 61–91.

PHILLIPS, A. and TAYLOR, B. (1980) 'Sex and skill: notes towards a feminist economics', *Feminist Review*, No. 6.

PURVIS, J. (1981) Towards a history of women's education in nineteenth century Britain: a sociological analysis, *Westminster Studies in Education*, 4, pp. 45–79.

REID, I. (1981) *Social Class Differences in Britain*, 2nd edition, Grant McIntyre.

RILEY, K. (1981) 'Black girls speak for themselves', *Multiracial Education*, 10, 3, pp. 3–12.

SARAH, E., SCOTT, M. and SPENDER, D. (1980) 'The Education of feminists: the case for single sex schools', in SPENDER, D. and SARAH, E. (eds) (1980) *Learning to Lose*, The Women's Press.

SHAW, J. (1974) 'Finishing school: some implications of sex-segregated education', in LEONARD BARKER, D. and ALLEN, S. (eds) (1976) *Sexual Divisions and Society: Process and Change*, Tavistock.

SHAW, J. (1980) 'Education and the individual. Schooling for girls, or mixed schooling–a mixed blessing?' in DEEM, R. (ed.) (1980) *Schooling for Women's Work*, Routledge & Kegan Paul.

STANWORTH, M. (1981) *Gender and Schooling: A Study of Sexual Division in the Classroom*, Women's Research and Resource Centre, Pamphlet No. 7, Hutchinson.

STEEDMAN, J. (1983) *Examination results in Mixed and Single Sex Schools: Findings from the National Child Development Study*, EOC, Manchester.

TAUNTON REPORT (1868) *Report of the Commissioners: Commission to Inquire into the Education Given in Schools*, Eyre and Spottiswoode for HMSO, *Schools Enquiry Commission*.

TAWNEY, R.H. (1931) *Equality*, Unwin Books.

WALKERDINE, V. (1981) 'Sex, power and pedagogy', *Screen Education*, No. 38, Spring, pp. 14–25.

WICKHAM, A. (1985) 'Gender divisions, training and the State', in DALE, R. (ed.) *Education, Training and Employment: Towards a new Vocationalism?* Pergamon Press.

WILLIS, P. (1977) *Learning to Labour*, Saxon House.

WOLPE, A.M. (1976) 'The official ideology of education for girls', in FLUDE, M. and AHIER, J. (ed.) *Educability Schools and Ideology*, Croom Helm.

WOLPE, A.M. (1978) 'Girls and economic survival', *British Journal of Educational Studies* 26, (2), June, pp. 150–62.

WOOD, J. (1984) 'Groping towards sexism: Boys' sex talk', in McROBBIE, A. and NAVA, M. (eds) *Gender and Generation*, MacMillan.

4 Women Health and Medicine
Lesley Doyal and Mary Ann Elston

Women and Medicine Today

During the twentieth century, the institution of Western scientific medicine has achieved considerable social and economic prominence. Throughout the world it is seen as the most effective means of dealing with ill-health, and this is reflected both in the power and prestige of doctors and in the vast sums that are spent each year on the provision of medical care. In Britain, for instance, we spent over £12,000 million, or almost 6 per cent of our GNP, on the National Health Service (NHS) in 1983.

This situation is usually regarded as entirely desirable. Medicine makes sick people well – it is argued – so surely we should provide as much of it as we can. But things are more complex than they might at first appear to be, and the value of modern medicine is now coming under increasing scrutiny.

On the one hand, there can be no doubt that medical scientists have developed valuable techniques to prevent or to cure some illnesses and to relieve suffering in others. Vaccination, antisepsis, anaethesia, antibiotics and pain-relieving drugs are all obvious examples. However, we cannot assume that all aspects of medical practice are equally beneficial. We know, for instance, that some widely used medical techniques are of very little therapeutic value, while others may even cause harm. The removal of a child's tonsils used to be a common practice, but is now regarded as being rarely of value and potentially dangerous. Doubt has also been raised about the efficacy and safety of some commonly used drugs. Reservations of this kind about the effectiveness of some aspects of medical care have become increasingly common in recent years, and they have been highlighted by rapidly rising costs.

But is it not just the technical and economic aspects of modern medicine that are giving cause for concern. The power of doctors extends beyond immediate decisions relating to diagnosis and treatment – beyond what could strictly be regarded as the clinical domain. This can be seen in the context of individual patient care when doctors will sometimes advise, or even exhort, their patients about non-medical aspects of their lives in much the same way as a priest might have done in the past. For instance, doctors will often involve themselves in discussions about whether or not a woman *should* have an abortion rather than simply making technical decision about the medical feasibility of such a procedure. And, in the broader social context, doctors often make judgements about a wide range of issues, for instance, on whether mothers should go out to work. This growth in the power of doctors has given rise to considerable criticism in recent years, and to discussions about how such power might be controlled (Kennedy, 1981).

Modern medicine has therefore become an immensely powerful and important institution, but one whose value has to be looked at very carefully. On the one hand, it is a useful resource, providing services which people undoubtedly need. However, it can also become a means of control, opposing or reinforcing wider social values. Questions about the nature of medicine are particularly important to women because, as we shall see, women are both the major consumers and also the major providers of health care in our society.

Women as Consumers of Medical Care
Women constitute the majority of NHS patients and use general practitioner, psychiatric, geriatric and most preventive services more frequently than men. This is often seen as a paradox because, on average, women live longer than men and therefore one might conclude that they are healthier than men and use medical services less. In 1981 a woman's life expectancy at birth was 76.2 years compared with 70.2 years for a man. At the age of 60, life expectancy was 20.4 and 15.9 respectively.

The practical result of these differences is that women need more medical care rather than less. Women now form a significant majority of the elderly in the population: among those over 75, there are now two women for every man. Since the very elderly always have great need of medical services, the longevity of women in obviously important in explaining their predominance among patients in NHS hospitals.

Another reason for women's greater use of health services is their reproductive capacity, which brings them into the medical orbit in a variety of different ways. Women are obviously the only users of maternity services, and they come into frequent contact with the health-care system during the processes of pregnancy and childbirth. They are also the most frequent users of services connected with fertility control, since women are increasingly taking responsibility for contraception, and most female contraception techniques involve some degree of medical intervention, whether in the prescribing of a pill or the fitting of an intra-uterine device (IUD). Finally, since women bear the major responsibility for childcare, they frequently accompany children on visits to the doctor.

Because women are often using medical services in connection with reproduction, they may well visit their doctors when they are perfectly healthy. They are not then 'patients' in the classic sense of the term, yet doctors and health workers often treat them as though they were sick and dependent and in need of medical intervention. As we shall see later, this problem of the healthy woman being treated as ill is perhaps at its most acute in the context of childbirth.

Generally speaking, women are treated for psychiatric problems rather more often than men, whether we compare GP consultation rates for 'emotional' problems, outpatient psychiatric visits or admittance to a psychiatric hospital. In 1970 it was calculated that one woman in six in England and Wales would enter hospital because of mental illness at some time in her life, compared with one man in nine. Psychiatric admissions have fallen considerably since then, largely because of changes in treatment policy (more people are treated as outpatients), but the difference between the proportions of women and men still remains.

The most obvious conclusion that could be drawn from these figures would be that women suffer from mental illness more often than men and this is reflected in a straightforward way in their greater use of psychiatric services. However, we cannot assume simple relationship between the use of medical services and the level of physical or psychological ill-health in a community. A great deal of illness is never brought before a doctor, so official consultation rates only represent the tip of an iceberg, with most illness remaining invisible.

On the other hand, many medical consultations do not arise directly from physical or psychological illness but are actually a response to a social or economic problem for which there appears to be no alternative source of help. Tranquilizer advertisements aimed at doctors show that this is well recognized by the drug industry. The companies that manufacture tranquilizers have realized that many women's unhappiness or 'depression' is caused by the circumstances in which they live, since women are pictured in advertisements in bad housing conditions, surrounded by piles of washing-up and screaming children. However, the answer shown is not to change the situation, but to prescribe a pill to dull the pain. Not surprisingly, problems presented to a doctor – whatever their origin – will usually be interpreted only in medical terms. This can lead to an overemphasis on the rate of illness in a community and an underestimate of other social and economic problems.

These difficulties of definition and measurement are particularly acute when we are trying to compare the frequency with which women and men consult doctors. This is because studies have shown that there are differences between sexes in what sociologists call 'illness behaviour', that is, the way people behave when they are ill. These are likely to lead to an overestimation of the amount of ill-health among women compared with that of men. First, it appears that women are more likely than men to express their problems though anxiety, depression or other symptoms of illness. In general, it is more socially acceptable for women to admit weakness and to seek help, particularly when their problems are emotional. Therefore, women may find it easier than men to take problems of this kind to a doctor. Moreover, the fact that psychological weakness is not only more readily tolerated but may even be expected in women, will affect the perceptions that doctors have of their patients. Hence doctors often interpret a woman's symptoms as psychosomatic (psychological in origin) when they might consider similar symptoms in a man to be physical in origin (Lennane and Lennane, 1973).

It seems then, that some of the greater use made of medical services, and psychiatric services in particular, by women can be explained by sex differences in attitudes towards illness and towards the seeking of medical care. However, it also seems likely that we cannot explain the entire difference in this way. If we cannot explain away the greater female use of psychiatric services, then we have to look at alternative explanations for why women should exhibit higher rates of certain kinds of mental illness than men.

Some of the excess, particularly in admission to hospital for senile dementia (a form of mental confusion that sometimes accompanies ageing), is again accounted for by the number of elderly women in the population. However far more women than men are also treated for anxiety and depression, and, despite the problems in interpreting the statistics, this does seem to reflect real differences between the sexes.

One argument that is frequently used to explain – implicitly or explicitly – is the suggestion that women are genetically (biologically) more prone to certain kinds of mental illness than men. That is to say, they are inherently more excitable and emotionally unstable, and are therefore more likely to to 'over the top' or 'off the rails' and find themselves in a doctor's surgery. The most important argument against this idea that all women have a genetic predisposition to mental illness is that it ignores all the social and environmental factors that also influence women's lives and inevitably affect their experiences of sickness and health. A more appropriate starting point for understanding female mental illness would not be women's genes but an analysis of the role of women in our society in order to ascertain whether or not it is liable to make them more likely than men to suffer from anxiety and depression.

Feminists have also pointed out that the role of a woman in our society is in many ways a 'sick' one – that femininity itself is somehow equated with sickness. Thus there is a sense in which to be a 'normal' woman is often to be a neurotic human being. Another suggestion is that the behaviour and attitudes expected of a woman may sometimes be so intolerable or contradictory that anxiety or depression become a reasonable response. The hysteria sometimes exhibited by middle-class women in the nineteenth century, for instance, has been described as an entirely understandable response to their sheltered lives – and possibly even as a form of protest. Finally, it is argued that the lives many women lead – the nature of their living and working conditions and the quality of their relationships with other people – will often be conducive to depression and/or anxiety. One example of this might be the middle-aged woman who is depressed because her children have left home, and who now has little sense of her own identity or worth. Another illustration would be the prevalence of depression among working-class housewives at home with small children. Obviously, the reasons behind this phenomenon are complex, but among the most important must be the social isolation of these women combined with the very low value placed on their work (Brown and Harris, 1978).

Women as Producers of Medical Care

Although medicine is usually thought of as a male sphere of activity, it is women who make up the majority of health workers. Over 70 per cent of people working for the NHS are female. But women are by no means evenly distributed within the health labour force. Only about 25 per cent of NHS doctors are women, and most female health workers are found low down in the occupational hierarchy, particularly in nursing and ancillary work. These involve the traditionally female task of caring for the intimate needs of the sick and the domestic duties of cooking, cleaning and laundering; thus the sexual division of labour in health care reflects that of the wider society. If we look at the relationship between doctors and nurses, for instance, we find that it often mirrors the relationship traditionally found between the sexes. That is to say, the (usually) male doctor makes the 'hard' intellectual decisions while the (usually) female nurse carries them out and provides 'tender loving care' for the patient. Most NHS work is therefore 'women's work' and this is reflected in the inferior status, low pay and often unpleasant conditions that characterize many jobs in the health service as well as women's work in other sectors of the economy.

But women's role in caring for the sick is by no means confined to the NHS. Women also provide a vast and largely invisible reservoir of care for those people who are in need but who are not deemed to be the responsibility of the healthcare system. In practice, most of the chronically sick and disabled, the mentally handicapped and the elderly are not cared for by paid workers either in institutions or in the community, but by individual women who feel morally bound to do so – usually by ties of kinship or marriage.

Women are also held responsible for maintaining the health of their families. This idea that women should look after the health of others is not a new one. If we go back to the nineteenth and early twentieth centuries we find that it was often mothers who were blamed for the high infant mortality rate. Rather than paying any serious attention to the problems of poverty, insanitary housing, and lack of medical attention during labour, most reformers blamed mothers themselves for their 'ignorant' and 'feckless' behaviour. In later years the content of this criticism of mothers has changed, but the logic remains the same. Thus the immediate post-war period was dominated by the notion of 'maternal deprivation' which was said to cause a wide variety of psychological problems in children whose mothers went out to work.

The Medical View of Women and Its Impact on Medical Practice

Medicine as a science
Modern medicine is usually described as a science. Indeed we often refer to it as 'Western scientific medicine', thereby differentiating it both from its supposedly less scientific predecessors as well as its present-day competitors – the various types of so-called 'alternative medicine'. Thus, doctors are seen as medical scientists who can be objective about their subject matter (the patients) in much the same way that other scientists can apparently be objective about fossils, mountains or molecules of gas. Medical progress is said to be achieved through the use of the scientific method, thus ensuring the acquisition of certain and unchallengeable facts, and an autonomous and value-free body of knowledge.

However, this belief in medicine (or any other science) as objective and unbiassed has come under critical scrutiny in recent years. Indeed there is a growing recognition that all scientific activities are inevitably influenced by the values of the society in which they are carried out. Moreover, it is argued that scientists themselves often play a major part in explaining – and ultimately in justifying – various aspects of the way in which society is organized. In what follows, we look in more detail at how this general discussion of the nature of science relates to medicine. This will involve, among other things, an examination of the underlying values that influence medical practice, particularly as they apply to women.

The origins of modern medicine can be found in the scientific revolution of the seventeenth century. These early investigations consisted mainly of attempts to describe the internal workings of the human body and they were founded on a mechanistic view of the nature of living things. That is to say, in the seventeenth century, people thought of human beings and animals as sets of mechanical parts rather than integrated wholes. Thus human bodies were assumed to funtion like machines (though with a soul added), and the task of science was to describe and understand the working of those machines in as much detail as possible. This mechanistic model formed the intellectual basis for the development of modern medicine and remains at the heart of most contemporary medical practice.

There can be no doubt that it was the adoption of the mechanistic model that ultimately made possible those medical techniques that have been of genuine value – the development of effective and safe surgery, for example. However, it is important to recognize that this is not the only way of thinking about human health and illness, and that the mechanistic model has also influenced the nature of modern medicine in ways that are coming under increasing criticism. For instance, ill-health is still defined primarily in terms of the malfunctioning of one part of a mechanical system. Little attention is paid to the prevention of illness, and treatment usually consists of surgical or chemical intervention to 'mend' the broken part of the machine and restore it to normal working order. This ignores the importance of emotional factors in recovery and encourages doctors to treat their patients as 'things' to be manipulated, rather than subjects to be understood. It also emphasizes the active role of the doctor who decides for passive patients both what they are suffering from and how it will be treated. As a result, patients are often regarded as objects rather than as unique human beings with their own wishes, needs, desires and feelings.

The unequal relationship between doctor and patient and the high degree of social prestige awarded to medicine means that a medical consultation often involves the reinforcement of particular beliefs and values. For instance, the idea that it is only the doctor who can make you better serves to reinforce the feelings of powerlessness that are so common in other areas of life. Thus people come to believe that they have little control over their own bodies, just as they often have little control over their housing conditions or their working lives. Obviously feelings of frustration, ignorance and fear in the face of medical expertise are experienced by both sexes. However medical ideology also contains ideas about the nature of men and women and their different roles in society. Because most doctors are men, the effects of these ideas are experienced particularly strongly by their women patients.

The medical view of women in the nineteenth century
This medical ideology can serve to justify the sexual divisions in society, a process seen clearly if we look at the medical attitudes towards women that were prevalent in the nineteenth century. Throughout this period medicine was developing rapidly, though its ability to cure remained very limited. During this time of rapid social and economic change, the question of the 'natural' status and duties of women was a matter for major debate. Traditional and religious justifications for the patriarchal authority of husbands and fathers were being undermined and the task of defining the position of women increasingly fell to the proponents of the new science and to doctors and biologists in particular.

One widely held medical view was that the potential of women was predetermined by their reproductive organs (Doyal and Doyal, 1984). This was not a new idea, but doctors were able to provide more complex and apparently more scientific explanations of this ancient 'truth'. A malfunctioning uterus or ovary was said to spread disease throughout the body. Doctors could provide no real evidence as to how this occurred, but it was assumed that the uterus, the ovaries and the nervous system were somehow connected so that the nervous system transmitted pathological impulses to the rest of the body. The healthy functioning of a woman's reproductive system was said to take up all her energies and women were warned against straining themselves any further.

However, women in different social classes led very different lives, a fact which was difficult to reconcile with the belief that women's biology determined their entire existence. Middle-class women conformed most closely to the medical image of the weak and dependent woman, and it was they who came into contact with doctors most frequently. Indeed they provided many doctors with the major part of their income, though the advice they received was usually as much moral as technical in character. Rest was frequently prescribed and most activities outside the home were frowned upon. Higher education in particular was seen as a danger and women who took it up were said to do so at the risk of both their health and their femininity.

Working-class women, on the other hand, spent their lives labouring extremely hard inside and outside the home. It was therefore difficult to describe them as physically weak and dependent. Despite evidence to the contrary, it was assumed that working-class women were actually healthy, despite their material conditions. The notion that women were destroyed by brainwork rather than manual labour could thus reinforce traditional ideas about the inferiority of women and at the same time justify the very different lifestyles of middle-class and working-class women.

The medical model of women today

The position of women of all social classes has changed dramatically over the past hundred years and the lives of most women in Britain today are far removed from the stereotypes of the woman fulfilling her entire potential in motherhood. A large proportion of women are now involved in waged labour outside the home. Women also have fewer children than they did in the past; most women spend only about four years of their lives either pregnant or looking after a child under the age of one. Women are now generally accepted both as waged workers and as housewives/mothers. However, they are often assumed to be less effective mothers because their work interferes with their mothering and less effective workers because their mothering interferes with their work.

These changes in the material position of women and in ideas about femininity are reflected in medical perceptions of women, and in contemporary medical education and practice. It is clear that during the twentieth century the Victorian belief in the physical weakness of women has waned but it has gradually been replaced by an emphasis on their psychological weakness. Two ideas in particular seem to be basic to contemporary medical definitions of women and can be found in medical textbooks and often in the attitudes and pronouncements of individual doctors. The first is the assumption that men are 'normal' whereas women are 'abnormal', and the second is the belief that this abnormality stems from the fact that a woman's natural role is motherhood. Thus the capacity to have children continues to be seen as the central characteristic of a woman's nature. This capacity to be a mother is no longer seen to make her physically weak, but it is assumed to render her intellectually and emotionally different, and, by implication, inferior.

Sexism in medical education

The medical view of women outlined above is reflected both in the way medical education is carried out and also in the content of what is taught. In lectures and seminars women can be treated by teachers as objects of ridicule – as a means to entertain male students. Feminist students frequently report the use of educationally irrelevant but sexually titillating slides, as well as the general denigration of women. Recent examples include menopausal women being referred to as 'prunes' and the removal of the ovaries being said to produce an immediate improvement in driving skills. For many medical students, stereotyped ideas of this kind about women's inferiority may be an extension of beliefs which they (and most of their friends) have held to a greater or lesser extent all their lives. As a result, they can be easily absorbed to form the basis for their future professional practice.

Medical textbooks are an important element in any doctor's training, yet most include 'facts' about women that turn out on closer examination to be little more than prejudice. In other words, they represent a less blatant but potentially more serious example of medical sexism. Furthermore, such books usually emphasize the inevitable superiority of the doctor's clinical experience over women's own subjective perceptions – even when it is a woman's own experiences that are under discussion. Little attention is paid in the medical curriculum to problems specifically suffered by women, unless they relate directly to pregnancy and childbirth. As a result, common problems such as thrush, cystitis (bladder infection) or vaginal infections may not be taken seriously, either by researchers or by doctors dealing with individual women.

We can examine some of these issues in more detail if we look at the portrayal of female sexuality in medical textbooks. Doctors are generally assumed to be experts on sexuality, and there are few other sources of help for those with sexual problems. However most doctors are given very little training to help them carry out this important task, and recent evidence about the nature of female sexuality has been virtually ignored by medical educators. This can be seen in the following extract from a standard gynaecological textbook published in 1975:

> In the woman sexual feelings are dormant compared with those of the man and only develop gradually with experience ... Some women never achieve vaginal orgasms and always depend on stimulation of the clitoris, vulva and extra-genital erogenous zones for satisfaction. Indeed one current view denies the existence of the phenomenon of the vaginal orgasm ... but most women with satisfactory sex lives have no doubt that vaginal orgasm is real and much more powerful than that induced by superficial stimulation ...The above views long established and confirmed by nearly all normal women are an anathema to small pressure groups, agitating for the liberation of women and equality of the sexes in all matters. They protest that the concepts of masculine initiation of sexual activity ... reflect the prejudice of males in general and of male gynaecologists in particular. And such protagonists maintain that the sex drive and desire are spontaneously just as strong in girls and women as they are in boys and men, being motivated by personal pleasure rather than by a procreational instinct or anxiety to satisfy their lover. If this is what they really believe to be true in general, rather in isolated cases, they deceive themselves, but not others, not even the majority of women. Sex equality in many respects is desirable; but equality in sex desire is unattainable, being contrary to an all-powerful inherent law of nature. (Jeffcoate, 1975, p.568)

It is striking that Jeffcoate continues to talk of the vaginal orgasm as a fact – as something women should strive for – whereas other researchers have shown that all women's orgasms are centred on the clitoris. He also continues to claim that 'healthy' women are interested only in heterosexual intercourse, have a 'weaker' sex drive than men and are motivated not by the desire for pleasure but by the wish for a child or the desire to please 'their' man. Above all, he is making definitive claims about the sexual desires and experiences of women that run counter both to women's own accounts (Hite, 1977) and also to the widely accepted research findings of Kinsey (1953) and Masters and Johnson (1966).

Two American sociologists, Diane Scully and Pauline Bart (1978), examined 27 general gynaecology textbooks published in the USA between 1943 and 1972, to assess how far they acknowledged the findings of Kinsey and Masters and Johnson. They found that Kinsey's findings made no impact whatever, and that the only effect of the massive Masters and Johnson study had been 'some changes in rhetoric'. This suggests that what passes for scientific evidence in other fields does not do so where female sexuality is concerned. As a result, women continue to be described in medical textbooks as basically reproductive creatures, 'real' sexuality continues to be defined in terms of vaginal orgasms only, and women's sexuality is still considered primarily in terms of their partners' sexual pleasure rather than their own. Scully and Bart summed up the implications of their findings in the following way: 'Gynaecologists, our society's official experts on women, think of themselves as the woman's friend. With friends like that who needs enemies?'

Two doctors, Jean and John Lennane (1973), have pointed out that many common female disorders are explained away as psychogenic – as 'all in the mind'. This occurs even when there is perfectly acceptable clinical evidence of physiological causes. This, they suggest, is not normal scientific practice, and stems from medical prejudice against women. More specifically, women's problems are often attributed to their refusal to accept their femininity. As the Lennanes point out, period pains in adolescence are seen as a sign of resistance of impending womanhood, and the mother who is sick during pregnancy is said to be failing to come to terms with motherhood. Many women's problems are therefore attributed to their deficiencies as women, rather than to physiological causes. The Lennanes do not suggest that women never experience psychosomatically caused illnesses, or that there is not an important relationship between mind and body. But they question the implicit assumption that *most* of women's problems are psychological in origin, and hence not to be taken seriously.

Women, doctors and fertility control

In the past, women have had their own ways of preventing pregnancy and causing abortion, though some of these methods were unreliable and others were certainly dangerous. Abstinence and withdrawal were the most common methods of birth control but, for many women, abortion, however dangerous, was probably the main method of preventing unwanted children.

Today, both contraception and abortion are safer, more effective and easier to obtain than ever before. Indeed women's improved ability to avoid unwanted pregnancies is probably the single most important reason for their increased emancipation during the last hundred years. However, the control of these improved methods has increasingly been allocated to the medical profession, giving doctors a new and important source of power. As a result, the *technical* potential for all women to control their own fertility has not been realized in practice, and decisions about what method of contraception a woman uses, whether she becomes pregnant or not, and whether she goes on with a pregnancy, are often made for her by others. We shall explore this situation in more detail by looking first at developments in contraception and then at abortion provision in Britain since the nineteenth century.

Policies relating to birth control are always formulated within the context of a wider set of ideas about women and their place in society. In Victorian Britain, women were seen above all as mothers, and both contraception and abortion were strongly opposed by the Church, the State and the medical profession. Any attempts to alter the 'natural' processes of pregnancy and childbirth were regarded with abhorrence, and most doctors emphasized the danger of all forms of contraception. They wrote about the terrible damage to health that was likely to follow from any interference with a woman's sacred duty; galloping cancer, sterility and nymphomania, for instance, were all cited as the likely consequence of birth control. Thus medical arguments based on the flimsiest of evidence, were used to justify what was essentially moral opposition to contraception. These same attitudes were reflected in the legislation of the period. Starting in 1803 a series of Acts were passed, making all abortions illegal, and people who wished to make contraceptive information more widely available were prosecuted under the laws against obscene publications.

However, by the late nineteenth century, the fall in the birthrate had shown that despite their public utterances, middle-class couples had been practising birth control for some time. During this same period, several groups with varying political beliefs were formed to campaign for the spread of information on contraceptives to the working class. Some were directly concerned with the welfare of working-class families. But others, such as the Malthusian League, saw population control as a cure for wider social problems, for example poverty and unemployment. Still others were concerned with eugenic questions, fearing that the physical and moral degeneration of the British population would soon follow if a high birth-rate were allowed to continue among the working class while that of the middle class declined.

Thus these different groups had very different attitudes towards contraception, reflecting the varying social and economic origins of their membership. But despite their differences, most had two things in common. First, they believed that decisions about the rights and wrongs of birth control were much too important to be left to women but had to be taken by experts, who were usually male. Second, most campaigners were less concerned with what we might call birth control, with the capacity of individual women to control their own fertility, than with population control, with enabling/ persuading women to act in certain ways in order to achieve a desired social change.

There is little evidence of what we would now call feminism among these early birth-control campaigners. Most women who saw themselves as socialists were suspicious of birth-control campaigns, believing that they were designed to reduce the size and political strength of the working class. Even those who would have called themselves feminists, most of whom were middle-class, appear to have been in favour of 'voluntary motherhood' only if achieved through abstinence. Most did not support contraception because they felt this would make it easier for men to seek sexual pleasure outside marriage without risking discovery. Few were concerned with the sexual liberation women themselves might have achieved through the use of birth control. Rather, they saw their task as improving women's legal and financial position within the family and ensuring the status and prestige of motherhood.

By the beginning of the twentieth century, attitudes towards birth control had begun to change. During the years between the two World Wars, the use of contraception gradually increased but although networks of help and advice existed in local communities, working-class women in particular still found it difficult to obtain either information or supplies, and many continued to rely on abortion as *the* form of birth control. The well-known campaigner for birth control, Marie Stopes, received thousands of letters from people in all social groups requesting information about contraception. The following letter written by a working-class woman in 1926 sums up the predicament of most:

> Could I hear from you personally. I sorely need advice concerning birth control. I have only been married Four years and have just given birth for the Fifth time and it has made us desperately poor financially as my husband's wages are but small. It is through my weakness of body that I become pregnant every time we submit to Marital Rights. I would be grateful to the end of my days if you would save me any further distress. Yours very truly. (Hall, 1978, p. 40).

When the National Health Service was set up in 1948, the ambivalence of doctors and politicians towards the provision of contraceptive advice continued. Immediately after the Second World War great emphasis was placed on building up the population, and birth-control clinics were not made an integral part of the health service. Instead, advice was provided – initially for married women only – by the Family Planning Association and other private clinics. In 1976 these services were integrated into the NHS but some women continue to experience difficulties in meeting their needs for contraceptives. Doctors themselves played very little part in the early development of contraceptive techniques or in campaigns to bring knowledge about contraceptives to women who needed it. Indeed, many actively opposed such work. However, in recent years, the medical profession has increasingly influenced both the methods of contraception available, and also the distribution of advice on contraceptives and supplies.

Like other fields of medical and scientific activity, research and development in the area of contraception continues to be dominated by men. Some feminists have argued that this has introduced a serious bias into decisions about which contraceptives should be developed and how they should be evaluated (Roberts, 1981). In particular, it is suggested that women's interests and feelings are not taken seriously and that what are called the 'side-effects' of particular methods are often ignored in a way in which they would not be if men were the users.

The case of the contraceptive pill provides a useful illustration of some of these questions of male bias. The 'Pill' was first introduced in the USA in 1960 and it is now used by millions of women throughout the world. Its attraction comes not just from its effectiveness but also from the fact that it appears to be the most modern and 'scientifically respectable' of birth-control methods. However, anxieties about the safety of oral contraceptives were first expressed in the latter half of the 1960s, when questions were raised about their possible implication in the causation of cancer and circulatory disease (heart disease and strokes). Attempts to assess the validity of these accusations soon revealed the disturbing fact that there were serious deficiencies in the testing of contraceptive drugs. Although they had all been carefully evaluated in terms of their contraceptive efficacy, much less research had been done to assess their impact on general health. In particular, there had been no research to show the effects on women who had taken the Pill over the whole of their reproductive cycle.

A study of some 60,000 women in Britain carried out by the Royal College of General Practitioners in 1974 showed that the risk of dying from circulatory disease is five times greater for women taking oral contraceptives. The greatest risk is for women over 35, women who have taken the Pill for five years or more and women who smoke. It seems certain then, that for some women, the Pill may pose a serious threat to health. In addition, it affects many women in ways that are less serious but nevertheless important. The 'side-effects' of the Pill are known to include depression, loss of libido (or sex drive), headaches, nausea and excessive weight gain. Significantly, these symptoms have received little attention from researchers and doctors, who often describe them as 'merely subjective' or 'all in the mind'. Indeed, some doctors have even argued that it is better not to warn women about them since the warning itself will make them more likely to develop them!

Attempts to liberalize the laws on abortion have faced even greater opposition than campaigns to extend the availability of contraception. Under the Offences Against the Person Act of 1861, all abortions were made a statutory offence – even when the woman's life was in danger – and it was not until the 1960s that abortion law reform was accepted as a serious possibility. The 1960s were a period of more general social reform, and the 1967 Abortion Act has to be seen within this wider context. Legislative provisions in the areas of juvenile delinquency, divorce, drug use and homosexuality were all being reappraised, and there was a marked liberalization in attitudes towards women. For many people the possibility of abortion (under medical supervision) no longer represented a threat to the social order and the majority of doctors (especially GPs) now supported the proposals for reform. However, they were also afraid that any automatic right to abortion would remove their freedom to practise medicine as they wished, and their support was therefore contingent on the decision about whether or not to grant an abortion remaining firmly in medical hands. There were also considerable eugenic overtones to much of the support for reform. Many of the campaigners saw the increased availability of abortion as a means of limiting the number of births to inadequate mothers who might later become dependent on the welfare state.

After considerable debate, the 1967 Abortion Act was passed, making it legal for a doctor to perform an abortion if two other registered medical practitioners agreed that the continuation of the pregnancy would be a greater risk to the life or health of the woman or her existing children, than an abortion would be, or if there was a serious risk that the child would be physically or mentally handicapped. This was a very important step forward in widening the availability of abortion. By 1973 the number of legal abortions performed on British residents had risen to nearly 120,000, perhaps giving some indication of the huge number of women who had been forced to obtain illegal abortions in the past. However, the aim of the Act was certainly not to make abortion available 'on demand', and many women who seek abortions still do not obtain them.

When the 1967 Act was passed, no extra resources were provided to enable the NHS to carry out abortions. Thus the legislation represented a commitment to the *idea* of abortion being more freely available but without the financial backing to implement it. As a result there are not enough facilities for all women requiring abortions to obtain them without delay. Only about half of all abortions are now performed within the NHS, the rest being mostly carried out in the charitable sector. This lack of resources is often exacerbated by the policies of individual consultants who have the power to decide how many abortions – if any – are performed within their area, and this leads to considerable regional variation in services. They are also able to determine the *type* of abortion that will be provided. As a result the simple abortions performed on an outpatient basis, which women themselves seem to prefer, are the least easy to obtain.

Of course, doctors are also in a position to make judgements about individual women and to decide whether or not they should be *allowed* to have an abortion. These judgements provide an important illustration of traditional medical ideas about the nature of female sexuality and reproduction, and about the moral issues surrounding them. Other things being equal, it is more difficult for a married women than an unmarried woman to obtain an abortion, since most doctors assume that having babies is a normal part of being married. Although they may make an exception for women who already have several children, few will be prepared to recommend termination for a 'normal' married woman on the grounds of what the doctor may regard as 'mere convenience', even if the woman herself feels it is essential to her health and well-being.

A medical sociologist, Sally Macintyre, (1976) carried out a piece of research to see what happened to a sample of single Scottish women who were pregnant. She found that when the doctors in her study dealt with requests for abortions from single women they appeared to classify them into three categories – the 'normal as-if-married', the 'nice girl who has made a mistake' and the 'bad girl'. The 'normal as-if-married' woman was someone who was in a stable relationship but had simply 'anticipated' the wedding. It was assumed that she would continue with the pregnancy as a married woman should, and an abortion was therefore less likely to be granted. The 'good girls' and the 'bad girls' were differentiated on the basis of their past sexual experiences as well as their present attitude towards the pregnancy. Thus the doctor would ask the woman about her relationship with the father of the child – 'is it "serious"? – her use of contraception and her previous sexual history. Both the content of the woman's answers and also her demeanour appeared to be important in determining whether she obtained an abortion. Another study of Scotttish women showed that doctors paid a great deal of attention to how much respect the patient showed in making her request. According to the author, Jean Aitken-Swan, 'the doctors respond best to a concerned approach and tears are never amiss' (Aitken-Swan, 1977). It is clear, then, that a woman needs to treat her doctor carefully and to present the right image if she wishes to obtain an abortion. 'Good girls' may be successful because they have just made a mistake and are sorry for it, but 'bad girls' may be required to continue their pregnancy because the doctor believes that an abortion would encourage them in their 'promiscuity'.

Childbirth

The changing experience of childbirth

So far we have looked at arguments concerning the status of medicine as a science and the significance of medicine in the lives of women in Britain. We shall now look at one particular area of women's lives affected by medicine, that of childbirth, a particularly useful example with which to illustrate some of the arguments made earlier. Many women have recently expressed their anger and disappointment with their treatment, particularly by the medical profession, during pregnancy and childbirth. Much of this anger focuses on the application of medical ideas that hold women to be sick to an event that is not a sickness.

It is interesting to compare the experiences of women today with those of a hundred or even fifty years ago. Perhaps the most important change in the last hundred years is that today more women are having children but individual women are having fewer of them. (This is discussed in Chapter 1, on the family.)

Another way in which childbirth has changed is that it has become much safer for both mother and baby, if we judge safety by the likelihood of one or other dying soon after birth. In 1901, for every 10,000 live births 48 women died; today, one woman does. This way of describing women's deaths in childbirth is called the *maternal mortality rate*. In measuring safety for baby, the usual indicator used is the *perinatal mortality rate* (PMR). This is the number of babies who are stillborn after the 28th week of pregnancy of who die in the first week of life, for every 1000 births. In 1931, the PMR in England and Wales was 62.1 per 1000; that is, one baby in every 16 was stillborn or died in the first week of life. in 1982 the PMR was 11.2 per 1000, that is, one perinatal death out of every 87 births. So there has been a considerable improvement. Nevertheless, over 7,000 babies in England and Wales were stillborn or died in the first week of life in 1982. Moreover, the national figures conceal considerable variation between different parts of the country and between different occupational classes. In 1982, babies born to women whose husbands worked at unskilled manual jobs were nearly twice as likely to die in the first week of life as those born to the wives of professional and managerial workers.

A third way in which childbirth has changed is in its setting and in the people likely to be involved. Three hundred years ago, childbirth was exclusively women's business, taking place in the home, with women in labour being assisted by other women. One hundred years ago the vast majority of all births still took place at home, but upper-class and middle-class women's deliveries were more likely to be attended by male doctors. Poor women were likely to be assisted by midwives alone. Today, almost all births (98 per cent in 1979) take place in hospital. Midwives still deliver about 75 per cent of normal deliveries in hospital but usually under doctors' supervision.

A fourth change in childbirth is that in the last fifteen years obstetricians have become more likely to practise 'active management' of labour. This means increased use of procedures like induction (artificial starting of labour), forceps deliveries or Caesarian sections, and of the use of technological aids like foetal monitors which check the baby's heartbeat during labour. These precedures are controlled or performed by doctors, not midwives.

The safety of childbirth

Two rather different explanations have been put forward with respect to the decline in maternal mortality. For example, in a book called *Prevention and Health: Everybody's Business*, published by the Department of Health and Social Security we find improvements are attributed to increased professional skills, deployed as part of a co-ordinated programme.

> The quite astonishing reduction in deaths of mothers during pregnancy and childbirth can most fairly be classed a victory for 'the system' . . . A planned attack, which included higher professional standards among doctors and midwives combined with effective use of the legislative and administrative machinery and the use of epidemiological techniques, was the key . . . The establishment of the Royal College of Obstetricians and Gynaecologists was an important feature of this period as was the Midwives Act of 1936. Midwives were given better training, better arrangements were made for the care of pregnant women and later fo their confinement, where possible, in hospital, and more hospital beds under specialist supervision were provided as quickly as possible. (DHSS, 1976, p.27).

In contrast, a recent study of the history of maternal and child welfare policies in the 1920s and 1930s concluded:

> It is by no means clear that child and maternal welfare policies were primarily responsible for the fall in infant and maternal mortality. Moreover, professional rivalries and political considerations placed considerable constraints on the range of services provided and limited the benefits that women gained from them . . . The real needs of mothers and infants were never addressed directly. In the light of the realities of childbearing and childrearing experience government policy often appeared contradictory: having professed a desire to improve maternal and child welfare, married women's national health insurance benefits were cut in 1932 and the need for both birth control and economic assistance denied . . . In the case of maternal mortality, it was easier to avoid arguments relating to poverty and class because large numbers of middle-class women died in childbirth. This made it possible for officials to argue that better maternity services alone were the answer and to ignore evidence that better nutrition, for example, also seemed to improve mortality figures. (Lewis, 1980, pp.219–20).

Here social factors are held to have been more important than medical and other professional services. Furthermore, this account suggests that, rather than being a 'planned attack', policies for maternal and child welfare were highly controversial politically.

Most historians would agree that the major improvements in health that occured in the nineteenth century were due to better sanitation, housing and diet, rather than to doctors' treatment of individual patients. The same is probably true for the improvements in rates of maternal and perinatal mortality in the early years of the twentieth century. This is partly because at the time the improvements took place most people did not receive much medical care and, if they had, they would probably have derived little benefit from it.

Earlier we noted that modern medicine has come under considerable attack, for, among other things, its failure to consider social factors in the causation of disease. Critics of modern medicine often draw upon the historical evidence that social changes brought about the improvement in health in the nineteenth century to support their argument for the importance of social factors such as housing and diet in determining ill health today. Many such critics believe that major social changes are necessary to prevent ill health. In their view medical intervention is of limited value, and some would go further, arguing that it can itself be a danger to health. In contrast, advocates of modern medicine point out that because social changes rather than medical intervention were crucial in the past it does not follow that this is so today. They stress the effectiveness of modern medicine, arguing the lack of resources to develop even better techniques and lack of appropriate utilization of existing services are barriers to the further reduction in ill health. These contrasting views of the value of modern medicine have been particularly prominent in recent discussions of perinatal mortality.

Thus, in some analyses, the nation's high PMR (relative to other western industrial nations) is attributed to a lack of appropriate medical services. For example, the House of Commons Select Committee on Social Services produced a report in 1980 on perinatal and neonatal (first month after birth) deaths. It concluded that 3000–5000 deaths a year could be avoided 'if modern knowledge and care were universally applied'. The solutions proposed for reducing perinatal mortality were for women to be encouraged to make more use of antenatal services and for more resources to be given to obstetrics. Critics of this view question the assumption that increased resources for antenatal, obstetric and perinatal medical intervention would improve infant health. They argue that social changes such as reduction in poverty or improved diet throughout a woman's life may be more important. Some express concern that attributing perinatal mortality to lack of use of services is often accompanied by blaming women for their failure to use services appropriately.

> Put crudely, the argument often seems to be that babies die because their mothers knowingly and wilfully put them at risk by smoking too much, choosing the wrong diet, refusing to attend for antenatal care, and even stubbornly, holding out for confinement in an unsuitable place – the home. The evidence points in a quite contrary direction: the behaviour of women as maternity patients or as the mothers of child patients is, like that of patients in general, often determined by

social and economic conditions over which they as individuals have little control, although they recognise their responsibility to their baby. (Chalmers *et al;* 1980, p.844).

These authors reject the assumption that not following doctors' advice is necessarily evidence of women not caring for their future babies. Pregnant women may see their own experience or the advice of other mothers they know as just as valid as doctors' advice. A number of surveys have shown tht women who do not come to antenatal clinics as early as doctors would like are more likely to be working-class and also more likely to be:

(i)   women who already have children to look after;
(ii)   women who live a long way from the clinic and who have no transport of their own;
(iii) women who are unhappy or ashamed about their pregnancy;
(iv)   women who do not trust doctors.

Most of these factors would be difficult for individual women to change. The authors quoted above, a team of researchers from Oxford, also express scepticism as to the proven effectiveness of some medical interventions in pregnancy and labour and suggest that more attention should be paid to evaluating services and to making those that are of value meet women's needs. Women are themselves claiming that their needs are not being met. Indeed, increased intervention in labour appears to have been accompanied by a marked increase in the complaints made by women about childbirth. Women have claimed that ritual preparations like shaving pubic hair are demeaning, uncomfortable and of no proven benefit for childbirth and that anaesthetics are sometimes forced on them without explanation and deprive them of the sensations of giving birth.

In 1967, 16.8 per cent of all hospital births were induced. In 1971 the figure was 26.3 per cent, and by 1974 it had risen to 39.9 per cent of all births (Chalmers and Richards, 1977). Over the same period, assisted deliveries (use of forceps and Caesarian operations) also increased. As induction rates rose, women complained of increased pain in labour and lack of control over contractions. In 1974 there were articles in the *Sunday Times*, television programmes and questions in Parliament on induction. This prompted a leading article in the *Lancet*, a major medical journal, to comment that 'the public might be right to express concern over the use of unproven procedures for convenience' (*Lancet*, Nov.16, 1974, pp.1183-4). But many women found that their doctors did not share this respect for public concern. Two years later a major study of births in Cardiff was published, reporting that there was no evidence that increased induction or other interventions led to improvements in perinatal mortality rates (Chalmers *et al.*, 1976). The authors of the report called for caution in the use of such procedures. Following this, some obstetricians have said they have changed their policy, and there has been some reduction in the routine use of induction.

Other issues concerning births have also generated conflict. Some women and their partners have sought to avoid the potential humiliation, loss of control and 'assembly-line' treatment of many maternity hospitals by seeking a home delivery attended by a community midwife and their general practitioner. The difficulty most of these women face is getting professionals to agree to attend home confinements. Without such attendance, a home birth may actually be illegal.

Some people have also fought for changes in the hospital organisation of childbirth, often against fierce resistance from professionals. Many have pressed for a move away from the compulsory 'stranded beetle' position for delivery (flat on your back, often with your legs in the air) in favour of women being allowed to adopt the positions they find comfortable, such as squatting or sitting. In 1982, the media gave considerable coverage to a maternity unit in France run by Dr Michel Odent where women gave birth in the positions they chose. At the same time the media also noted that a ban on 'natural childbirth' practices in 'his' unit had been made by the professor of obstetrics at a London teaching hospital. The reason he gave for the ban was that 'natural' childbirth practices such as squatting had not been scientifically proved to be safe.

Both 'sides' in this dispute seem to be making the same claim, that their opponents' favoured methods are of unproven effectiveness. The professor of obstetrics justified his reliance on medical intervention on the grounds that all births are potentially unsafe. His critics question this, and the assumption that medical intervention is necessarily safer. It seems that the two 'sides' have quite different ways of looking at childbirth, and may interpret events in the pregnancy or labour in quite dfferent ways.

Medical and maternal perspectives on pregnancy
Two sociologists, Hilary Graham and Ann Oakley, have described this difference in medical and maternal perspectives on pregnancy and the resulting conflict they observed in their research as follows:

(a)   Most women see pregnancy as a normal health process. Doctors tend to treat pregnancy *as if* it were actually or potentially an illness.

(b)   Most women see themselves as having expert knowledge as to what is happening to their bodies and in their lives. Doctors appear to consider that all useful knowledge about pregnancy is medical knowledge. They are the experts.

(c)   Women express a wish to control what happens to them in childbirth. Doctors usually act as if all decisions are for them to make. For some women, the use of technology in childbirth involves loss of control and clashes with the view that pregnancy is a normal process. For the doctors, technology appears to be an important aid in controlling a potentially pathological process.

(d)   Women complain of unsatisfactory communication. For example, questions are difficult to ask, and, if asked, are not answered or are interpreted as requests for reassurance. Doctors appear to consider women as anxious rather than wanting information, and either do not volunteer explanations or give vague or trivial answers when pressed.

Treating pregnancy *as if* it were an illness means, according to Graham and Oakley, that doctors make decisions about intervention in pregnancy in the same way as they do in other branches of medicine. Medical decision-making is strongly influenced by the view that it is a lesser error to treat a well person as sick than a sick person as well. Applied to pregnancy, this decision-making rule justifies intervention 'just in case'. This is the view expressed, for example, by the London professor of obstetrics mentioned earlier.

Graham and Oakley attribute the increased use of induction and other technological interventions to doctors using this *as if* rule. That is, doctors treat every pregnancy *as if* it were potentially pathological. A 'normal' birth – that is one in which no medical intervention was necessary – can therefore only be recognized in retrospect.

The *as if* rule is operated particularly for 'at risk' women. If a particular woman is in a category in which there is statistical evidence of increased risk (by medical standards) to mother or baby, she is likely to be regarded as 'at risk' prior to delivery. In such cases, particular management procedures may be decided on in advance; for example, in some hospitals all women in a particular 'at risk' category might be induced after forty weeks of pregnancy. Among the 'at risk' factors currently identified by doctors are being a primagravida (having your first baby); being a multipara (having already had three or more babies) and being younger or older than the medically defined optimal age for childbirth (early to mid-twenties).

In many hospitals, the use of technology is not confined to women previously identified as 'at risk'. For example, foetal monitors, which record the baby's heartbeat during labour, may be used routinely for all births. Many women have found being attached to the monitor uncomfortable and restrictive. Critics also argue that the reliability and accuracy of the information given by such machines has not been sufficiently investigated.

It has also been suggested that contemporary doctors' training make them value technologically advanced practice in general. 'Normal' childbirth, in which women do all the work and the timing is out of doctors' control, gives doctors little opportunity to use their technical skills. Active management of labour enables doctors to use their skills and to attempt to control the timing of birth. For some women such medical intervention brings reassurance that their pregnancy is being expertly looked after, but for many others there is no such reassurance. Rather, as Graham and Oakley suggest, there is conflict over the use of technology in childbirth. The conflict comes about because of the different place technology has in medical and maternal frames of reference. The use of technology follows from the medical frame of reference, through the use of the *as if* rule. If women do not share this frame of reference but see pregnancy as a normal biological process and also as a social event of great significance, then they may perceive the use of technology as a violation of their bodies. Conflict in the underlying frame of reference means that some women will experience conflict with doctors even if there is no technological intervention in their pregnancy or labour. For women who share the medical frame of reference, conflict over technology may be much reduced. The medical frame of reference sees each individual woman's pregnancy as a 'patient episode', terminated by discharge from maternity care. The maternal frame of reference sees pregnancy, especially with a first baby, as having major and long-term implications for other aspects of a woman's life.

In childbirth, it seems, many women feel they are doubly 'at risk' from medicine. In the medical perspective pregnancy is approached as if it were an illness, and, as we have seen, women's illnesses are likely to be inappropriately treated. Women's illnesses are often explained by reference to their actual or potential motherhood, yet becoming a mother is treated as if it were an illness.

Women as health workers

Where are the women?
When we think about health care in the 1980s, it may be a picture of doctors working in a hospital that first comes to mind.

> Consider a patient in his bed on a ward in a modern general hospital. Every member of the staff in the hospital must successfully perform his or her function. The patient's food has to arrive at the right time (cooks, porters), it must be of the right sort (dieticians), clean linen must be available (launderers, porters), supplies of drugs must come up to the ward (pharmacists, porters), materials must be sterilised (porters, sterilisers), laboratory tests must be completed (technicians, pathologists), X-rays must be taken (radiographers), records of the patient's past treatment must be available (clerical staff), orders for food and equipment must be prepared (administrators), nurses must be available night and day to monitor his condition and tend to him in emergencies. In order to carry out his role in the way he expects, a doctor in a modern hospital needs all these different workers to be functioning effectively. (Tuckett, 1976, p.225)

This is an extract from a textbook on sociology for medical students, which seems to suggest that *all* the other workers (male and female) do their work *in order that* the doctor (male) can get on with his work. In this complex division of labour there is a high degree of occupational segregation by sex, and men are more likely than women to be in positions of control. 75 per cent of doctors and 95 per cent of senior administrators are men. Much of women's work, cooking, cleaning and caring, is similar to women's domestic work, and is often done part-time. 90 per cent of nurses and most catering staff, launderers, cleaners and sterilization workers are women. Women's position in the NHS labour force is typical of their situation in paid employment today.

But this kind of hospital is of relatively recent origin, emerging only in the last fifty years. (And, of course, even now, hospitals provide only a tiny fraction of the total health care in the community.) A brief review of the history of women's place in health care will indicate how this occupational segregation developed alongside the growth in hospitals.

The history of women and men as healers in Britain
The situation of doctors and their patients was very different before the nineteenth century. There were few hospitals, and those that existed had few workers. Doctors had lower social status and power than they have today and there were few of them. Indeed, the word 'doctor' did not come into regular use

as the generic term for those who practised medicine until well into the nineteenth century. Until 1886 there were three formally separate categories of *qualified* medical practitioners, physicians, surgeons and apothecaries, as well as unqualified healers, though the boundaries between the work of the three classes of qualified practitioners had blurred over the century. (*Qualified* in this context refers to the possession of a certificate from a recognised institution, not to the quality of the training received.)

In 1858, an Act of Parliament established the Medical Register (a list of qualified medical practitioners), made it an offence to claim to be a qualified practitioner without being one and restricted public medical appointments to qualified medical practitioners. The Act did not actually make it illegal to practise 'medicine' without being on the Register, although it limited opportunities to do so in the long run. The Act did not specifically mention women, but access to the Register for women was difficult because they were excluded from the institutions (e.g. universities) that awarded the necessary qualifications.

However, one women was entitled to have her name on the Medical Register from the start. Elizabeth Blackwell qualified at an American medical school in 1849 and subsequently returned to practise in her native England. Having practised for more than two years before 1858, she was entitled to be on the Register. Her example inspired Elizabeth Garrett (Elizabeth Garrett Anderson after her marriage), the daughter of a wealthy Suffolk businessman, to pursue a career in medicine. After a long struggle she qualified in 1865 with the Society of Apothecaries. (It promptly changed its rules to prevent such a thing happening again.) These two, then, were the first *qualified* women doctors in Britain, unless we count Dr James Barrie, said to have been found to be a woman after 'his' death, having served for more than 30 years with the Army medical department in the first half of the nineteenth century!

After the Apothecaries' door was shut firmly against women it took a decade for more women to get on the Medical Register, and much longer before all legal barriers were dismantled. From 1869 to 1874, Sophia Jex-Blake and other women struggled to be allowed to qualify at Edinburgh University and, when they failed, they established the London School of Medicine for Women in 1874. Even when access to the Medical Register was achieved, later in the 1870s, women were not accepted into all sections of the profession. Early women doctors confined their practice almost entirely to women and children, often working in hospitals and dispensaries they themselves established, or as medical missionaries, particularly in India.

The history of qualified women doctors in Britain begins in the mid-nineteenth century, but this does not mean that the history of women as healers begins then. Recent historical studies have suggested that until well into the last century most people, especially the poor, received their 'medical care' not from qualified practitioners but from members of their family or community who had knowledge of healing. Barabara Ehrenreich and Deirdre English, two American feminists, have argued that:

> Women have always been healers. They were the unlicensed doctors and anatomists of western history. They were abortionists, doctors and counsellors.

They were pharmacists, cultivating healing herbs and exchanging the secrets of their uses. They were midwives travelling from home to home and village to village. For centuries women were doctors without degrees, barred from books and lectures, learning from each other, and passing on experience from neighbour to neighbour and mother to daughter. (Ehrenreich and English, 1973, p.19).

There is other evidence to support their claim. Before, and even during, the eighteenth century the unqualified (but not necessarily unskilled or unpaid) healers were often and, possibly, mostly, women. Nor did they only come from or serve the poor. An eighteenth-century memoir describes Lady Ann Halkett, born in 1622, daughter of a Provost of Eton College:

Next to the study of Divinity she seems to have taken most delight in those of Physick and Surgery, in which she was no mean proficient; nay, some of the best physicians in the kingdom did not think themselves slighted when persons of the greatest quality did consult her in their distempers, even when they attended them as ordinary physicians. Many from England, Holland and the remotest parts of the kingdom have sent to her from things of her preparing; and many whose diseases have proved obstinate under all the methods of physicians, have at length, by the physicians' own advice been recommended and sent to her care, and have been recovered by her. (Quoted in Jex-Blake, 1886, p.27)

If, as seems likely, healing was mainly women's work until the eighteenth century, then how is it that by the middle of the nineteenth century we see an entirely male medical profession being besieged by ladies wishing to practise 'petticoat physic', as it was sometimes derisorily called?

One explanation is that the untrained women disappeared because male doctors' knowledge and skill were superior to theirs. But as there is little evidence of qualified doctors having effective treatments before this century, it is unlikely that all qualified practitioners displaced women healers because their skills actually proved to be superior. Of course, their *claims* to superior skills may have been believed. Better explanations consider the social changes that took place in Britain during the Industrial Revolution and their effect on the lives of women and on the position of qualified male healers. Discrimination against women healers by medical guilds (the precursors of the Royal Colleges) was part of the process whereby skilled work in general was moved out of the family into the market place.

Before the middle of the eighteenth century, medical men treated only a small sector of society and most of their patients were their social superiors, far less subservient to doctors than patients today. But, towards the end of the century, hospitals began to be built in Britain's growing towns. These hospitals, known as 'voluntary hospitals', were built with funds donated by the wealthy for the exclusive and free use of working-class patients. (The wealthy continued to be treated at home.) It was in these hospitals that medical men began treating patients who were socially inferior to them. Some historians have suggested that this development was crucial. Doctors were able to develop skills and test ideas on these non-paying patients. At the same time the growth of the middle classes increased the number of lucrative patients for doctors to treat at home. Thus a growing clientele and claims to new scientific knowledge provided a base from which qualified doctors pressed for elimination of their unqualified rivals (many of them female).

However, women healers did not disappear completely. Childbirth remained primarily women's business for much longer, although from the 1660s a very few men offered women their services as 'man midwives' in childbirth. This development was initially greeted with opposition from much of the public as being indecent, from female midwives as a threat to their livelihood and from established medical men, especially physicians, as degrading. For the latter had long regarded midwifery as dirty work, women's work, not part of medicine at all. But (from the late eighteenth century onwards) providing services for middle-class women was a possible way for aspiring medical men to acquire patients. The problem male midwives faced was gaining sufficient skills to have services to offer. Here again, the development of the first hospitals for lying-in (childbirth) was crucial. Female midwives were initially excluded by medical men from some of these hospitals, which were used only by poor women. There is no evidence that the skills developed by the male midwives were greater than those of many women. The death rate among mothers in hospitals was probably higher than in home confinements because of greater risks of infection. But the men's claims of a superior service, of scientific and surgical obstetrics, may have been believed. Doctors gradually became the preferred attendants for upper-class and middle-class women, but female midwives remained the normal attendants in childbirth for working-class women until after the beginning of the twentieth century. Since then, the autonomy of midwives has been increasingly circumscribed by doctors, and hospitalized childbirth has become the norm for all women.

Nursing was something women did (and, of course, still do) in their homes long before it became a distinct and paid occupation. Its emergence as a specialized paid occupation for women was linked to the development of the hospital, and the growth of 'scientific medicine'. In the infirmaries attached to pauper workhouses in the beginning of the nineteenth century, nursing care was provided by able-bodied inmates of the workhouses, strictly segregated by sex: women looked after sick women and men after sick men. In the voluntary hospitals (the charitable foundations), employed nurses were usually women. The stereotype of the gin-drinking Sairey Gamp was not necessarily accurate, although these women were not especially trained.

The reform of nursing into a trained and skilled occupation suitable for ladies is often associated with Florence Nightingale in the second half of the nineteenth century. It is interesting that training and higher status for nurses was intially opposed by some of the more insecure medical men in the mid-nineteenth century. A popular picture of Florence Nightingale, both during her lifetime and now, is that of 'the Lady with the Lamp', the ministering angel who brought solace and healing to British soldiers in the Crimea. She is seen as having been caring, compassionate, soothing, the qualities acceptable in the Victorian woman. But this is not an accurate picture. She was neither particularly good at bedside nursing nor enjoyed it greatly. She was, first and foremost, a shrewd politician and administrative reformer. Her main contributions to nursing reform was organizational; for example, the development of nursing training on the wards and changing the role of hospital matrons who had previously been primarily housekeepers. Florence Nightingale's training school produced matrons of a different sort who went on reorganizing nursing in other hospitals. She wrote:

> ... the whole reform in nursing both at home and abroad has consisted in this: to take all power over nursing out of the hands of men and put it into the hands of one female trained head and make her responsible for everything. (Nightingale, 1867: letter quoted in Abel-Smith, 1960, p.25).

In suggesting that it should be taken out of the hands of men, Florence Nightingale was concerned about how nursing itself should be organized, but not with changing the subordination of nurses to doctors. For she wrote as follows:

> To be a good nurse one must be a good woman, here we shall all agree ... What is it like to be 'like a woman'? 'Like a woman' is sometimes said as a word of contempt: sometimes as a word of tender admiration ... What makes a good woman is the better or higher or holier nature: quietness-gentleness-patience-endurance-forebearance, forebearance with patients, her fellow workers, her superiors, her equals ... You are here to be trained for *Nurses-attendants* on the wants of the Sick-*helpers* in carrying out Doctor's orders ... Then a good woman should be thorough, thoroughness in a nurse is a matter of life and death in a patient, or rather without it she is no nurse. (Nightingale, 1881; quoted in Garmarnikov, 1978)

Nightingale proposes an equation: good nurse = good woman. Eva Garmarnikov, a sociologist studying the history of nursing, has argued that this equation is a recurrent theme in writings on nursing in the late nineteenth century. In the early twentieth century a second equation was increasingly drawn. For example, from a 1905 nursing journal:

> Nursing is distinctly woman's work ... Women are peculiarly fitted for the onerous task of patiently and skilfully caring for the patient in faithful obedience to the physician's orders. Ability to care for the helpless is women's distinctive nature. Nursing is mothering. Grown up folks when very sick are all babies. (Hospital, 8 July, 1905; quoted in Garmarnikov).

Here, good nurse=good mother; patient=child. Garmarnikov suggests that analogies were frequently drawn between the nurse-doctor-patient relationship and the wife/mother-husband/father-child relationship, an ideology that served to reinforce the relationship of subservience of (female) nurses to (male) doctors. This ideology of nursing perhaps helps to explain the persistence of the popular image of Florence Nightingale. Within this ideology, male nurses and female doctors are anomalous, though both existed in small numbers in the nineteenth century. In the twentieth century there are rather more male nurses and female doctors but the imagery described by Garmarnikov is still potent.

Women as health workers today

Most health work today still takes place not in hospitals, nor even in general practitioners' surgeries, but in the home. 'Health-keeping' is part of women's normal domestic work for their families. For some women (and some, but fewer, men) this health work goes much further. Some children never recover their health.

> Dorothy is 48. She cares for her 29-year-old daughter, Jill, who has a muscle disease.
>
> 'My daughter has a muscle complaint which affects all the muscles ... She is in the house all the time, and can only go out when I take her. We can't lie her down, if we did she can't breathe, so she has to be propped up.
>
> 'I get up at 6 o'clock and by the time I get her downstairs and have attended to her, it takes about two hours. It's a full-time job for me ...
>
> 'I have to cut her food up very fine and I have to make different food for her ... I do all the washing, I couldn't afford to go to the laundrette. Well, she wets the bed because she can't get up.
>
> 'I am caring for her because there is no-one else to do it for her ...
>
> 'My family life has been affected a lot. My husband and I have to go out separately. Caring has caused tensions in the family, we fall out. The other kids say "you'll do it for our Jill, but you won't for me." ... I can't go out and leave her, I take her with me, but only to the shops and back. I don't have friends coming to the house, I used to have a lot of friends but they don't come now ...
>
> 'I work picking and counting cones in a mill. I used to work 30 hours a week, but they said, even if it's only an hour a day to come in, as long as I don't leave. The doctor says I should be at home with her all the time, but I need the money ...
>
> 'I've never asked for help from the Social Services, I have no help at all, I don't know about any help. I only get her tablets for nothing. I would like financial help so that I can pack in work. When I asked the doctor if I could get night allowance he said I hadn't been looking after her long enough. If she gets worse I couldn't do my job. I'd have to give that up – but I do everything as it is.' (Equal Opportunities Commission, 1980, pp.41–2)

Hilary Land, a researcher into social policy, argues that services for the long-term sick are organized around two assumptions: (i) that most people have female relatives to care for them; (ii) that women have no other competing claims on their time (Land, 1978). From the account of Dorothy's life, the second assumption seems open to doubt. It is hard to know whether the first is true because the work done by women such as Dorothy is hidden from official statistics. What we do know is that Dorothy's experience is shared by thousands of women. She was interviewed for a survey carried out by the Equal Opportunities Commission on women's caring work in the home. In 1981 the EOC estimated that there are about one and a quarter million 'carers' in Britain, most of whom are women.

The number of carers in the population is likely to grow in the future for two main reasons. First, the growth in the numbers of very elderly people during the next thirty years will in itself bring increased need for caring by relatives, many of whom will themselves be over retirement age. Most elderly people live at home or with family members, not in institutions. Welfare State services have not replaced the family over the past forty years but mainly provide services for those without families, or where relatives can no longer cope. These services, such as home helps, always in short supply, have been further reduced in recent years.

The second reason is that a reduction in institutional provision is an explicit aim of current Government policy. The reasons behind this are complex. One factor is that during the 1960s and early 1970s, research and a number of public enquiries showed that conditions in some of the large institutions for the long-term sick, handicapped or elderly, were nothing short of scandalous, often exacerbating rather than relieving the suffering of their patients. 'Community care' has since been promoted as an alternative. But what exactly is meant by community care? One of the key figures in the development of post-war social policy, Richard Titmuss, wrote of the dangers in using the term unthinkingly. It conjures up a sense of warmth and human kindness, essentially personal and comforting ... [so that] what some hope one day will exist is suddenly thought by many to exist today' (Titmuss, 1968, p.104).

Titmuss is pointing to the gap between rhetoric and reality, between ideals and actual facilities and support. Moreover, as two writers on social policy, Janet Finch and Dulcie Groves (1980), have pointed out, there has been a subtle shift in policy emphasis since the early 1970s from care *in* the community to care *by* the community. Care *in* the community focused on the establishment of small homes and hostels with care provided by paid workers. Care *by* the community means care by family and neighbours, usually care by women 'for love'. Finch and Groves suggest that, in part, it is public expenditure cuts that lie behind this shift. In 1982 the EOC described the present policy of commuity care as a euphemism for an under-resourced system which places a heavy burden on individual women.

In the recent past, many individual women like Dorothy have been faced with two alternatives: placing a loved relative in an institution lacking in care, comfort and stimulation; or devoting their lives to the care of someone else, involving much personal sacrifice and loss. Policy-makers concerned with eliminating the first unacceptable alternative seem to give less consideration to the unacceptable aspects of the second.

Women as nurses today

The following extracts are from the newsletter of the Radical Nurses' Group. Founded in 1980, this is an informal group for nurses to discuss their experience of and feelings about nursing work and to challenge the traditional 'handmaiden' relationship of nurse to doctor.

> There were many times when I loved our patients ... But what they did to make me sometimes hate them, was to bring their stereotypes of nurses into hospital with them. To some men, the ideal nurse seemed to be Barbara Windsor in a 'Carry On' film. Pert, pretty, always good for a naughty giggle, but at the same time, chaste little servants without too many brains. The women were more apt to play up the 'blessed virgin' aspect, sometimes almost extolling us as saints minus our haloes ...(J. Wilson, *Radical Nurses' Newsletter*, 1981).

> There is no concept of our Nurses' role as anything distinct in its own right, and therefore men can and do define our role for us to suit their own needs. They can

define us as their skivvies. As a result, nurses carry on the bulk of doctors' work, implementing their orders, gather inforation about their patients etc. so that doctors can swoop in on their rounds, rush around the ward, while still believing that they are in control. *All* nurses, as *all* women, know that the men they service (their husbands, doctors, etc.) could not cope without them and yet, despite this knowledge, there is a conspiracy of silence, a fear of saying outright, 'you couldn't survive without me'. (Kath, Report of a Workshop, *Radical Nurses' Newslatter*, 1981).

It seems that the Victorian image of the 'ministering angel' and the equating of nursing to womanly qualities and tasks in general lives on.

Table 1 shows the representation of women and men in different grades of hospital nursing in 1983. There are two kinds of qualified nurses; registered nurses with at least three years' training, and enrolled nurses with two years' training. Those training to be registered nurses are classified as student nurses; pupil nurses are training to be enrolled nurses. Table 2 shows the most senior grades of nurse administrators. It would seem that the higher grades of nurses are more likely to be occupied by men than the lower grades. Up till the middle of the 1960s, men in nursing were mainly to be found in psychiatric nursing. They were rarely found in the position of matron, abolished in the late 1960s. Is there a link between the abolition of the position of matron and the entry of more men to senior nursing administrative positions? One sociologist, Michael Carpenter, suggests that there may be. The replacement of the matron system by the hierarchy of administrative grades followed the recommendations of a Committee of Inquiry (known as the Salmon Committee after its chairman). Although the Committee's report says very little explicitly about gender and nursing, Carpenter suggests that it is an implicit critique of female authority. Matrons are seen as unable to delegate and to lack skills appropriate for management and decision-making (Carpenter, 1977).

So, it seems that even within nursing, traditionally regarded as *the* female occupation, there is now a tendency for men to be found in the senior posts.

Table 1 also suggests that there is a higher proportion of women among 'other nursing staff' than in any other category. The number of 'other', i.e. untrained, nurses has grown in recent years, along with the modern hospital. These nurses now perform much of the 'basic' nursing work such as the washing and feeding of dependent patients, work that may be seen as inferior to the 'real' nursing work of helping doctors cure patients. Perhaps this is an example of the 'deskilling' process whereby work is subdivided, unskilled labour, being substituted for highly trained workers. And, as often happens, women seem especially likely to be in the de-skilled jobs.

Women doctors today

Women doctors are a relatively privileged minority among women in Britain. They are qualified to work in what has become a profession carrying high status, and highly paid. However, this does not exempt them from some of the problems that face women workers in general. In 1983 there were about 19,000 women qualified as doctors in Britain, and they made up about 25 per cent of

Table 1 Hospital Nursing Staff by Grade and by Sex as at 30 September, 1983: England (Source: DHSS Annual Census of Non-Medical Manpower) Whole Time Equivalents[1] [2]

Grade	Female	Male	Total	% Female
Total Registered nurses	87,340	18,540	105,890	82%
Enrolled nurses	59,490	5,910	65,400	91%
Student nurses	48,280	5,890	54,170	89%
Pupil nurses	17,000	1,330	18,340	93%
Other nursing staff[3] (inc auxil iaries)	79,670	6,500	86,170	92%
ALL GRADES	291,780	38,190	329,970	88%

Table 2 Senior administrative nursing staff at regional, and below regional level as at 20 September, 1983: England (Source: DHSS Annual Census of Non-Medical Manpower) Whole Time Equivalents[1] [2]

	Female	Male	Total	% Female
Regional level	30	20	50	67%
Below regional level	140	100	240	58%

Notes:
1 Figures are rounded to the nearest 10, therefore the sum of the component figures may not add up to the total shown. Percentages calculated on unrounded figures.
2 Excludes agency nursing staff.
3 Includes cadets.

the total practising medicine. There has been an increase in the numbers of women in medicine and also in the proportion of women within the profession over the last thirty years. In 1951 there were about 7,500 working women doctors (according to the 1951 Census), representing 16 per cent of all doctors. So the number (although not the proportion) of women doctors has more than doubled over thirty years, a period of rapid growth in the total number of doctors. The proportion of those entering medical schools in Britain who are women varied between 22 and 25 per cent overall from 1948 to 1968; since then it has increased fairly rapidly and by 1982 was over 40 per cent.

Where do these women doctors work? Just under 30 per cent of them work in NHS community medicine and health services. These are the doctors in child health and family planning clinics, the school health service and administrators in community medicine, and about 56 per cent of them are women. It is a field of medicine that carries little prestige or public visibility. Another thirty per cent (approximately) of women doctors work in general practice, about 20 per cent of all general practitioners in England and Wales in 1984. Most of the remaining women doctors work in the NHS hospital service, making up about 20 per cent of medical staff in this sector. Within hospitals, women are less likely than men to be consultants, the only hospital doctors with full legal responsibility for patients. This is partly because a higher proportion of women than men in hospitals are recent entrants, still in training, but there are indications that women face more obstacles than men in getting consultant posts, and they are not evenly distributed across the different specialities of hospital medicine.

Table 3 shows the hospital specialities in which women are most likely to be consultants (here called the 'most feminine') and those in which they are least

Table 3 NHS hospital consultants, England and Wales, 1984: most 'feminine' and most 'masculine' specialities* (Source: *Medical Staffing Statistics*, 1985: this is an amended and updated version of a table that first appeared in A. Oakley, (1981) *Subject Women*, Martin Robertson.)

Speciality	% Women consultants	Total no. consultants (men and women)
Most 'feminine'		
Child and adolescent psychiatry	37.7	350
Mental handicap	27.6	163
Medical microbiology	22.0	308
Haematology	20.3	354
Anaesthetics	19.3	1878
Radiotherapy	17.6	204
Dermatology	17.2	221
Histopathology	16.7	599
Mental illness	16.4	1168
Radiology	16.0	940
Most 'masculine'		
General medicine	4.1	1141
Nephrology	3.2	63
Ear, nose and throat surgery	2.9	375
Cardio-thoracic surgery	2.6	117
Neurology	2.3	171
Plastic surgery	2.2	93
Urology	1.1	182
Neurosurgery	1.1	92
General surgery	0.6	947
Traumatic and orthopaedic surgery	0.4	679
All specialities	12.5	13942

*Specialities with fewer than 50 consultants have been excluded.

likely (the 'most masculine'). The latter are also those in which there has been most competition for posts in the past. So, even among this relatively privileged group some of the features that characterise women's work in general are to be found.

The women's health movement

Health issues have been a major area of concern for feminists both in the past and in the contemporary women's movement. The feminist health campaigns of the late 1960s and early 1970s were concerned mainly with the identification and elimination of sexism in medical practice. There was also a growing emphasis on self help and on the need for women to take care of themselves and each other. Starting from critiques of medical knowledge and practice, feminists concentrated on four main activities; redefining women as healthy; overcoming women's ignorance; attacking sexist beliefs and practices; and 'seizing the means of reproduction' for themselves. A starting point for many of these activities has been the formation of women's health groups in many parts of the country. These groups are based on the principles developed in other parts of the Women's Liberation Movement of collectively sharing knowledge and experience. A core activity in many of these groups has been self-help health care, often involving self-examination of the vagina with the aid of a plastic speculum (the instrument used by doctors for examining the vagina), a lamp and a mirror. By looking at this previously hidden part of their bodies, women can learn about the normal and healthy changes that take place, for example, in vaginal secretions or the position of the cervix over the menstrual cycle, in pregnancy, or at the menopause.

Some health groups have gone on to develop more self-help skills, for example in pregnancy testing and fitting diaphragms and IUDs. In the USA and some other countries, one of the most controversial of these groups' skills has been menstrual extraction. This is a procedure whereby the lining of the uterus, which is normally discharged slowly as the bleeding of a period, is removed all at once by vacuum suction through a slim plastic tube (a cannula) inserted through the cervix. It can be a safe and effective abortion technique and it is identical with the procedure used by doctors in early abortions. This has been one of the means by which feminists 'seized the means of reproduction' for themselves, for example, in the USA and in France before abortion was made legal there.

One extension of the self-help movement especially in the USA has been the development of women's health clinics which provide much-needed feminist health care. Some of these have been organized by workers doing most of the examination and treatment and women who attend the clinics participating actively in their own health care. Not surprisingly, such clinics frequently meet with strong opposition from established medical interests and there are only a few of them. In practice, therefore, they have been unable to provide a full alternative service for all women.

The organization of health care in Britain and the USA is quite different. In

Britain most people rely on the National Health Service, the State-run system. Feminists wanting to establish separate and special facilities for women have therefore been faced with a dilemma. On the one hand, it is argued that the State is an important factor in the subordination of women in Britain so that to press for more State services for women might lead to an increase rather than a decrease in the State's control over women. On the other hand, to establish services outside the NHS would mean that women would have to pay directly for health care, a situation many feminists find unacceptable. Many women's groups in various parts of the country have pressed for the increased provision of 'well-women clinics' within the NHS. These clinics may be run by general practitioners or by the community health services and provide a range of services concerned with reproductive health, such as cancer screening and counselling. The majority are organized along fairly traditional lines, with doctors (often women) doing the examinations, and giving advice and treatment. Some feminists, might consider that well-women clinics run by doctors still use a model of medicine that is inappropriate to women's needs. Others consider that the provision of any kind of well-women service is better than none.

One feminist health service that has been successfully established in London outside the NHS is the women's Therapy Centre, which provides a referral and treatment service for women seeking feminist psychotherapy. Psychotherapy of any kind is difficult to obtain on the NHS, so the Women's Theraphy Centre provides a service most women would have to pay for anyway. The Centre also runs courses of NHS staff and other working for the State in the field of mental health.

As part of the process of redefining women as healthy, feminists in the Women's Health Movement have been active in providing women with information about health and health care. For example, the magazine *Spare Rib* regularly carries articles on the causes, symptoms and treatment of particular conditions, such as genital herpes, or on the pros and cons of procedures such as hysterectomy. These do not start from the view that 'doctor knows best' that is often a feature of medical advice pages in other women's magazines but from the experience of women themselves. A similar perspective is taken in feminist books on women's health. One of the best-known of these is *Our Bodies, Ourselves*, first produced in 1971 by the Boston Women's Health book Collective, and now an international bestseller. The book's title aims to convey the connection between women's control over their bodies and over their lives. It deals with such issues as the functioning of the reproductive organs, the diagnosis and treatment of women's disorders, contraception, pregnancy and childbirth and sexuality, by integrating scientific information with accounts of women's experiences. These educational efforts were taken a step further in 1982 with the setting up of the Women's Health Information Centre in London, and in many parts of the country, women and health courses have been developed as part of local adult education provision.

Public campaigns concerning particular medical practices have been another aspect of feminist health activism. As we have seen, the medicalization of childbirth has been opposed by many women (and men) including both feminists and those who might not see themselves as such. The campaign to preserve women's rights to abortion has involved more women than any other in the 1970s. It was waged against a series of Parliamentary Private Members' Bills that sought to reform the 1967 Abortion Act. The National Abortion Campaign (NAC) was formed in 1975 and differs from earlier abortion reform groups in that it was explicitly concerned with women's rights to abortion – a concern reflected in slogans such as 'A Woman's Right to Choose'. NAC played an important part in mobilizing opposition to restrictive legislation on abortion.

So far, we have looked at the activities of the women's health movement mainly in relation to women as users of health care, particularly those concerned with reproduction. This reflects the main emphasis in the Women's Health Movement, at least in the early 1970s in Britain. However, in recent years, women health workers have also begun to organise and campaign.

Women working for the NHS are now questioning the vocational ethos that has underlain so much low-paid health work. They have joined trade unions in ever-increasing numbers, playing a major part in the health workers' strike of 1982, and have also formed new groups based on their particular occupations. Nurses and midwives, in particular, have experienced a de-skilling process in which their abilities and knowledge have been down graded and the work that many of these women do has been criticized by feminists because it supports a system that oppresses women. To resolve this paradox, feminist health workers have been fighting for their rights at work, for better pay, and against reductions in health services, and have also been querying the way their work and training are organized and the effects these have on patients. Thus, as well as working with their trades unions, feminists in health work have also formed consciousness-raising and support groups.

The first of these groups was the Association of Radical Midwives (ARM), started in 1976. The aims of the group included re-establishing the confidence of midwives in their own skills and encouraging midwives to support women's active participation in pregnancy. Similar associations include the Radical Nurses' Group, the Radical Health Visitors' Group and Women in Medicine (a group for feminist doctors).

From the mid-1970s onwards, women users and women workers have become increasingly involved in campaigns to defend the National Health Service. This is not surprising, since they have been hit especially hard by the cutbacks of recent years. As we have seen, they use most services more than men and the community services used frequently by women and children have been major targets for 'economies'. Since women fill the majority of health service jobs they have also been severely affected by reductions in staffing levels and deteriorating conditions. In addition, of course, they have to bear the burden of looking after those for whom the NHS will no longer take responsibility. As a result of these pressures, many women have fought to save hospitals, jobs and services and to oppose moves towards the privatisation of medical care. At the same time they have campaigned to make the NHS more responsive to the needs of users, stressing the importance not just of defending services but of moving towards more humane, participatory and non-sexist models of provision. One example has been the long running campaigns to keep open the Elizabeth Garrett Anderson Hospital and the South London Hospital for Women (two hospitals staffed only by women and serving only women). Feminist groups campaigned with trades unionists not just to keep the hospitals open but to provide new services in which women would have a real say in the care they were receiving.

Finally, and most importantly, women have begun to challenge those aspects of social and economic life that make them sick. They have looked at the health risks run by women in their reproductive lives; the hazards of contraception, for instance. But they have been especially concerned to show how women's work can affect their health. While few women are in the most dangerous industries such as mining and construction, many face hazards in their own, typically female, sectors of the economy – hairdressing, clerical work, hotel and catering work, textile production and electronics manufacturing. Ironically, even hospital work has been shown to be potentially dangerous to health, with nurses at risk from lifting heavy weights, from infection and from chemicals and radiation. In the light of this knowledge, more women have become involved in health and safety campaigns, trying to reverse the bias that has led to an almost exclusive concern with male issues in these campaigns in the past (Chavkin, 1984, Kenner, 1985).

Domestic labour – housework and the physical and emotional care of others – can actually damage a woman's own well-being. Damp and overcrowded housing, for example, can have a particularly serious effect on women who spend so much time within the confines of their own home. They also suffer higher rates of domestic accidents than men. This has led feminists into campaigns for better housing and improved social security benefits. Domestic violence can also be a serious health hazard and women have set up refuges to help others threatened in this way.

Recent research has confirmed what women have long suspected, that mothers who stay at home with small children are more vulnerable to depression than other groups in the population (Brown and Harris, 1978). This stems in large part from the low status of their work, the loneliness and isolation that often accompanies motherhood and the economic dependence on a man or the state than enhances their feelings of vulnerability. Paid employment appears to protect many women from depression, but it may do so at the cost of the physical and mental stress brought on by the double burden of work inside and outside the home. Thus, the health of many women continues to be damaged by the sexual discrimination that structures their lives, and they are unlikely to attain a state of true well-being until these inequalities are removed.

Grateful acknowledgment is made to Rosy Daley for typing this chapter.

References and further reading

The references listed below that are marked with an asterisk are those which would be most useful for further reading if you want to follow up particular issues.

ABEL-SMITH, B. (1960) *A History of the Nursing Profession*, Heinemann.

AITKEN-SWAN, J. (1977) *Fertility Control and the Medical Profession*, Croom Helm.

BROWN, G.W. and HARRIS, T. (1978) *The Social Origins of Depression*, Tavistock.

CARPENTER, M. (1977) 'The new managerialism and professionalism in nursing', in STACEY, M., REID, M., HEATH, C. and DINGWALL, R. (eds) *Health Care and the Division of Labour*, Croom Helm.

CHALMERS, I., LAWTON, J.G. and TURNBULL, A.C. (1976) 'Evaluation of different approaches to obstetric care', *British Journal of Obstetrics and Gynaecology*, 83, pp. 921-9 and 930-9.

CHALMERS, I., OAKLEY, A. and MACFARLANE, A. (1980) 'Perinatal health: an immodest proposal', *British Medical Journal*, 22 March, pp. 842-5.

CHALMERS, I. and RICHARDS, M. (1977) 'Intervention and causal inference in obstetric practice', in CHARD, T. and RICHARDS, M. (eds) *Benefits and Hazards of the New Obstetrics*, Heinemann Medical.

CHAVKIN, W. (1984) *Double Exposure: Women's Health Hazards on the Job and at Home*, Monthly Review Press.

CLARK, A. (1919, repr. 1982) *Working Life of Women in the Seventeenth Century*, Routledge & Kegan Paul.

DEPARTMENT OF HEALTH AND SOCIAL SECURITY (1976) *Prevention and Health: everybody's business*, HMSO.

*DOYAL, K., and DOYAL, L. (1984) 'Western scientific medicine: A philosophical and political prognosis', in BIRKE, L. and SILVERTOWN, J. (eds) *More than the Parts: Biology and Politics*, Pluto Press.

*DOYAL, L. (1983) 'Women, health and the sexual division of labour: a case study of the Women's Health Movement in Britain', *Critical Social Policy*, No. 7.

EHRENREICH, B. and ENGLISH, D. (1973) *Witches, Midwives and Nurses: A History of Women Healers*, Old Westbury, New York. (Published in England by Writers' and Readers' Publishing Cooperative.)

ELSTON, M.A. (1980) 'Half our Future Doctors?', in SILVERSTONE, R. and WARD, A.M. (eds) *Careers of Professional Women*, Croom Helm.

ELSTON, M.A. (1981) 'Medicine as Old Husbands' Tales: the impact of feminism', in SPENDER, D. (ed.) *Men's Studies Modified*, Pergamon.

EQUAL OPPORTUNITIES COMMISSION (1980) *The Experience of Caring for Elderly and Handicapped Dependants; Survey Report*, EOC.

ERNST, S. and GOODISON, L. (1981) *In Our Own Hands: Book on Self-Help Therapy*, Women's Press.

FINCH, J. and GROVES, D. (1980) 'Community care and the family: a case for equal opportunities?', *Journal of Social Policy*, 9, 4, pp. 487-511.

GARMARNIKOV, E. (1978) 'Sexual division of labour: the case of nursing', in KUHN, A. and WOLPE, A.M. (eds) *Feminism and Materialism*, Routledge & Kegan Paul.

*GRAHAM, H. (1984) *Women, Health and the Family*, Harvester.

*GRAHAM, H. and OAKLEY, A. (1981) 'Competing ideologies of reproduction: medical and maternal perspectives on pregnancy', in ROBERTS, H. (ed.) *Women, Health and Reproduction*, Routledge & Kegan Paul.

HALL, R. (ed.) (1978) *Dear Dr Stopes: Sex in the 1920s*, Deutsch; Penguin, 1981.

HITE, S. (1977) *The Hite Report: A Nationwide Study of Female Sexuality*, Collier-MacMillan.

HOUSE OF COMMONS SELECT COMMITTEE ON SOCIAL SERVICES (1980) *Perinatal and Neonatal Mortality*, HMSO (Short Report).

JEFFCOATE, N. (1975, 4th edn) *Principles of Gynaecology*, Butterworth.

JEX-BLAKE, S. (1886) *Medical Women: A Thesis and a History*, Hamilton, Adams and Co.

JORDANOVA, L. (1981) 'Mental illness, mental health: changing norms and expectations', in CAMBRIDGE WOMEN'S STUDIES GROUP', *Women in Society*, Virago.

KENNEDY, I. (1981) *The Unmasking of Medicine*, Allen & Unwin; rev. edn Paladin, 1983.

KENNER, C. (1985) *No Time for Women*, Pandora Press.

KINSEY, A. *et al.* (1953) *Sexual Behaviour in the Human Female*, Simon and Schuster.

LENNANE, K.J. and LENNANE, R.J. (1973) 'Alleged psychogenic disorders in women: a possible manifestation of sexual prejudice', *New England Journal of Medicine*, vol. 288, pp. 288–92.

LAND, H. (1978) 'Who cares for the family?' *Journal of Social Policy*, 7, 3.

LEWIS, I. (1980) *The Politics of Motherhood*, Croom Helm.

*LLEWELLYN-DAVIES, M. (ed.) (1915) *Maternity Letters from Working Women*, Bell for the Women's Co-operative Guild; reprinted Virago, 1978.

MACINTYRE, S. (1976) 'Who wants babies? The social construction of "instincts" ', in LEONARD-BARKER, D. and ALLEN, S. (eds) *Sexual Divisions and Society: process and change*, Tavistock.

MASTERS, W.H. and JOHNSON, V.E. (1966) *Human Sexual Response*, Little, Brown.

OAKLEY, A. (1980) *Women Confined*, Martin Robertson.

PHILLIPS, A. and RAKUSEN, J. (1979) *Our Bodies, Ourselves*, Penguin.

ROBERTS, H. (1981) 'Male hegemony in family planning' in ROBERTS, H. (ed.) *Women, Health and Reproduction*, Routledge & Kegan Paul.

ROYAL COLLEGE OF GENERAL PRACTITIONERS (1974) *Oral Contraceptives and Health*, Pitman Medical.

SCELLY, D. and BART, P. (1978) 'A funny thing happened on the way to the orifice: women in gynaecology textbooks', in EHRENREICH, J. (ed.) *The Cultural Crisis of Modern Medicine*, Monthly Press.

TITMUSS, R. (1968) *Commitment to Welfare*, Allen & Unwin.

TUCKETT, D. (ed.) (1979) *An Introduction to Medical Sociology*, Tavistock.

VERSLUYSEN, M. (1980) ' "Old wives tales?"? women healers in English history', in DAVIES, C. (ed.) *Rewriting Nursing History*, Croom Helm.

VERSLUYSEN, M. (1981) 'Midwives, medical men and "poor women labouring of child' ", in ROBERTS, H. (ed.) *Women, Health and Reproduction*, Routledge & Kegan Paul.

WILSON, E. (1978) *Women and the Welfare State*, Tavistock.

YOUNG, G. (1981) 'A woman in medicine: reflections from the inside', in ROBERTS, H. (ed.) *Women, Health and Reproduction*, Routledge & Kegan Paul.

The chapters in this book have been adapted from the Open University course U221: *The Changing Experience of Women*. The units forming the course are called:

Unit 1 *The Woman Question* by Veronica Beechey and Richard Allen

Unit 2
Unit 3} *Nature and Culture* by Lynda Birke

Unit 4 *Sexuality* by Sonja Ruehl

Unit 5 *Reading Women Writing* by Richard Allen

Unit 6 *Femininity and Women's Magazines* by Janice Winship

Unit 7 *Women in the Household* by Rosemary O'Day

Unit 8 *Development of Family and Work* by Catherine Hall and Susan Himmelweit

Unit 9 *The Family* by Diana Leonard and Mary Anne Speakman

Unit 10
Unit 11} *Women and Employment* by Veronica Beechey

Unit 12 *Economic Dependence and the State* by Susan Himmelweit and Sonja Ruehl

Unit 13 *Educating Girls* by Madeleine Arnot

Unit 14 *Health and Medicine* by Lesley Doyal and Mary Ann Elston

Unit 15 *Violence against Women* by Jalna Hanmer

Unit 16 *Moving Forward* by Diana Leonard

In addition, there are 8 television programmes made specially for the course. They are entitled:

TV1 Women speaking
TV2 Women and sport
TV3 Sexual identity
TV4 Public place and private space
TV5 Working for love
TV6 An office career
TV7 Raising sons and daughters . . .
TV8 Everyday violence

For general availability of material referred to above, please write to Open University Education Enterprises Limited, 12 Cofferidge Close, Stony Stratford, Milton Keynes, MK11 1BY, Great Britain.

Further information on Open University courses may be obtained from the Admissions Office, The Open University, PO Box 48, Walton Hall, Milton Keynes, MK7 6AB.

Index